THE SHOCK OF COLONIALISM IN NEW ENGLAND

The Shock of Colonialism in New England

Fragments from a Frontier

Meghan C. L. Howey

The University of Alabama Press *Tuscaloosa*

The University of Alabama Press
Tuscaloosa, Alabama 35487-0380
uapress.ua.edu

Typeface: Minion

Cover images: Background, Pascatway River in New England, by J. S., c. 1670, courtesy of Maine State Archives; foreground, seventeenth-century artifacts recovered in the Great Bay ([top] Westerwald stoneware tankard fragment, [middle] Staffordshire slipware fragment, [bottom] seal-topped spoon), photographs by Ron St. Jean, courtesy of GBAS
Cover design: Lori Lynch

Cataloging-in-Publication data is available from the Library of Congress.
ISBN: 978-0-8173-2222-9 (cloth)
ISBN: 978-0-8173-6185-3 (paper)
E-ISBN: 978-0-8173-9544-5

To the teams that made this project and book a reality: the Great Bay Archaeological Survey (GBAS) team and Team Howey-Clark

CONTENTS

ILLUSTRATIONS

Figures

Table

ACKNOWLEDGMENTS

THE GREAT BAY ARCHAEOLOGICAL SURVEY (GBAS) has been a true team effort. I am deeply grateful to the many people who have been involved over the years helping to advance this incredible project. The words that I share here are certain to fall short in expressing the depth of my gratitude.

To all the community volunteers and students who spent time out in the field surveying and excavating sites with GBAS, please know the time that you spent sweating, soaking, getting sunburned, checking for ticks, or suffering from poison ivy helped shine a light on stories from colonialism that have gone overlooked for too long. Those especially dedicated GBAS field and lab crew—including Caroline Aubrey, Ryi Friese, Ryan Rybka, Rachel Chaney, Brooke Laskowsky, Hannah Corrow, Audrey Waterman, Callie Pray, Will Shine, and Nan Nutt—deserve an extra thank you.

Over the years, a particularly tight-knit group came to form the heart and soul of GBAS. While we may look ragtag, do not be fooled; we are a crack team. Dick Lunt, a retired naval shipyard engineer turned amateur historic archaeologist, always held us to the highest standards in our fieldwork. Dick sadly passed away before he could see this book released, but I know he would say a gruff but heartfelt "good job" and then ask me when he could expect the full field report. Our team will not be the same without him. Laura Wolfer (aka Cousin Laura) was also there from the start, patiently teaching me, a long-time precontact archaeologist shifting gears, so much about colonial material culture and lifeways while also tolerating me as her constant and chatty shovel test partner. Jordan Fansler, a historian who came to volunteer one summer to get a little archaeology experience, is now here every season, getting much more archaeology than he ever bargained for. Emily Mierswa joined GBAS when she was a University of New Hampshire (UNH) anthropology undergraduate and quickly came to fill an essential role as lab manager (and paperwork wrangler). I am especially thankful to Emily for being willing to spend the summer of 2020, at the peak of the pandemic, traversing a hot, tick-filled field along the Oyster River with just me, leading to the discovery of one of the most important sites in all our years of fieldwork. Alyssa Moreau also first joined GBAS as a UNH anthropology undergraduate. After just a few weeks in the field, she was teaching others and soon formally became the GBAS field crew chief and lab manager. She continues to advance our work even as she has started her own graduate education and the start of what I am sure will be an illustrious career in archaeology. And that brings me to the incomparable Diane Fiske, a retired paralegal who serves as GBAS's community historian. Diane's archival research has been a kind of forensics work, sleuthing in the most obscure places to chase down early colonial deeds and then following the transfers of properties (many of them complicated and poorly documented) over many generations, all to make sure GBAS was working in the right places and putting together the right stories. Diane's relentlessly high research standards uncovered fragments in the archives that led us to overlooked histories of Indigenous peoples and enslaved Africans; she has worked to bring forward these stories that are ever present in colonial era documents but that were pushed to the side, often quite literally. Diane has not just been in the archives; she has also been out in the field almost every day of GBAS. Diane is a gift to GBAS but also to me as a person and the rest of the GBAS team.

GBAS has also benefited tremendously from community support and collaboration, most notably with regional Indigenous knowledge keepers Paul and Denise Pouliot, the Sag8mo (Head Male Speaker/Grand Chief) and Sag8moskwa (Head Female Speaker) of the Cowasuck Band of the Pennacook-Abenaki, who worked with GBAS from the start to develop research questions and plans. Because of this collaboration, GBAS never approached the colonial sites we were looking for as English-only spaces, something that opened up valuable new research horizons. Michael Palace and Frankie Sullivan of UNH's Satellite, Airborne, and UAV Remote Sensing Lab have generously used these technologies to help GBAS improve our survey and documentation of sites. The Durham Historic Association provided enthusiastic support for the project in its early development phases and made key introductions to local landowners. To the landowners who have let us traipse all over your properties, I thank you, especially the Lockhart family and the First Parish Church of Dover.

UNH has provided me with an enriching academic home for many years. GBAS was supported by the James H. Hayes and Claire Short Hayes Professorship in the Humanities at the UNH Center for the Humanities. Becoming the Hayes Chair transformed my career trajectory, and the generous funding allowed me to make GBAS a true community project by creating opportunities for fieldwork at no cost to participants and avenues to pay supervisory crew. I thank those who served as directors of the Center for the Humanities through my tenure as Hayes Chair: the late Burt Feintuch and Stephen Trzaskoma and current assistant director Katie Umans, for all of the support then and now (something I especially appreciate as I have now become director of the center myself). For most of GBAS, I was also serving as chair of the Department of Anthropology. It is a testament to my department colleagues that I could serve as their chair and still advance such an active field-based research program. There is a much longer list of people at UNH who have also given me encouragement, friendship, and, critically, the space to vent and laugh along the way, and I hope they know how much I appreciate them.

In April 2020, home in lockdown in the very early phases of the COVID pandemic, I learned that I had been named an Andrew Carnegie fellow. The plans and timeline I had laid out in my application all had to shift as I learned to accept a different scholarly pace, teaching and chairing online while trying to help our two elementary-aged kids navigate remote school. Living day to day through something global and so beyond my personal control gave me a wholly different appreciation for what it may have been like for the ordinary people living through an extraordinary time who left behind the fragments at the core of this book. I hope I have done some small justice to humanizing their stories, and I am grateful to the Andrew Carnegie Fellowship (Carnegie Corporation of New York) for giving me the opportunity to focus on those stories in producing this book.

A deep thank you to Karen Alexander, my copy editor, who came to fill a much more important role as my constant advocate during those times, reminding me not to let circumstances stop me from sharing these important stories and pushing me closer to the finish line. Done with the draft, I found myself nervous to send it out to presses. My wonderful dad, Mike Howey, told me to send it to him. He made copious comments (and caught numerous typos), but his emphatic message was this: he could not put the book down and he was confident others would feel the same. I started contacting presses the next day and knew I found a good home when I connected with

Wendi Schnaufer, a senior acquisition editor at the University of Alabama Press, who, like my dad, said she could not put the draft down and has supported from that moment on my vision for a book that is academically rigorous yet accessible to a broad audience. Thank you to the two anonymous reviewers for also appreciating that vision and providing important feedback that helped me improve the final manuscript.

To close, I want to thank the most important team of all, Team Howey-Clark: Melissa and our amazing kids, Jack and Beatrix. GBAS meant lots of time out in the field, and Melissa took on a ton of summer childcare during my field seasons, balancing that with her full-time career. This was especially true during the pandemic summers of 2020 and 2021 when childcare options were nearly nonexistent. With GBAS's fieldwork funding running out, I knew I had to push those field seasons forward even with the stressors of the pandemic, and she made that possible. For all of it, Melissa, I am profoundly grateful. And Jack and Beatrix, what generous and kind kids. They are subjected to a tremendous amount of me doing and talking about archaeology (and, yes, making us visit sites on our vacations), but they never give me a hard time. In fact, quite the opposite, they seem proud, even voluntarily attending some of my public talks. It is my great hope that they know how proud I am of them and how much joy, light, and fun they bring to my life. Everything matters more because of them.

THE SHOCK OF COLONIALISM IN NEW ENGLAND

INTRODUCTION

It was 6:00 a.m. in June in New Hampshire, and it was hot. Our Great Bay Archaeological Survey (GBAS) team was gathered out in a field along a tidal river that forms part of the Great Bay Estuary, an incredibly unique ecosystem in the Northwest Atlantic Ocean, or as referenced from land, northeastern North America (fig. I.1). This was a kind of hot that you just do not expect during early June in New Hampshire. Only a few weeks earlier, there were snow flurries. Our team had met early to avoid the crushing heat, but the air was already thick, and the field had no shade in sight. As hot as it was, as many ticks as there were, and as much poison ivy we had just trod through, we were out in this field for a good reason. We were here to open that summer's field season of GBAS.

Looking at our group, you might not guess that we were archaeologists. There was no Indiana Jones or Lara Croft. Instead, you would see me, a chunky middle-aged lady, wrangling the crew and fieldwork plans; a bunch of people in their seventies looking like they might fall over (but they are tougher than looks indicate, trust me); a couple of other middle-aged types; and a motley mix of college students (many of whom looked even more exhausted than the seventy-plus-year-olds). You would not be alone in feeling disappointed looking at us. That hot morning, a PBS film crew had followed us out to film the opening of our field season for a documentary on the arrival of the English in New England, and it was to air around Thanksgiving. I am

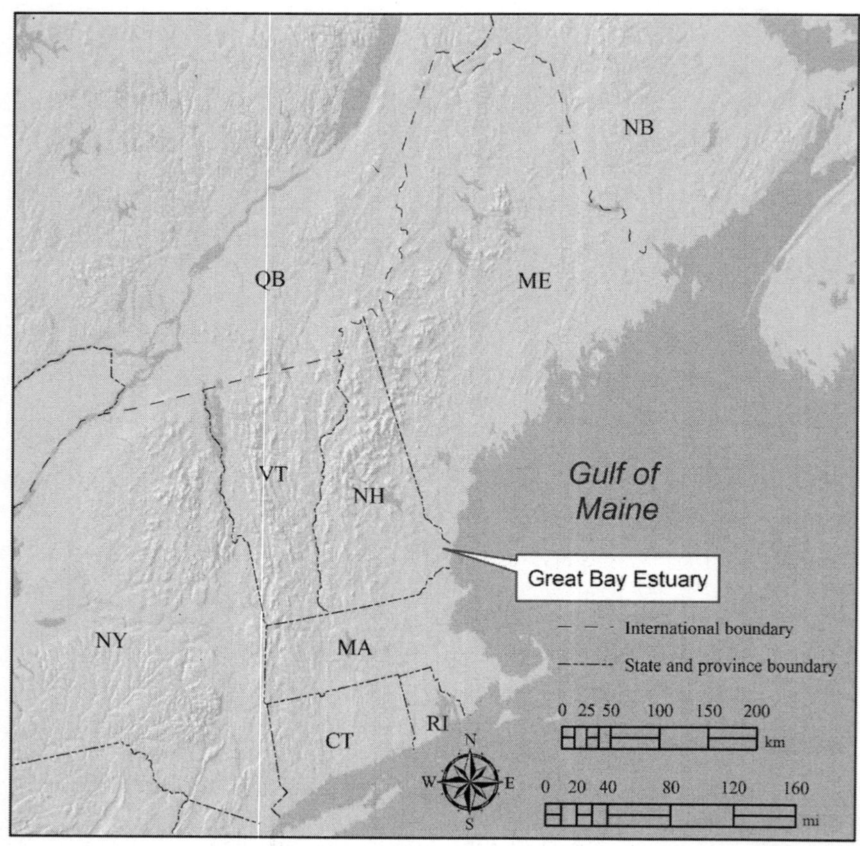

Figure I.1. A map of the Great Bay Estuary, a unique ecosystem on the Atlantic Ocean in the part of northeastern North America known today as New England, which encompasses the states of Maine (ME), Vermont (VT), New Hampshire (NH), Massachusetts (MA), Rhode Island (RI), and Connecticut (CT). (Canada's Quebec [QB] and New Brunswick [NB] provinces are also shown.) P8bagok, pronounced P-ohn-ba-gock, is an ancestral term for bay in the Indigenous Abenaki language that would have been used to refer to this ecosystem. (Base map from Esri.)

quite certain they felt let down looking at our ragtag bunch. How would we play on TV?

Despite our ragtag appearances, we are an archaeological research team working tirelessly to help bring forward new understandings of the socioecological shock of colonialism in the region. Contributing to our motley look is the fact that, on GBAS, expertise comes from people from all walks of life, not just from professors and students. When I launched GBAS, I went out to find people with knowledge about the ecology and history of Great Bay, regardless of their formal positions or titles. Community members from all kinds of backgrounds became essential team members. From local church historians to vital Indigenous collaborators, we are creating a community of practice that weaves diverse knowledge strands together in powerful ways.[1]

We have spent years going any- and everywhere our research suggested that we could find sites dating from the early colonial period, between circa AD 1600 to 1750, when the English first came to the area. We survey for, map, and excavate seventeenth- and early eighteenth-century residences (e.g., "garrisons" and homesteads), resource extraction sites (e.g., sawmills and dams), and shared civil and religious places (e.g., meetinghouses and cemeteries) across the Great Bay Estuary. We also share our findings widely.

This early June heat wave would turn out to be the first of a summer of record-setting weather events. At the end of June, a second heat wave broke eighty-year-old heat records. That July would prove to be the rainiest July on record ever in New Hampshire (and most of the rest of New England). The excavation units that we were digging in flooded regularly. These unexpected field conditions are hardly exceptional, and they are happening more and more here and everywhere. Record-setting weather events and climate extremes are constantly in the news: deadly heatwaves, crushing droughts, massive wildfires, unprecedented hurricanes, and the list goes on.[2]

A MESSY ANTHROPOCENE

Ever-increasing human population pressure has undercut the resilience of social and ecological systems in a variety of ways, from overexploitation of natural resources, nutrient runoff leading to decreased soil fertility, sprawl and development, chemical pollution, dangers caused by atmospheric accumulation of CO_2 emissions, catastrophic weather events, global warming, sea level rise, and ocean acidification.[3] Recently, the Intergovernmental Panel on Climate Change (IPCC) released their sixth assessment report, *Climate Change 2021: The Physical Science Basis.*[4] This report is incredibly informative and quite devastating.

The report explains that it is "unequivocal that human influence has warmed the atmosphere, ocean and land" and done so at unprecedented rates. While we watched it in live time from our small vantage point of trying to dig during extremes in the Great Bay Estuary, the IPCC confirmed that "human-induced climate change is already affecting many weather and climate extremes in every region across the globe." In their assessment of climate futures, the picture they lay out thoroughly and scientifically is, in a word, grim. Changes in the climate system will become bigger: there will be increases in the frequency and intensity of hot extremes, heavy precipitation, droughts in other regions, increased tropical storms and reductions in Arctic sea ice, snow cover, and permafrost (with associated ripple effects across the globe). Recently, a group of scientists identified another somber transition, and that is human-made mass now exceeds living global biomass.[5] Stated more simply, the stuff we have made and discarded, such as roads, buildings, plastics, and cars, now weigh more than all living things, like trees and animals.

Given the major impact of human activities on Earth and the atmosphere, many climate scientists agree that we are living in the Anthropocene, a human-dominated geological epoch supplementing the Holocene.[6] The term *Anthropocene* does not exactly roll off the tongue, but breaking it down is clarifying and shows why it is increasingly being turned to as an explanatory term for the degraded state of the Earth. Anthropocene derives from two Greek terms, *anthropos* and *kainos*.[7] *Anthropos* is Greek for "human being." Kainos is Greek for "new" or "recent." Charles Lyell, a nineteenth-century scholar foundational to the discipline of geology, used the Greek *kainos* and transformed it into the geological suffix -cene to help distinguish rock layers, or strata, indicating changes over time.[8] With this, whatever word is added to -cene marks how recent geological strata are and the fossils (and forces) responsible for them.[9] *Anthropocene* then, by this standard geologic nomenclature, means a geological stratum in which human beings are most recent and dominant.

While this term is broadly used in popular and scientific discussions of human-environment interactions, the Anthropocene has not yet been formalized as a geological epoch. This is, in large part, due to focused, technical debates over identifying the golden spike, a boundary in the sedimentary rock record, for the start of the Anthropocene.[10] Multiple human-led transformational events, such as the origin of agriculture or the Industrial Revolution, have been put forward as the one when humans changed from being biological agents to geological agents. The Working Group on the Anthropocene at the thirty-fifth International Geological Congress, in August 2016, proposed the relatively recent date of 1950 and radioactive elements as the necessary stratigraphic signature for an epoch declaration (and reaffirmed this date with a binding vote in 2019). However, continued disagreements over the golden spike, and its measurement geologically, led to a hotly contested vote recently at the International Commission on Stratigraphy (ICS), the global governing body that formally names geological eras, against declaring the Anthropocene a geologic epoch. Many of the no votes see the

Anthropocene, in geologic terms, as an event, not an epoch, events being a looser term in geology although still significant planetary happenings.[11]

Such an intensely focused search for, and debate over, the golden spike obscures the fact that the question of "when" is far from the only question of the Anthropocene. There are the other "w" questions that are as, or more, compelling to consider—who, what, why, and where.[12] The emphasis on finding a singularly significant tipping point for declaring a planet wide epoch prioritizes physical phenomena at the expense of cultural, lived experiences. This vote does not change the reality that humans have profoundly altered, and continue to alter, Earth systems, and it should not detract from the concept of the Anthropocene, which does useful work for us toward answering these questions.[13] The Anthropocene is a new conceptual reality; it requires us to look in new ways at the deep history of interconnections between humans and the environment.[14] The Anthropocene as a new conceptual reality means that we, as scholars and citizens alike, have to grapple with the enormous complexity of interactions between humans and their environments across space and time if we want to make better sense of where we are today and to imagine possible futures.

For example, we did not just end up one day with an ocean full of plastic or living on a planet where more human-made stuff exists than natural stuff.[15] This has a historical trajectory.[16] To understand it, we must break up the Anthropocene.[17] We have to appreciate the Anthropocene is patchy.[18] As humans, we live on a planet but we do not live at the planetary level; rather, we have been and continue to be situated in multiple places, times, and societies.[19] It was not an undifferentiated, symmetrical, singular *anthropos* that led to the Anthropocene, nor is it one that occupies it today.[20] Historically and culturally contextualized, humans have had varied power and responsibility for altering the Earth system in irreversible ways.[21] The world we occupy today is not the product of one geologically distinguishable event (i.e., the golden spike). Rather, it is the product of numerous social, economic, and ecological ruptures, the burdens of which have been carried differently, and often inequitably.[22]

THE SOCIOECOLOGICAL SHOCK OF COLONIALISM

One of the ruptures that is inextricably linked to the crises we are living through today is European global colonialism.[23] While human modifications of the Earth had been ongoing for thousands and thousands of years, the rise and spread of European global colonialism starting at the end of the fifteenth century/start of the sixteenth century differed in scale, intensity, and ideology. A series of developments in Europe, including advances in sailing technology, enabled European explorers to spread across vast reaches of the globe. The start of this period is often marked by the infamous date of 1492 (and a famous children's song and years of erroneous idealizations), and it is often called the Age of Discovery as it began globalization in the West.[24] Calling this time the Age of Discovery centers on European colonial powers setting out across the globe "discovering" new places. If one wants to keep with naming ages, European colonialism could more usefully be termed the Age of Disruption as some of its most lasting legacies are the radical transformations to peoples and ecosystems it ushered in across the globe.[25]

Driven by global capitalism with an extractive imperative, this era of colonialism cut across both flesh and earth.[26] The violent disruption of human relationships to the environment was central in the unfolding of the colonial era across the globe.[27] Viewing nature and humans as commodities, market incentives came to dominate interaction with the environment, leading to an intensive exploitation of natural resources as quickly as possible and an attendant demand for (often forced) labor to support resource extraction. This led to commercial land use practices and ultimately fueled the development of industrial societies.[28] The mad dash of extraction and industry took a terrible toll.[29] People lived and died, often at astounding rates. Through it, natural ecologies previously managed sustainably were decimated, and social and economic worlds were transformed forever.

This age of European global colonialism may seem far removed from us, but today's environments, both natural and human, were shaped by decisions made centuries ago during this period. Our degraded environment is not a simple by-product of colonialism; instead, a damaged environment was colonialism's very aim. Colonizing powers always sought to change the land, everything and everyone upon it, and to reengineer the climate for their own prosperity.[30] I find the term shock useful here—the socioecological shock of European colonialism remade the globe and it is a collective inheritance still playing out today.[31] We live in the wake of global colonialism and its wake lives in us.[32] The present and past do not, and cannot, exist independently. Even as we may want to silence the uncomfortable realities of the past, the past is not silent.[33]

THE SHOCK OF COLONIALISM EMBEDDED IN PLACE

Building better understandings of these transformative processes and their lasting legacies today requires detailed research on the ground where these histories played out. The socioecological shock of European global colonialism is not just recorded in written archives; it is embedded in place. And that is why in heat and in rain our GBAS archaeology team treads through fields and forests full of ticks and poison ivy chasing down seventeenth- and early eighteenth-century archaeological sites in the Great Bay Estuary—these sites hold material evidence of people living on the ground, in place, through global colonialism's unfolding. I have also focused on this ecosystem because it is in New England, a region, which evidenced in its continued contemporary name, figured prominently in the rise of European global colonialism and continues to be important in how we think about our shared colonial past today. However, understandings of this period have been dominated by research on the political power center of colonial New England—Boston and Massachusetts Bay. As an early colonial frontier landscape of New England, the Great Bay Estuary holds overlooked stories of what it meant to live, in real time, through the shock of colonialism.

THE NORTHEAST

Sculpted by the retreat of the glaciers at the end of the Pleistocene, northeastern North America's landscape is characterized by interlocking ecosystems. Freshwater streams and rivers meet the Atlantic Ocean in large coastal bays and sprawling estuaries, of which the Great Bay Estuary is one. Forests extend inland along the waterways, eventually meeting mountains deeper in the interior.[34] With multiple ecosystems, the Northeast holds a diverse natural resource base that can be bountiful, but seasonal fluctuations are also a major aspect of the region's climate. Winter is significant, always a time of colder temperatures and snowfall, but also a season of especially unpredictable conditions and one that can be long.[35] The Northeast's changeable environment makes it a place aptly characterized as one of want and plenty.[36]

In the early 1600s, English colonists arrived and set out reinscribing a large swath of northeastern North America into New England. For English settlers this was very much a "new" England that "would provide a fertile ground in which to plant their fields and raise their sons."[37] There were, of course, already peoples planted and planting here.[38] Long before colonists came, Indigenous peoples had stewarded the Northeast's lands and waters for millennia and knew their home (and continue to know it today) as N'dakinna—"our land," the place "to which we belong." It was and remains the homelands for an array of Indigenous communities who are culturally diverse, yet who also share in a spectrum of eastern Algonquian languages. With communication possible across vast distances, the Indigenous groups living in homelands they referred to as N'dakinna developed and sustained an extensive network of mutual responsibilities, obligations, and kin relations between themselves, nonhuman inhabitants, the forests, the rivers, the estuaries, the coasts, and the ocean.[39]

The region's coastal geography has lands extending easterly out into the Atlantic Ocean, and so using a north–south orientation is a somewhat limited way of explaining location in the Northeast. However, it is a commonly used way of referencing, and, if one roughly follows a regional map north–south down the Atlantic Coast, Indigenous communities include the Mi'kmaq, Malisseet, Passamaquoddy, Penobscot, Abenaki, Pennacook, Nipmuc, Massachusett, Wampanoag, Narragansett, Pequot, Mohegan, and Schagticoke.[40] The east is the land where the sun is born in a startling array of light every day as it rises over the Atlantic Ocean, making this the land of the dawn, or dawnland. Native peoples have a deep embeddedness in this land; they are "the people who, like the sun, are continually born in this easternmost place."[41]

The English sought to inscribe their own homelands over these deeply Indigenous homelands, this kind of cultural, ecological, and territorial dispossession being a hallmark of European colonialism across the globe.[42] The English undertook a persistent transformation of the landscape with little consideration for the consequences, environmental or otherwise.[43] English settler colonists dammed rivers, planted and pastored their foreign crops and animals, and cleared forests at astonishing rates; upward of 55 percent to 80 percent of New England was completely deforested by the end of the 1700s, and other natural resources were likewise depleted.[44] The capital success of the commercial extraction of the region's resources made this an important colony in the broader British colonial enterprise (on which it came to be said the sun never set). Indeed, New England was so important that the British would fight against many groups many times before ultimately losing it in the Revolutionary War in 1783.[45]

New England is remarkable in the unfolding of global colonialism not just for the transformations that took place here in this time but also because it continues to hold a prime position in collective memories and celebrations of European colonialism today. New England and colonialism in America tend to be synonymous, and colonial New England is understood as the canvas of early America.[46] Prevalent Euro-colonial narratives of New England's origins have long valorized an image of the region as arising from innocent, morally upright ambitions and actions carried out by English arrivals. English colonists tend to be remembered as settling the region through a rather benign process, one in which they developed just property deals and legal systems and had friendly relations with Native peoples, only to have them turn hostile and unleash violence which the English had to defend themselves against.[47] This has been coined English "firsting" and Indigenous "lasting," and it is inscribed everywhere in New England's landscape—from monuments to roadside markers to town welcome signs to school, stores, and place names.[48] This

"New" England imposes a history of what is said to have happened rather than engaging with what actually happened.[49]

Such imposed notions of colonial New England history are projected broadly across collective rememberings. Each November, people across the United States celebrate Thanksgiving where simplified narratives of innocent, devout Pilgrims in search of religious freedom and helpful Indigenous peoples gathered to consume the day's feasts. These are reaffirmed without reflection on the dynamic experiences of those who actually lived through colonialism. For most school children, this sanitized Thanksgiving narrative is one of the first, and often only, things they learn about colonialism in what became the United States. Such storytelling leaves us with silenced pasts that haunt and limit our present.[50]

Research on colonialism in New England has had a heavy focus on Boston and southern New England, areas that were politically dominant places during English colonialism and with well-known colonial era archives. New England's farther afield northern colonies have seen many fewer studies.[51] Stories from the erstwhile colonies of northern New England offer the chance to diversify and reshape collective understandings of our shared colonial past.[52] I will explore how here, in these spaces, English and Indigenous peoples alike were part of becoming that which had never existed before: New World people.[53]

During the early colonial period, the Great Bay Estuary was part of New England's two erstwhile northern colonies, Maine and New Hampshire (and is located in these states today, with two-thirds of the ecosystem's watershed falling in New Hampshire; see fig. I.1). These northern colonies occupied a distinctive frontier space in New England's story of colonialization, removed from New England's power center in Puritan Boston, in a position that made New France's power center in Quebec accessible, and in the heart of what, over the colonial period, became even stronger Indigenous power-scapes.[54]

The Great Bay Estuary, this bay referenced as P8bagok for millennia (see fig. I.1), is one of the most complex and recessed estuaries on the entire Atlantic Ocean.[55] As a place where freshwater rivers and tidal ocean water mix, the Great Bay Estuary is a sensitive ecosystem. The recessed nature of the estuary offers important buffering from ocean storms, providing protective places for diverse plants and animals to flourish as well as a safe haven for people to live in a coastal setting.[56] This distinctive ecosystem falls in the traditional territories of Abenaki and Pennacook peoples and was used by them as well as other regional Indigenous communities on their seasonal harvesting, visiting, and ceremonial rounds for millennia. English colonists were likewise attracted by its rich and diverse natural resource base. Its sensitive ecology and distinctive position in a colonial frontier make the Great Bay Estuary/P8bagok an understudied yet robust "laboratory" to study the socio-ecological shock of European global colonialism. GBAS has been amassing a collection of early colonial period (ca. AD 1600–1750) artifacts, ecofacts, and geospatial data to this end.

THE BOOK'S PATH

What we do now to repair our relationship with the Earth is one of the most compelling questions of our time, but taking this on at the planetary scale is overwhelming. This is not a scale we can relate to as humans. My aim in this book is to ground us in lived experiences of threshold change embedded in place, stories that are little streams into the river that is the messy Anthropocene. In the Great Bay Estuary/P8bagok, the global colonial project played out, but on-the-ground, real people lived in and had to navigate the starts and stops and disconnects of colonial encounter. I started GBAS with this idea at the front of mind. As an archaeologist, my aim was to explore colonialism—its social dynamics and ecological impacts—from a material perspective first, to prioritize not the written record, but the fragments left behind by ordinary people living through the extraordinary shock of colonialism here in this place.

Across the globe, the archaeological record holds data and information that can be harnessed to track how people experienced changing socioecological systems over time.[57] Key categories consist of (a) settlement patterns: where people lived in a given landscape, and when and how locations changed over time; (b) culturally modified features: houses and hearths; (c) material artifacts left behind and/or discarded in these features (e.g., dishes, tools); and (d) ecofacts or detritus of everyday life (e.g., plant remains, animal bones, and shells from food procurement or other routine activities). When exploring early colonialism, such material fragments display remarkable candor. Unlike maps and other written records, these fragments are not consciously or subconsciously edited to reflect what stories should be told and how they should be documented.

Chapter 1 opens with colonial maps to situate us in the colonial transformation of New England, and the Great Bay Estuary/P8bagok ecosystem specifically, and how English colonists in the seventeenth century perceived it and promoted it. I explore colonial maps as important for what they tell us but also for what they do not. And it is these untold stories I center in the following five chapters of the book by featuring tangible fragments explored and discovered in GBAS. Chapter 2's fragments show us the deep connections Abenaki/Pennacook peoples had here and how they creatively navigated colonial encounter and the process of becoming that which had never existed before: New World people. Chapter 3's fragments show local English colonists were also becoming New World people and reveal dynamic, and unexpected, interactions with Indigenous peoples. In chapter 4, I explore fragments from tensions between those living in this northern colonial frontier and the colonial New England's power center in Boston. Chapter 5's fragments track the shifting social, ecological, and economic realities of local colonists in the Great Bay Estuary, people who were at once global and local, at once English and not. In the last chapter, chapter 6, I look at the violence that eventually came to the Great Bay Estuary/P8bagok during the early colonial period and reenvision how we tell and remember stories of colonial violence based on fragments recovered by GBAS. To conclude, I discuss how sea level rise is threatening to destroy Indigenous and English colonial cultural heritage sites across this ecosystem (and beyond). I emphasize the need to recover more fragments from the lived experience of colonialism before the messy Anthropocene that we occupy today quite literally washes away the evidence of the varied trajectories that led us here and the important lives and stories overlooked along the way.

Bringing forward the stories of what it meant to live through global colonialism, in place, is the central focus of the book. But these stories did not just appear; the hard work and tremendous efforts of students, community volunteers, scientists, and Indigenous collaborators made the discovery and interpretation of these fragments from a colonial frontier possible. At specific moments in the book, I share brief stories of our fieldwork, how we made our discoveries, and how moments of discovery resonated among our collaborative team. These will be called out in parts titled "Finding."

Each chapter's fragments hold the stories of people immersed in a landscape of threshold change; they resonate from the past to us today, and they gesture toward our uncertain future.[58] They offer us glimpses into the diversity and enormity of our relationships with the Earth and each other. As we move through this exploration, I invite you to ask what fragments might we leave behind and what stories will they resonate forward about how we navigated our contemporary world's challenging, extraordinary circumstances, especially as we face the realities presented by a messy Anthropocene. I am not arguing for direct parallels between the past and the present, but I am suggesting that in sharing stories of our intervulnerability over time and space, we may find something uniquely connective there among the fragments of our varied tribulations.[59] And so, it is to the fragments we turn.

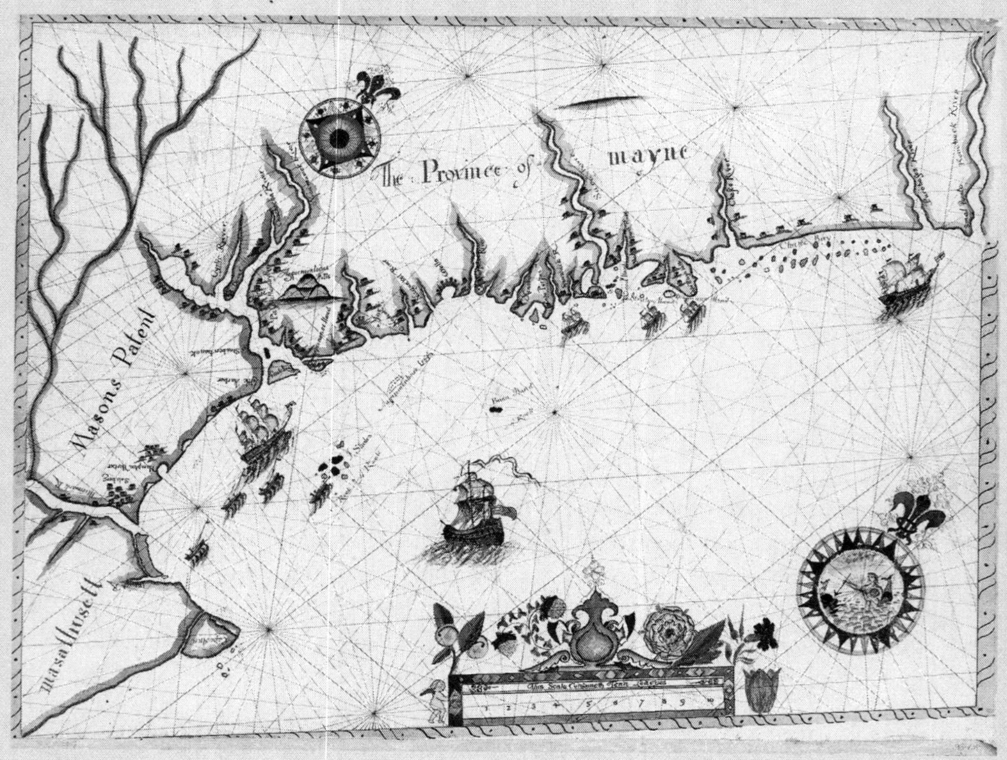

Figure 1.1. Fragment: *The Province of Mayne*, circa 1650. (Map courtesy of the Maine State Archives, Baxter Rare Maps Collection.)

1

FRAGMENTS FROM MAPPING

MAPS ARE IMPORTANT TOOLS IN most aspects of our work in the Great Bay Archaeological Survey (GBAS). We use maps and mapping technology to try to predict where colonial-era dating archaeological sites might be found still intact in the Great Bay Estuary/P8bagok amid the area's modern development. When we find sites, we map them and everything we find in them. Just as maps are key tools in our contemporary archaeological research into colonialism in the region, maps were tools used by colonial powers themselves to portray their specific interests and aims in colonizing the region during the seventeenth century. Colonial-era maps, like all maps, are symbolic simplifications of incredible complexities, but when available, these historic maps offer us a springboard back into the context of the time and offer insights into the unfolding of colonialism.

Maps and nautical charts produced by colonial entities expressed their knowledge, supposition, and speculations about the geographical distribution of things in the places they were trying to colonize. They were essential tools of European global colonialism. This was a time when, among other developments, the transformative technology of open-ocean sailing enabled the spread of Europeans and an extractive economy across all parts of the world. In deciding what to depict and how to depict it, European colonial-era mapmakers instilled priorities, social context, and allegiances into their workmanship. It was a long time before maps were things that people could easily use to get from place to place. Cartography was an inherently cultural endeavor.[1] Mapping allowed lands to be sketched, sovereignty staked, and ambitions articulated.[2]

This is certainly true for the map that is our opening fragment, *The Province of Mayne* (see fig. 1.1). It has quite a bit of decorative flair, which is typical of many seventeenth-century English maps of North America. While having decorative flair, most of the map navigational conventions we have come to expect had not yet been established. The scale is highly embellished but rudimentary. Two colorful compass roses point north, but the top of the map points north–northeast, probably because most European vessels approached the coast from east–southeast. The map's only real geographical information is its coastline contour broken by rivers penetrating the continental interior, potential highways into an unknown land. From the early 1500s to the end of the seventeenth century, most maps of the New World "delineated the sea from the shore with a single line, revealing little detail of the interior landmass, but highlighting the shoals, islands, ocean basins and river mouths in which European mariners encountered right whales, haddock, mackerel, and herring."[3] One unique elevational feature in this coastal setting, Mount Agamenticus, stands out as a landmark in an otherwise blank landscape with its exaggerated size. Small squares indicate the rough positions of coastal settlements and fishing stations along rivers and the coast.

To modern eyes, the map seems somewhat uninformative. Yet it is one of the earliest colonial representations of the two erstwhile northern New England frontier colonies, Maine and New Hampshire. Although it shows a broad swath, given the Great Bay Estuary's location in a distinctive boundary position between these colonies, some of its key features are illustrated. These include the mouth of the Piscataqua River (Pis-cat'-a-qua), the river connecting the Great Bay estuarine system with the Atlantic Ocean, which is marked by another exaggerated feature, a mound representing the island at its mouth known today as New Castle. One of the map's three large-sailed ships is shown approaching this important port of entry (see fig. 1.1). The inland compass rose almost touches the Newichawannock, the Abenaki name for the Salmon Falls River, the river forming the boundary between the two northern colonies featured in this map. Dover, New Hampshire, one of the earliest permanent colonial settlements in Great Bay, appears as a small square on the tip of the dark grey peninsula to its left, and the Oyster River lies just west of Dover.

Probably drawn and painted in London based on earlier maps,[4] firsthand descriptions, and client specifications, this odd-looking map, in fact, represents a clandestine plot of economic, political, and religious takeover. One English colony was preparing to absorb another for its profitable fisheries. Interestingly, Indigenous peoples appear nowhere on this map (see fig. 1.1). To pull out its story, we need to start with how and why the Northeast was colonized.

FROM AND FOR THE SEA: EARLY EUROPEAN EXPLORATION IN THE NORTHEAST

In Europe, fish had long played an important role in the everyday diet. One important fish, Atlantic cod, was in such high demand in Europe that, as early as the fourteenth century, cod stocks were overfished in northeast Atlantic Ocean waters along the European coast.[5] By the end of the fifteenth century, fishing was second only to farming as an occupation in Europe.[6] Europeans first came to the Atlantic seaboard of northeastern North America as their fishing practices were exhausting marine resources in Europe's eastern Atlantic waters. European fishers were moving farther and farther afield in search of fish. In 1497, England officially sponsored John and Sebastian Cabot to explore the "eastern, western, and northern sea," and, while not the mission of their expedition, they are credited as the first European's to find and bring word back to Europe of rich fishing grounds at Grand Banks, a series of underwater plateaus off what Europeans came to call Newfoundland (New-Found-Land).[7]

Fifteen years after the Cabots confirmed New-Found-Land's rich cod fishing grounds,[8] "fifty vessels of different nations were employed" fishing for cod and drying it on the big island's rocky shore.[9] While many different nations had boats here, during the 1500s, fishers from the Iberian Peninsula (Spanish, Portuguese, and Basque) were the most commonplace in these waters.[10] By the early 1600s, however, the French had come to dominate the Grand Banks fishery. Unlike other European fishers in these waters, the French kept pushing farther south/west down the Atlantic Coast. Samuel de Champlain, who would come to found Quebec in 1608, reached the Gulf of Maine in 1604.[11]

The Gulf of Maine is a large gulf of the Atlantic Ocean that reaches from the Gaspe Peninsula in Quebec to southeastern Massachusetts. The Great Bay Estuary/P8bagok is one of many ecosystems that feed into this massive gulf. The Gulf of Maine is one of the most diverse, productive, and complex marine temperate areas in the world, sometimes called a "sea within a sea."[12] A complex array of basins, channels, and banks creates habitats that bring together a rich confluence of marine species. The French, once here, quickly claimed the territory and called it Acadia. They traded regularly with Native tribes of the northern Gulf of Maine and Bay of Fundy.[13] The richness of these waters attracted more European attention, and English explorers were close behind the French, pushing into the Gulf of Maine in the early 1600s.

Most early English explorers were looking for extractable resources, although even then, some of these early Englishmen envisioned future settlements along its shores.[14] Looking for sassafras (thought to cure syphilis) in 1603, Martin Pring was the first known European to explore the Piscataqua River, but he stayed for only a short time.[15] Capt. John Smith voyaged along the Gulf of Maine coast in 1614 and coined the region's lasting Euro-American name, New England, by publishing *A Description of New England* two years later. It was the most well-known promotional tract of its time. Smith was an advocate for settlement. His prediction that Gulf of Maine cod would eventually bring England more riches than the gold of Mexico proved prescient when the fish his sailors caught that summer made their voyage profitable.[16]

As the French and English moved into Gulf of Maine waters and explored its coast in the early 1600s, they routinely marveled at the diversity, abundance, and size of the marine resources there compared with conditions in Europe and even on the Grand Banks, which at that time had been fished for about one hundred years. Early accounts describe enormous "shoals" of monstrous cod as big as men (that is, about five feet in length) in the Gulf of Maine and exclaim how much bigger, more plentiful, and closer to shore they were than in Newfoundland.[17] Smith calculated that "each hundred [of Gulf of Maine cod] is as good as two or three hundred in the New-found Land. So that halfe the labour in hooking, splitting, and turning, is saved."[18] After almost three hundred years of fishing, the Gulf of Maine still produced 142 million pounds of menhaden in 1876, 43 million pounds of cod in 1889, and 153 million pounds of Atlantic herring in 1902.[19]

Two Englishmen, John Mason and Sir Ferdinando Gorges, interested in establishing cod fisheries in New England, obtained a royal charter from King James I in 1622 granting them a vast amount of land for a northern New England colony.[20] The King's Great Council for New England was established in 1620 and started making sweeping land grants like the one given to Mason and Gorges. Accounts indicate that land grants were quite vague and disorganized as the council knew very little about the actual lands it was granting.[21] Although Mason and Gorges were loyal Anglicans, they differed in critical ways. Gorges was an older knight who longed for a return to feudalism, while Mason had governed the English colony on New-found-land and aimed to personally manage his New World possessions.[22] Within a few years, Mason and Gorges divided their land, creating New England's two northern frontier colonies: Mason's Patent (indicated on the map, outlined in the colored original map is a somber grey), which he called New Hampshire after his English home, and Gorges's Province of Mayne (indicated on the map, outlined in the colored original map in yellow, the color of desire and riches, and today part of Maine).

Much like fishing companies had done in Newfoundland, these two proprietors sent over employees to establish fishing stations and larger trading posts (see the small dark squares around the Great Bay Estuary and to the northeast on fig. 1.1). These employees were some of northern New England's earliest English colonists, and they were far from a united bunch, except in shared expectations of the colony as a place for economic gains. Investment funded colonization and investors had to be repaid with interest. Provincial settlers quickly established export fisheries to pay their debts and accrue capital.[23]

New England merchants became major suppliers of salted fish and fish oil into what is known as the West Indies trade, the emerging international system of commercial exchange based on transactions funded by promissory notes called bills of credit.[24] European demand for salt cod remained strong and expanded as Catholic colonial populations grew around the globe.[25] The Isle of Shoals, offshore in the Atlantic Ocean from the Piscataqua River, was an important hub for English fisheries in the Gulf of Maine. These islands are depicted on *The Province of Mayne* with fishing boats nearby (see fig. 1.1).

The three large-sailed ships on this map, one seeming to be headed to "Masathusett" (Massachusetts Bay Colony), one, again, headed toward the mouth of the Piscataqua, and another in Casco Bay, the edge of English colonial holdings in the Gulf of Maine, likely transported cod, salt, and other cargo to and from these colonies. The four small boats near the Isles of Shoals were engaged in fishing, and the coaster boats off the northern coast either fished for cod or carried goods to scattered northeastern settlements. *The Province of Mayne* is a map about the commercial importance of the cod fishery in New England and the particularly important marine resources swimming in these erstwhile northern colonies' waters.

COLONIAL SETTLING IN NEW ENGLAND

Over the course of the first decades of the seventeenth century, the nature of colonialism shifted in New England. The "extractive colonialism" of proprietors and employees intending to gain wealth and eventually to go home evolved into "settler colonialism" where families came to permanently stake their futures in a new place.[26] Settler colonists are migrants who do not just move to a different country; rather, they move to places they want to remake in their idealized image of home.[27]

The most well-known group of settler colonists in New England are the 102 Pilgrims who came on the Mayflower and founded Plymouth Colony. While school children across the United States learn about the Pilgrims each fall, it was really a different group of much more powerful English migrants, the Puritans, who arrived in New England in 1630, who made the shift toward settler colonialism stick in the region. By 1630, England was increasingly fracturing due to civil strife. Wealthy and connected, Puritan religious zealots deplored the excesses of English life, its monarchy, and its Anglican Church, which, although Protestant, they thought retained too much Catholic ritual.

Arriving in 1630 with seventeen ships with one thousand passengers, they established the Massachusetts Bay Colony, its capital Boston, and quickly transformed their colony into the population center and political power base of New England.[28] They believed that it was God's will that they establish permanent sanctified settlements, succeed financially, create a pure English church, and live in a covenanted society.[29] As their leader John Winthrop said in his well-known city on the hill speech in 1630, they would be such a model that others would say of succeeding plantations "may the Lord make it like that of New England."[30] The Great Puritan Migration brought thousands of believers to Massachusetts Bay during the next decade, further solidifying this colonial power base. Between 1630 and 1690, the colonial population of Massachusetts grew from one thousand to fifty thousand, dwarfing all other colonies in New England.[31]

As Winthrop did, early English colonists also routinely referred to their settlements as plantations and themselves as planters to indicate their intent to stay permanently and transform the land, via planting, clearing, and harvesting, into landscapes resembling their former homes.[32] By the eighteenth century, Portuguese, Dutch, French, and British plantations growing sugar, tobacco, rice, and other bulk commodities were large agricultural complexes reliant on African chattel slavery. This is what comes to mind when we hear the term *plantation*.[33] However, in its earlier colonial context, including in New England, *plantation* referred to where planting took place, a term used to delineate defined colonially settled areas (often loosely delineated). *Plantation* is a term that comes up over the course of this book, and so it is important to clarify its seventeenth-century meaning here.

Massachusetts Bay quickly established a commercial cod fishery along its coast, and Boston merchants profitably marketed their salt cod to London distributors. But in the late 1640s, Massachusetts fisheries hit a snag. Heavy cod fishing in coastal waters, along with habitat degradation due to a proliferation of planting activities from forest clearing, agriculture, animal husbandry, road and dock building, and human household activity, caused catches to rapidly decline. Suddenly, some Boston merchants could not fulfill their London contracts and risked default and bankruptcy.[34]

Yet just a day's sail north lay the rich fishing grounds off the Piscataqua River and the Isles of Shoals. John Mason had died in 1635. His erstwhile colony, haphazardly run by employees and servants, was a haven for people who broke with the stringent Puritanism of Massachusetts Bay. Religious apostates settling here included Rev. John Wheelwright, the brother-in-law of Ann Hutchinson, who was one of the most powerful religious reformers at odds with Puritan Massachusetts Bay (she and many of her supporters moved to Rhode Island). Reverend Wheelwright brought his dissident congregation to Exeter on the Great Bay Estuary. On pretext of providing orderly government, Massachusetts Bay Colony absorbed Mason's Patent, New Hampshire, in 1640 (a move that we explore more in chapter 4). The English Civil War, which involved multiple prolonged conflicts between Royalists and Parliamentarians and saw the seating of the Long Parliament, which could not dissolve, or effectively govern, for close to twenty years (ca. 1640–60), meant that no one in higher authority was paying attention. This is why in *The Province of Mayne* this area is outlined in the same darker somber grey as Masathusett (see fig. 1.1). Sir Ferdinando Gorges died in 1647, and King Charles I of England was beheaded two years later.

This then left the Province of Mayne and its fisheries without a protector and placed the loyalist colony square in the sights of whoever commissioned this map. And in 1652, Massachusetts Bay expanded again and took over Gorges patent, the Province of Mayne, by fiat. It "extended its charter" up to the Kennebec River, the border with New France, a move that gave them authority over fish-rich Casco Bay.[35] That this map terminates abruptly at the Kennebec River appears an intentional move to avoid depicting New France's territory. France and England fought frequently, and these tensions overflowed in various ways into these two bordering colonies on this other side of the Atlantic Ocean. In this map, we see Massachusetts Bay political calculations: they saw economic potential in taking over the valuable assets of weak frontier colonies, while not antagonizing a powerful one, Catholic New France (with strong alliances with many of the northern Indigenous communities). Of course, these were political calculations in that moment, and they did not last.

INDIGENOUS PLACE-THOUGHT

Our opening fragment is a map that puts in material form something at the heart of the entire global colonial enterprise—waterways, landscapes, and their natural resources were rendered commodities, items of colonial possession. In New England, fish were some of the first natural resources to become commodities. Those sailed ships at the mouth of the Piscataqua and in Casco

Bay tell us Massachusetts Bay knew full well where rich fisheries were in the northern New England colonies (see fig. 1.1). At the same time, the almost complete lack of information beyond the Atlantic Coast in this map, and many other colonial-era maps, shows us how little colonists actually knew about the lands, and peoples, that they were trying to usurp.

Maps may have been introduced during the colonial era, yet previously these lands were layered with geographic knowledge. For thousands and thousands of years, Indigenous peoples who referred to their larger homelands as N'dakinna anchored knowledge to geographic features, those "continually woven into the fabric of social life."[36] In colonial maps, place is inert and so possessable; in Indigenous knowledge systems, land and waterways are symbols *of* and symbols *for* a way of living; Indigenous peoples both inhabit the land and are inhabited by it, creating lasting relationships.[37] A helpful frame for explaining Indigenous geographies is the concept of Place-Thought. As the "non-distinctive space where place and thought were never separated because they never could or can be," Place-Thought is a physical embodiment of knowledge and holds that the land (and everything it subsumes) is alive and sentient.[38]

The "empty" lands in the *Province of Mayne* map were hardly empty; these lands were Indigenous power-scapes. English colonists remained tethered to New England's coast due, in part, to their use of marine resources but also because it was hard for them to move over land to interior places, especially in winter. The English had migrated from a small island with a temperate climate and mild winters. The Northeast, in contrast, has a continental climate with significant annual temperature variation. English migrants had difficulty managing the region's harsh, unpredictable winters, winters exacerbated during their arrival by a circa five-hundred-year global cold snap called the Little Ice Age.[39] They could not really move overland through snow. In contrast, Native peoples moved across the heartlands of their homeland N'dakinna with ease, including during winter on snowshoes. The English did not adopt Indigenous snowshoe technology until the early eighteenth century. Indigenous place-based knowledge and mobility created important power-scapes in interior and frontier landscapes for them during early colonialism.[40]

While colonial maps obfuscated Indigenous relational geographic knowledge systems, these were still inscribed upon the land and so were then, and remain today, unerasable. Maps continue to resonate as difficult, colonially imposed products among Indigenous communities in New England. In a recent major anthology of Indigenous writing from New England, *Dawnland Voices*, the anthology's coordinating editor explained that no map of

Indigenous groups in New England would be provided in the book because mapping is "tricky and political business and in the end, the tribal editors were unable to agree on a single map of Indigenous homeland in the northeast."[41] But maps are this book's first fragments precisely because maps are tricky and political, reflecting broader social contexts and priorities, as well as knowledge, supposition, and ignorance.

OUR "LABORATORY": THE GREAT BAY ESTUARY/P8BAGOK

Pascatway River in New England is another colonial map, this one mapping in more detail the late seventeenth-century Great Bay Estuary, the joint hub of Mason's and Gorges's earlier colonies, and a large natural harbor that remained navigable in winter and so hosted the largest aggregation of English settlements north of Boston in the seventeenth century (fig. 1.2). The map's maker, John Scott, called this ecosystem Pascatway, this being one early English translation of the ancestral Abenaki name for the English entry point

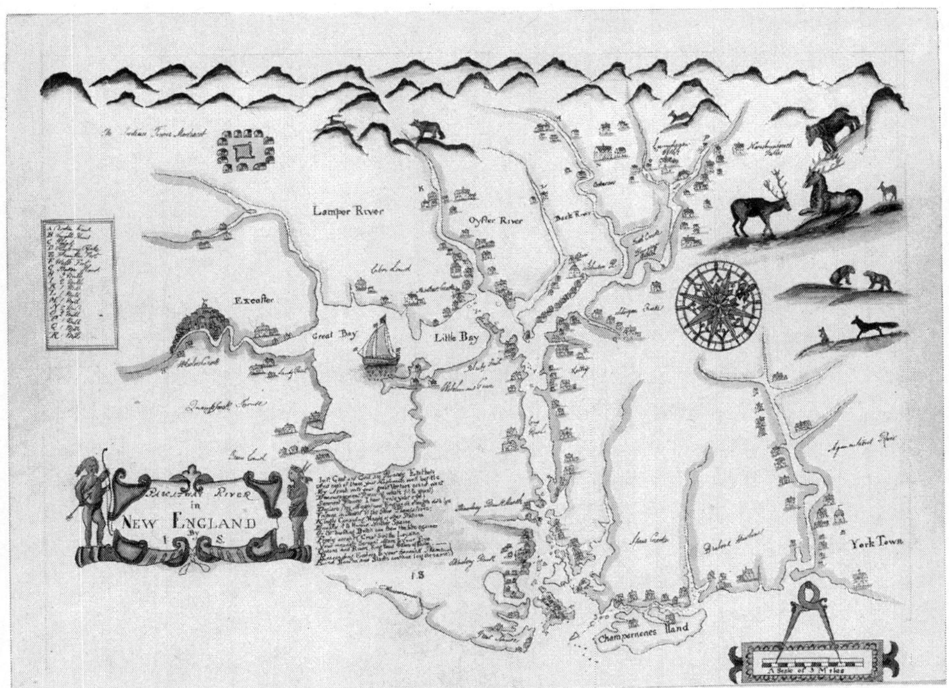

Figure 1.2. Fragment: *Pascatway River in New England*, John Scott, 1660–70. (Map courtesy of the Maine State Archives, Baxter Rare Maps Collection.)

into the ecosystem known today as the Piscataqua River (in Abenaki, Paskataquauke, pronounced peske-tegew); other iterations in English include Pascataquak and Piscataqua.[42] Today, the ecologically based name of the region is the Great Bay Estuary, one of the most complex and recessed estuaries on the entire Atlantic Ocean. The estuary was likely referred to as P8bagok (pronounced P-ohn-ba-gock), an Abenaki word to describe a bay, and when different parts of the vast ecosystem were being referenced attached to these place names (for instance, if talking about traveling the bay toward the Piscataqua River, it was probably connected as P8bagok Paskataquauk).

The river that connects the recessed Great Bay Estuary system to the Atlantic Ocean and the Gulf of Maine retains the name Piscataqua, and it is one of the fastest navigable tidal currents in the United States.[43] As the Piscataqua River runs inland, it splits at a neck of land called Dover Neck and/or Point today. To the south, it enters Little Bay, which tightens at a strait before opening into the Great Bay, the broad inner bay of the whole system. North of the split, the Piscataqua River meets two of the estuary's seven inflowing rivers. The first is the Salmon Falls River. This is, again, the erstwhile northern colonies boundary, and it is shown on this map extending toward the mountains, near the wild animals in the upper righthand corner (see fig. 1.2). Next, the Cochecho breaks off to the east. These rivers are followed by the other five inflow rivers, which, moving north to south around the bays of the system, are the Bellamy, Oyster, Lamper (Lamprey), Squamscott, and Winnicut Rivers. Several smaller tributaries also flow into the system.

The Great Bay Estuary/P8bagok contains a meshwork of jutting land features (necks, points, and peninsulas), inlets, harbors, confluxes, wetlands, waterfalls, and mixed forested uplands. Five different aquatic habitats form the estuary itself: eelgrass, mudflat, salt marsh, subtidal, and rocky intertidal.[44] The Great Bay Estuary/P8bagok hosts high biodiversity, including abundant marine and freshwater fish, shellfish, migrating waterfowl and mammals, and despite centuries of ecological degradation, its biodiversity remains significant enough that it is one of only twenty-nine National Estuarine Research Reserves in the United States.[45] Its complexity also makes Great Bay/P8bagok an important bellwether of anthropogenic ecosystem change.[46]

Pascatway River in New England was hand-painted on vellum between 1660 and 1670 by John Scott, an English adventurer, tradesmen, sometimes spy, and swindler who, for a time, was royal cartographer to King Charles II.[47] Like *The Province of Mayne*, northwest is at the top, and the size of figurative symbols convey their importance. Scott dedicated his map to King Charles II's brother, James, Duke of York, who was interested in colonies.[48] Scott left off Puritan Massachusetts Bay, even though they ostensibly governed this place at the time. In making it for the king and his brother, leaving off the powerful Puritan colony was probably a way to curry some personal favor. After all, Massachusetts Bay harbored two of the regicides who had executed Charles II and James's father, King Charles I.[49] Perhaps Scott meant to remind the royals that there were New England colonies who harbored more loyalist sentiments.

Boston has been a dominant political force in New England since its founding in 1630, and Massachusetts Bay history has often been a proxy for New England history. But not all New England colonies were Puritan. *The Province of Mayne* showed us that Massachusetts Bay was calculating and set on absorbing dissenting rival colonies. *Pascatway in New England* hints at lingering tensions in provincial governance and highlights that there were places where the outcome of colonialism was not foretold by Puritan Boston. Looking deeper into the nested layers of the colonial project in this contested frontier region offers new opportunities to understand that not all of early New England experienced the socioecological shock of colonialism in the same ways; there were multiple lived experiences. The Great Bay Estuary/P8bagok, with its distinctively sensitive ecology and early colonial frontier status, offers us a kind of "laboratory" to investigate and bring forward untold stories of early colonialism embedded in place here and to consider colonialism's lasting legacies today.

GREAT BAY'S EARLY COLONIAL VALUE

Early colonial cartographers did not have Google Maps. Even the simplest house lot sketch required physical work (walking property lines to estimate the extent of land), skill (use of a compass; basic reading, writing and math; drawing identifiable geographic and human-made features), and research (understanding past ownership and usage). It involved marshaling resources and it took time.[50] Time was invested in this map because the seventeenth-century Great Bay Estuary had critical value to the colonial enterprise in New England.

Scott's map situates the major water features that form Great Bay/P8bagok with fair accuracy. The estuaries' water resources were the initial draw for the English. The Laconia Company sent people "for the purpose of fishing, and of trading with the natives."[51] Early settlers reported that the head of tide at all of Great Bay Estuary/P8bagok's seven major freshwater rivers were so crowded with alewives and shad during spawning season that one could walk across them.[52] Other fish reported by colonists include salmon, cod, haddock, bass, mackerel, bluefish, herring, sturgeon, and pollock.[53]

The first permanent colonial investment in this area is debated, but one of the leading contenders is at Dover Neck, where Edward Hilton established a cod fishing station perhaps as early as 1623.[54] Both Edward and his brother William were members of London's Fishmonger's Guild, and William joined him in New Hampshire within a few years. This neck of land is bordered by the Bellamy River to the west and the Piscataqua to the east. Although it was long known as Wecannacohunt or Wecohamet, colonial occupation saw it re-inscribed as Hilton's Point.[55] Today it is called Dover Neck and/or Point. The Hiltons focused on fishing and trade and did little to improve or modify their tract of land, and they moved off of the point by 1633.[56]

The Great Bay Estuary/P8bagok's prolific environment offered an array of other marketable species that also played important ecological roles. Shell-fish in dense beds rapidly filtered a multitude of organisms, some potentially hazardous, from the estuary's brackish water. The most important species filling this critical role were the eastern oyster and softshell clam.[57] Wading birds and diving ducks fed in the estuary's plentiful eelgrass beds and salt marshes. Its large bays offered safe inlets for large flocks of migrating birds, including eider ducks that produce valuable down. English colonists noted remarkably dense migratory flights in the seventeenth century. Edge zones, particularly the large salt marsh fringing the Great Bay Estuary, host deer, mink, beaver, and otter. English colonists turned most everything harvestable into commodities: shellfish for food, eider ducks were sold for down, and mammals for hides and fur; salt marsh grasses were harvested for hay; and clay from mudflats was extracted for bricks.[58]

On *Pascatway*, Scott shows houses and settlements following the waterways, dispersed clusters of large and small English-style houses, white with red roofs (see fig. 1.2). "Excetter" (Exeter, New Hampshire), a town settled by refugees from Puritan persecution, appears larger and more tightly settled than other villages, even more so than "Strawbery Banke," which in 1653 had been incorporated as Portsmouth, named after John Mason's hometown. One more large "towne" on this map is found in the upper left-hand corner—here is an "Indian towne" by the Lamper (Lamprey) River near distant mountains.

Unlike *The Province of Mayne*, where Indigenous people are absent, the Scott map openly acknowledges a presence, although he makes it a peripheral one. This "towne" is depicted on the fringe of English settlement, along with wild elements such as wolf, bear, and deer (see fig. 1.2). A vague mountainous wilderness lies beyond. This illustrates the important point raised before about how little early English colonists knew about the region's landscapes. What the English knew about the interior, particularly in winter, likely came from Native peoples themselves or from colonial trappers and hunters who had ventured inland and spent time with them. Beyond the Great Bay's waterways, English power dropped off quickly. This ecosystem was a frontier to the continental interior and, at the time, a frontier zone between French Quebec to the north and English Boston to the south. Both its English and Indigenous inhabitants would be drawn in unwelcome ways into conflicts that broke out between the French and English colonial powers.

With this "Indian towne" placed far from any colonial structures, this map creates an impression that colonial structures and Native villages did not overlap, mapping the dendritic spread of colonial settlement along the estuary's rivers a rather neutral matter. As we explore fragments that people living in this ecosystem left behind in subsequent chapters, we will see it is clear that colonial and Native villages did indeed overlap. This was a tidy colonial mapping maneuver that obscures much more complex realities on the shores of Great Bay/P8bagok's waterways. In addition to this "towne," Indigenous people appear on the Scott map as decorative elements flanking the colorful map title, with stylized colonial representations of an Abenaki male and female (see fig. 1.2). This map acknowledges Indigenous presence yet minimizes it. The map pushes (literally and conceptually) to the side the fact Abenaki/Pennacook peoples and their knowledge had been emplaced here for thousands of years.

Although fishing was the initial draw of colonists to Great Bay/P8bagok, there is no indication of fish or fisheries on this map. As noted, this Scott map would not have been made if there were not some critically valuable colonial resources here. In the early 1600s, the estuary's lands were thickly forested with towering coniferous and deciduous trees.[59] On the far left of the map, a red outlined rectangular box is a letter key identifying the locations of fifteen water-powered sawmills throughout the network of rivers. Great Bay/P8bagok had various natural resources that attracted English colonists, but its forests held a special place as valuable sources of lumber.

GREAT BAY'S FORESTS

By the seventeenth century, England was already largely deforested due to centuries of demand for wood as fuel, clearing for pasture lands, and for wood products such as construction lumber for buildings and ships.[60] In England, the use of water- and wind-powered mills was restricted to slow deforestation as well as to ensure manual sawyers (woodcutters) would not lose their jobs to mechanization. The rich forests of Great Bay Estuary/P8bagok stood in stark contrast to the cleared landscapes English colonists had come from; finding themselves here in a place with lush forests and without regulations, lumber was an appealing extraction opportunity.[61] In addition to the forests, Great Bay's tidal rivers, each with multiple waterfalls, made lumbering even more appealing and accessible, as the falls offered significant power sources for tidal river mills to process, cut, and export lumber.

Correspondences among merchant patentees of the Piscataway Grant place the construction of the earliest water-powered sawmill around 1634 along the Newichawannock River, today's Salmon Falls River.[62] Between that first mill and Scott's map, fifteen water-powered sawmills had been constructed along the estuary's tributaries; by 1705, the number topped seventy.[63] Many early colonial dams were placed near the most powerful waterfalls in the ecosystem, the falls at the head of tide (the farthest point upstream where a river is affected by tidal fluctuations). Today, we know that these dams at the head of tide were particularly damaging because they stopped the ebb and flow between the freshwater rivers and the estuary's brackish tidal water, meaning that fish who migrate between fresh and salt water could not complete their life cycles. So, not only did colonial dams precipitate the removal of Great Bay/P8bagok's forests, they dramatically impacted fish as well.[64]

Shipbuilding was a driving force behind the estuary's lumber activity.[65] Again, over the course of the 1600s, global markets and trade systems expanded, and, with this, competition increased and there were frequent wars among European colonial powers. The towering white pines of Great Bay Estuary/P8bagok's forests were a key source for ship masts and were vital to keeping English Royal Navy warships afloat. The eastern white pine of precolonial New England could exceed 220 feet in height,[66] and its tall, straight trunks made exceptionally strong masts without having to splice spars. In 1681, the Piscataqua region's economy was described as wholly based "in masts, planks, boards and staves. . . . Ships usually come empty to fill with lumber."[67]

As the colonial lumber industry grew, moving large bulky materials through the estuary's shallow tidal landscape to wharfs where larger seafaring vessels could dock and load with exports posed logistical challenges. On Scott's *Pascatway River in New England* map there is only one boat depicted sailing in the inner bay of the ecosystem (see fig. 1.2). This is neither a fishing boat nor a seafaring trade boat; rather, it is a specialized flat-bottomed boat called a gundalow, which colonists developed in the mid-1600s specifically to maneuver in shallow water, "take the ground" at low tide, and refloat heavy loads with the incoming tide.[68] Gundalows capitalized on the region's strong tides to move the ever-more commodified natural resource base of Great Bay Estuary/P8bagok in and out.

Lumbering for masts was highly destructive because removing large white pines required cutting down a host of smaller trees to cushion the giant's fall. Logging mast trees created substantial collateral damage.[69] Other trees found in the ecosystem's diverse forests, including oak, cedar, chestnut, pitch pines, and hemlock, also had uses in shipbuilding as well as other productive activities. House frames, clapboards, shingles, barrel staves, tools and utensils, furniture, wagons, and even firewood went to West Indies sugar colonies such as Barbados and Jamaica. Occasionally, recipients complained about the quality of these products.[70] And forests here faced other pressures beyond commercial lumbering. To plant themselves and reproduce an English way of living, colonial settlements needed to clear land to farm and pasture livestock. Woodfires heated homes, cooked meals, and fired kilns. Wood made colonization possible.

Most English settler colonialists were unrepentant about the extreme damage their industries and extraction practices were causing to forests. Most saw "new" England's natural resources as boundless and rightfully *theirs*. However, this frustrated the Crown, who felt they were not getting their due from the resources of the colonies. The strategic importance of New Hampshire's forests made protecting valuable timber from poaching a matter of national security that required special scrutiny. The first White Pine Act was established by royal decree in Massachusetts in 1691. All timber trees on Crown lands "over two ft in diameter 12 inches from the ground were reserved for the use of the Royal Navy."[71] This brings us to another colonial map, *A Survey of Piscataqua Riv*, by Jonathan Bridger about 1700 (fig. 1.3). It was drawn to map timber resources of the Great Bay Estuary. Bridger,[72] was the first royal officer assigned to protect mast trees, and he drew *A Survey of Piscataqua Riv* as surveyor general of the King's Woods to map timber resources. Bridger and his two deputies had the authority to arrest and punish poachers. It was dangerous work and the surveyors' lives were frequently threatened by belligerent colonial woodcutters.

The contours of the Piscataqua River are executed with special care. Across the map, the land contains the names of types of forests found in those locations (see fig. 1.3). Mills and waterfalls are identified. In one spot, Bridger notes that "Great Masts floted down here," indicating that the pines in this area were particularly large, fine, and vital naval material—and that tidal rivers were essential to their harvest. An enigmatic comment appears on the right side of *Piscataqua Riv*: "A Large Swamp of White Pine Burnt by the Indians." By 1700, when he was making this map, there had been some violent clashes between English colonists and raids by Indigenous peoples (with their French allies) in the area that involved targeted burning of houses and infrastructure. No accounts indicated these raids burned huge swaths of forests, so this comment is confusing and misleading; where Bridger got this cryptic information and why he included it on this map is lost in history. In the long-term, despite decrees and the presence of royal surveyors, colonial

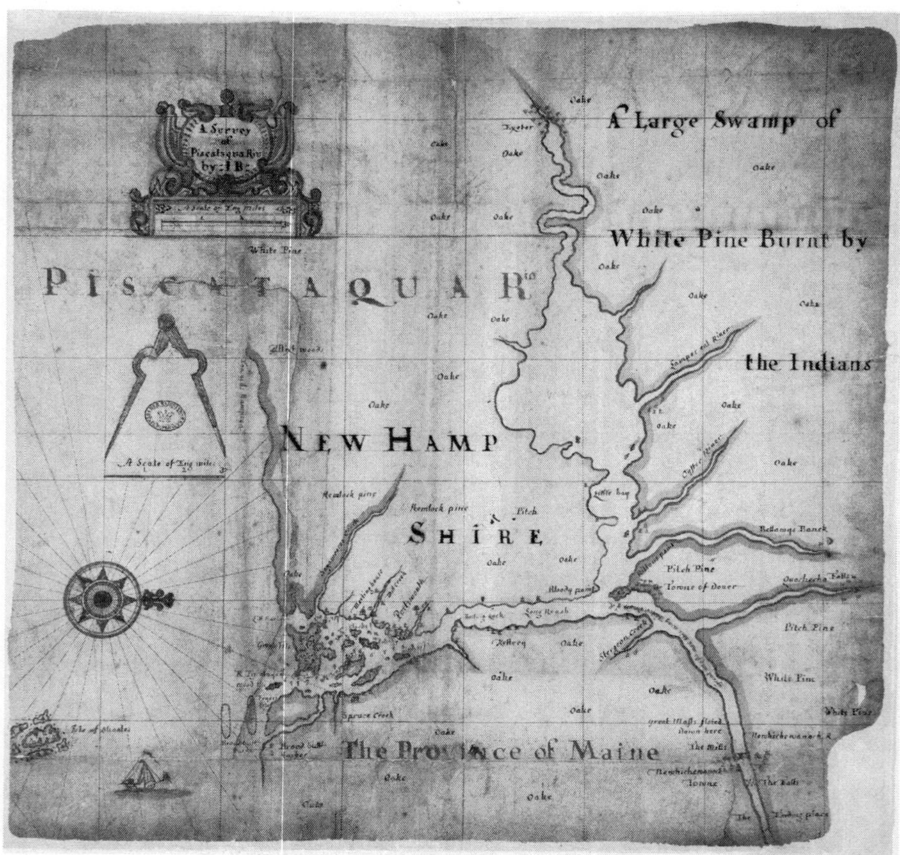

Figure 1.3. Fragment: *A Survey of Piscataqua Riv*, by Jonathan Bridger, surveyor of the King's Woods, 1700. (Courtesy of the National Archives of the UK, CO700/NEWHAMPSHIRE7.)

forest extraction continued largely unabated. Across New England, an estimated 55 percent to 80 percent of old-growth forests were cut down by the end of the eighteenth century.[73]

FINDING: FRAGMENTS FROM THE SHOCK OF COLONIALISM

In the introduction I suggest that it is useful to think about early global colonialism as socioecological shock. Every aspect of the Great Bay Estuary/P8bagok was affected by this shock. For thousands of years, Abenaki/Pennacook Indigenous communities mapped the Great Bay Estuary/P8bagok with

Place-Thought concepts that considered it and everything in it to be alive and sentient. They followed the rhythms of the ecosystem, planting and harvesting the estuary's natural resource base in times of abundance following seasonal rounds. But within decades of English arrival, almost every natural resource in this ecosystem had been transformed into a commodity. We have seen how English colonists mapped this transformation across the three colonial maps, from fish and farmland to forests.

Pascatway River in New England by Scott (see fig. 1.2) provides particularly valuable insight into how the colonial transformation of the Great Bay Estuary/P8bagok landscape was perceived and promoted by English colonists in the mid- to late seventeenth century. The English-style houses he maps spreading up the rivers are evidence of colonial permanence and prosperity. Carefully documenting the sawmills shows these were understood as important engines of that prosperity. Scott's map presents a somewhat sentimental idyll of prospering English settlement, industry, trade, and pastoralism. I emphasize in this chapter that colonial maps are important for what they tell us but also for what they do not. Scott's map does not tell us any stories about struggle and hardships that were undoubtably part of colonial life. Those stories do not fit under those red roofs on his tidy map. Nor are dynamic interactions and relationships with Indigenous peoples accurately captured by one "Indian towne" pushed off to the side. What stories, lived experiences, interactions, and impacts of global colonialism in this ecosystem are missing from accepted historical canon and how we remember this time? What is waiting to be recovered?

As explained in the introduction, I started GBAS with these questions at the forefront and a focus on the archaeological record and a material perspective to answer them. GBAS started by defining and then narrowing our research universe. The Great Bay Estuary/P8bagok drains over 2,400 square kilometers. It would be nearly impossible for one research group to survey this entire region. Time and labor are limiting realities—our field seasons run six to eight weeks and most of GBAS's team are volunteers. So we georectified Scott's *Pascatway* map (see fig. 1.2) by overlaying a scan of the historic map on corrected contemporary geospatial orientation and coordinates. This showed me where early colonial English structures were relative to the contemporary landscape. I removed all areas where modern land use/disturbances would make it impossible to find an intact site.

Next, we identified a set of environmental and spatial parameters relevant to colonial era occupation (historic land cover, soil type, temperature, topographic roughness, aspect, distance to fresh water, distance to shellfish beds, distance to river mouths, and distance to ports) and input them into an ecological habitat suitability model, maximum entropy modeling.[74] Working with presence-only datasets, the model accepts any number of environmental and spatial parameters that are relevant to habitat suitability, and so we used it to identify areas with high probability for finding early colonial sites. A very large research universe remained, so we started where GBAS's team had the strongest community and landowner contacts, as it is ultimately up to landowners to let archaeologists onto their land. We talked to community members and knowledge keepers in towns and in historic societies. We knocked on landowners' doors when we thought there was a high probability for a seventeenth-century site on their property. For each potential survey target, GBAS's community historian Diane Fiske went deep into the archives to chase down deeds reconstructing land transfers back in time to try to confirm that the land traced back to seventeenth-century residents.[75]

In all, we surveyed seventeen different early colonial archaeological targets. Some were quick surveys as land conditions made it clear we would not find anything. Others were more intensive. Today, most undeveloped land across the estuary hosts regrown forests, meadows, and hay fields with little to no surface visibility. This means that to determine whether an archaeologically significant site is present, we have to conduct systematic shovel test surveys to assess what cultural remains might be below the surface.[76] Shovel testing starts with laying out a grid across a determined area of interest. Next, shovel test teams are evenly spaced in the transects (spacing depends on how much area to test) (fig. 1.4). Teams use shovels to dig 50 × 50 centimeter square holes in the ground, screen the dirt for artifacts, collect the artifacts, and fill the holes

Figure 1.4. Finding: GBAS volunteers laying out shovel test transects and a dug and empty shovel test (before it is backfilled) along the Great Bay Estuary.

back in until all transects are completed (see fig. 1.4). After the grid is tested, the locations of all shovel tests that produced artifacts are mapped to determine whether there is enough cultural material present to conduct expanded archaeological excavation. Excavation involves opening larger areas, working in 1 × 1 meter square units, and digging slowly, typically by hand with a trowel, so artifacts and features can be found in situ (in their original place).

Of the seventeen early colonial sites that we tested, we conducted expanded excavations at five. One site proved to be an incredibly well-preserved early English colonial homestead site. We did extensive excavation there, the results of which are featured in subsequent chapters. We also conducted a shovel test survey across the landscape surrounding this colonial homestead to determine what other activities and/or structures might have been associated with it in the 1600s. In doing this, we found a site that was not on Scott's map, one we did not anticipate finding. We continue to work at this unexpected site. Material fragments found there are presented in the next chapter. Even though we found this site last, it is the first one we will visit. I present it first because this site has pushed us to reframe how we think about GBAS and our findings. Let us see why.

Figure 2.1. Fragment: Worlds collide. A broken, unfinished arrowhead recovered from a seventeenth-century Abenaki/Pennacook site on the Oyster River. It is made of English flint, a material brought to this river's shores during colonialism.

2

FRAGMENTS FROM BECOMING

The shorthand "Old World" and "New World" continues to circulate to distinguish Europe and the Americas. Europeans first developed this particular dichotomy to reflect what they knew about world geography before 1492 and the large, utterly perplexing landmass they found that blocked their westward way to Asia. While this divide may have emerged out of European ignorance, it became helpful in reinforcing ideas of European entitlement and colonialism as a preordained process whereby an "Old" world, one with real history, improved a "New" one lacking such depth and sophistication.[1] Of course, the "New" world was hardly new, having been peopled some fifteen to twenty thousand years ago.[2] Like Europe, its Indigenous inhabitants lived in an "Old" world ripe with history and traditions.[3] However, this shorthand divide has sticking power that limits a more expansive view of colonial encounter, one that lets us really grapple with global colonialism as a dynamic, nonlinear, and downright messy process.[4]

European global colonialism created novel situations, opportunities, and dilemmas as people from very different cultures, often with minimal understanding and erroneous assumptions about each other, negotiated new relationships, navigated an influx of foreign objects, and tried to traverse alien systems of value, economic and otherwise.[5] For European colonists and Indigenous peoples alike, colonial encounters were relational and intimate experiences that created a "third space," a place of expression where dialogues and negotiations of difference occurred.[6] In this third space, people had to actively navigate impossible things every single day, including the especially complex "need to register both sameness and difference, of being like and of being Other."[7] Indigenous peoples and colonial Europeans both had to figure out how to be themselves while also becoming what had never existed before the two old worlds collided: New World people.[8]

Complicated, extended processes of identity formation—of becoming New World people—did not alter peoples' humanity of who they were before, but it did alter their frames of reference.[9] Whether they knew it or not, New World people were living through threshold change, a new era where values, identity, and rules were in flux. Today, we look back on this threshold and see it as a clear demarcation between very different societies, but in the lived experience of encounter, exactly what becoming New World people meant was not so clearly demarcated. Instead, peoples, places, and things were drawn into all kinds of entanglements where difference, contradiction, and ambivalence, but also creativity and adaptation, swirled.

And this is where we meet the fragment that starts this chapter, in the swirl of encounter, of the third space, in the process of becoming (fig. 2.1). This unfinished stone tool was on its way to becoming an arrowhead when it broke. You can see little ridges on the bottom edges, scars from its maker trying to make the side notches of an arrowhead. Even the most skilled stone tool maker (called a knapper) can face unexpected issues that compromise the final product. This stone appears to have snapped, likely on a natural weak spot in the stone. If completed, the arrowhead would have been hafted to a wood arrow shaft and used with a bow, likely for hunting, a technology used across New England for thousands of years.

This broken, unfinished arrowhead was recovered at an archaeological site GBAS found on the Oyster River in the Great Bay Estuary/P8bagok. This particular fragment came from a hearth dating to the seventeenth century. Its maker was crafting something Abenaki/Pennacook peoples had a long history with; however, the material of this arrowhead was shockingly new—English flint. This material fragment could not have existed until the third space of colonial encounter became a portal of material exchange in this region. Like this stone tool, many of the entanglements of colonial encounter were mediated through material things given the early phases of global colonialism witnessed a near-constant influx of foreign goods being acquired and exchanged, valued and destroyed, produced and consumed. Objects had important social lives in colonial encounter.[10]

The Abenaki/Pennacook person who shaped this stone on the shores of the Great Bay Estuary/P8bagok was in the process of becoming a New World person but also was anchored to a place where generations of ancestors had lived as far back as circa AD 1200, a precontact time period designated by archaeologists as the Late Woodland period. In this chapter, I frame out briefly the Northeast's precontact setting and Great Bay/P8bagok's particular deep-time trajectory. This sets us up to explore GBAS's important findings from this significant site. This archaeological site is so important because it is a precontact site that became a postcontact site, spanning over the threshold of colonial encounter. This place was occupied up to and through much of the seventeenth century, and so this stone tool and other material fragments we will meet are from the context of colonial encounter. This means that they have much to tell us about what it was like to live through the process of becoming New World people.

A BRIEF PRECONTACT CHRONOLOGY

Before explorers imposed the concept of "New England" on maps to make it inviting to colonists, the Northeast was the homelands for an array of Indigenous communities who are culturally diverse but who also share in a spectrum of eastern Algonquian languages and so maintained close connections across vast spaces. As introduced previously, the Indigenous peoples who had stewarded the Northeast's vast lands and waters for millennia knew it as N'dakinna (and continue to know it today) as their home—"our land," the place "to which we belong," understanding themselves and their ancestors as the people who have always inhabited this place. Across the Northeast, Indigenous communities have their own versions of their creation histories, and they tend to share two key features. One, their peoples' origin was in place; they did not migrate here from elsewhere. Two, this origin occurred at a time beyond memory and recordable time.

This visceral sense of belonging instills a shared sense of connection that transcends boundaries between human and nonhuman elements of deep homelands. Across the Northeast, communities share concepts of the universe and everything within it as filled with an animating spirit called *manit* (also *mantu, manitou, mntu).*[11] Since everything is filled with animating spirit, interactions between any elements, not just between humans, are relationships. This foundational concept is embedded in the phrase "all my relations," which is pervasive across the regional languages of those who share in the homelands of N'dakinna.[12] For some Native peoples, signifying their origins and tracking temporal trajectories of change can feel like a denial of their way of knowing their own origins, betraying their place in and relations with their homeland. These ways of knowing and experiencing time are valid and valuable. While gaps cannot be fully reconciled, limitations are important to acknowledge, as we saw when comparing European mapmaking and Place-Thought systems that create and record spatial knowledge.

To explain what life was like before colonialism washed onshore, I, as a Western-situated and trained archaeologist, refer to this time as precontact and rely on Western-calendric dates.[13] Archaeologists break the precontact Northeast down into three major periods: Paleo-Indian, Archaic, and Woodland (further broken down into Early/Middle/Late divisions).[14] These periods are useful for providing broad brushstrokes for the patterns of precontact life in the region, but each period contained wide-ranging variations as local communities, responding to specific circumstances, made their own social and economic decisions.

Paleo-Indian Period

From the Western-scientific perspective, the first humans are documented as coming to the Northeast during the Late Pleistocene, around thirteen thousand years ago, when the great Laurentian ice sheet covering the entire Northeast had retreated enough for people to venture into and then inhabit the area. This is what archaeologists call the Paleo-Indian period, which dates from circa 11000 to 8000 BC, or thirteen thousand to ten thousand years ago. As the ice melted in stages, it sculpted regional topography. A variety of glacial landforms were left in its wake, including terminal moraines, recessional moraines, drumlins, eskers, kames, and glacial outwash plains. During the Late Pleistocene's glacial retreat, the region looked like an Arctic landscape. Large glacial lakes and rivers, fringed by patches of conifers, dotted wide expanses of open grassland.[15]

Across North America, Paleo-Indians' primary subsistence focus was hunting big game. People lived in small groups that moved frequently to follow mammoth, mastodon, and caribou herds. In New England, caribou was the focus.[16] Caribou migrate seasonally, and Paleo-Indian peoples moved with agility to exploit this important food source. Most Paleo-Indian sites in New England reflect seasonal hunting occupation by small, mobile family bands; however, some sites seem to be the result of larger communal hunting gatherings as well.[17] Paleo-Indians' flexible, sophisticated organizational strategy was eminently suitable for occupying the region's harsh postglacial landscape.

Archaic Period

The Archaic period dates from circa 8000 to 1000 BC or ten thousand years ago to three thousand years ago. Its start is marked by the start of the Holocene, the geologic epoch we live in today. The Holocene began when large Pleistocene mammals became extinct or, like caribou, retreated north with the glaciers as modern landscapes emerged. Loss of these megafauna herds meant that inhabitants of the Northeast could no longer rely so much on one food resource (caribou) that hunters could follow. Instead, groups adopted subsistence practices that took advantage of a range of new opportunities.[18] Expanding mixed deciduous forests harbored a greater diversity of animal and plant species. Communities developed broad, generalized hunting-gathering-fishing economies with assorted strategies to harvest, consume, and conserve an array of seasonal food resources, including small and large wild game, fish, shellfish, nuts, berries, and aquatic tubers.

Evidence indicates that regional communities actively consumed marine species by the Middle Archaic period (ca. 6000 to 3000 BC). Fishing continued through the Late Archaic (ca. 3000 to 1000 BC) and Woodland periods (ca. 1000 BC to European contact at ca. AD 1500–1600).[19] Faunal remains from precontact archaeological sites demonstrate that Indigenous populations routinely harvested a diverse mix of marine mammals, fish, shellfish, and seabirds during all seasons.[20] Anadromous fish, those migrating upriver to spawn, were particularly important, as multitudes could be procured near estuaries and in rivers in seasonally predictable patterns. Recent research has shown that shellfish contributed substantial amounts of meat protein to Indigenous diets by the Late Archaic period, in some places, possibly becoming a staple food in the Woodland period.[21] As Holocene forests developed more hardwood and nut-bearing trees, nuts became a more common food source during the Archaic period.

Woodland Period

The Woodland period lasted from circa 1000 BC to European contact at circa AD 1500–1600 (or three thousand to five hundred/four hundred years ago). Archaeologists use the appearance of pottery as the chronological marker between the Woodland and Archaic periods. While this technological development is used to break the time periods, there was not a stark break in lifeways signaling the end of the Archaic (Late Archaic) and the start of the Woodland period (Early Woodland). The technological innovation of ceramics was connected to already evolving subsistence practices, including an increased use of nuts and starchy seeds. Ceramics allowed people to extract oils by simmering them in pots over fires.

Over the course of the Woodland period, local resource exploitation intensified and diversified to include both wild and domesticated foods. Communities engaged in more specialized subsistence strategies that led to population growth and more sedentary lifeways. While general trends are understood, subsistence and settlement patterns of the Woodland period pose complicated questions that archaeologists have not yet fully answered. The degree of sedentism (frequency of movement, length of stay in one place) in Woodland sites remains unclear. The importance of seafood versus terrestrial foods is also not entirely clear. Heated debates churn on the how much farming was actually done in regional landscapes and the importance of domesticated crops in diets.[22]

Maize was introduced to the Northeast around AD 800, toward the later part of the Woodland period.[23] Two hundred years later, corn-bean-squash horticulture had become part of Indigenous subsistence practices in southern parts of the region. Although there is no consensus on how significant farming was, more specialized, mixed hunter-gatherer-fisher-horticulturalist economies did develop in southern New England after domesticated crops were introduced. Growing seasons farther north in New England were short, limiting the growing of Indigenous crops; here communities persisted in hunting-gathering-fishing practices with minimal influence from horticulture.[24] Even so, more specialized resource exploitation, such as shellfish harvesting, seems to have expanded over the course of the Woodland period.[25]

Farther inland to the west in what is today New York, there was large-scale adoption of agriculture by the Iroquois during the Late Woodland period (ca. AD 1000–1500/1600) and this led to increased sedentism, population increase, a rise in conflict, and the construction of fortified villages.[26] Archaeology in southern New England has not found the same kind of evidence of large village settlements and intensive agriculture.[27] Some suggest that this is because horticulture was practiced on a smaller scale and incorporated into existing seasonal rounds, and that the importance of horticulture observed by Europeans developed postcontact.[28] Others argue that large village sites may have been obscured by early colonial settlements built on or near them, or they may lie undiscovered below alluvial sediments.[29] This perspective points to the incorporation of maize into some regional Indigenous communities' calendars. Creation myths also support early European explorers' observations of deeply ingrained Indigenous horticulture, suggesting corn was a significant food resource in parts of New England before contact.[30]

LOCAL GREAT BAY/P8BAGOK PRECONTACT TRENDS

There has been limited archaeological work in Great Bay/P8bagok. A few Paleo-Indian sites have been recorded, but the record really starts with Archaic precontact sites, which are the most frequently discovered.[31] Known Archaic sites seem to cluster along freshwater tributaries and in inland and upland locations. The Middle Archaic (6000–3000 BC) is well represented. Notable sites lie at the head of falls of Great Bay Estuary tributaries, prime spots to capture spawning anadromous fish, which were widely exploited during this period.[32]

Woodland period sites (ca. 1000 BC to AD 1500/1600) have been found less frequently. The best known of those that have been found are located on Great Bay and Little Bay. Some have shell middens, which are shell trash heaps left over from harvesting shellfish.[33] A compact cluster of Woodland period sites is found along Furber Strait, connecting Little Bay to Great Bay, and inland along Great Bay. Interestingly, the largest shellfish beds in the estuary today correlate spatially with this cluster of sites, indicating that the sites were well positioned long ago vis-à-vis the bays' distinctive natural resource base.

Compared with Archaic sites, the lower number of Woodland sites could reflect decreased occupation during this period. However, it is important to consider that this reflects other factors. It likely reflects, in part, damage from substantial colonial and postcolonial settlements built to take advantage of the same landscape features Indigenous Woodland people valued. Another factor is the relatively limited archaeological research in the area. Local amateur collectors recorded most of the precontact sites in the Great Bay Estuary.[34] They focused largely on finding attractive stone tools, artifacts that were more common in the Archaic period, and they may have overlooked Woodland period ceramics.[35] Our GBAS survey for postcontact, early seventeenth-century English colonial sites discovered a substantial Indigenous occupation site dating from circa AD 1250 to 1680 (the later part of the Woodland period into early contact). This suggests that colocation, limited fieldwork in the area, and other factors likely explain the paucity of Woodland sites, rather than reduced Indigenous use of the Great Bay's prolific ecosystem.

FINDING: UNEXPECTED FIELD SURVEY OUTCOMES

The broken arrowhead of English flint that opens the chapter was recovered at the archaeological site on the Oyster River that we unexpectedly found in a shovel test survey as part of GBAS (see fig. 2.1). As I have explained, our primary focus in GBAS was surveying for English colonial sites from the seventeenth and early eighteenth century and conducting archaeological excavations when we found potential to recover important materials. One early colonial homestead, known as the Burnham garrison, proved to be especially well preserved, and we conducted extensive excavations there. I explore those in the next chapter. Given the significant finds from our dig at this colonial homestead and that GBAS archival research indicated there were various structures/outbuildings and activities associated with this homestead, we expanded our survey far beyond the location of the colonial stone house foundations.

Located on the south side of the Oyster River, the seventeenth-century English colonial homestead, known as the Burnham garrison, was built on a large rock outcrop set back from the river about three-quarters of a mile. Looking westward from the outcrop, a creek flows quite close to it and this creek flows into the Oyster River. On the other side of this creek, there is a large flat expanse of meadow. This meadow is bounded on its other side by a small inlet to the Oyster River. This meadow is quite large, covering about twenty acres. We started with a systematic walkover of this field looking for obvious surface indications of an early colonial site, such as a cellar hole or other depressions or stone features. We found none.

The size of this field was daunting. This was the summer of 2020 and COVID had turned everything upside down, including our research plans for that summer season. Normally, GBAS has several community volunteers, team members, and students participating in fieldwork. This summer, we were only authorized for me and two core community team members to work together.[36] Shovel testing was explained briefly in the last chapter; doing this survey testing is physically hard work and time-consuming. We knew this field had to be surveyed, and so we got to it the best we could. Recognizing that we had to prioritize our limited crew's time, we started close to the Oyster River and tested all along the larger creek that flowed into it. Working outward from the outcrop the Burnham homestead was on, this larger creek closer to the site seemed the logical place for associated activities. All of these shovel tests were empty.[37]

After seven weeks of empty shovel tests, we were nearly ready to give up. For the last planned week of testing, we decided to put in a few shovel tests along the smaller inlet on the farther side of the meadow. We decided to do this just to cover our bases, not expecting any specific outcomes. On what we had decided would be our last shovel test of that survey and the season, we found one small chip of flint, its distinctive caramel color indicating it was French in origin (fig. 2.2). Since we were looking for English colonial materials, this French flint was most certainly an intriguing find.

This one little artifact foretold more than we could have imagined; it was the first clue to the threshold spanning Late Woodland through colonial encounter site underfoot. After finding the chip, we realized that the topography got subtly flatter as we approached the smaller inlet. We also realized that this flatter topography separated the inlet from a small wetland area on this meadow. In subsequent seasons, GBAS has systematically shovel test surveyed this entire flattened area, expanding testing until we stopped recovering cultural materials.

After we determined the density and distribution of cultural materials

Figure 2.2. Finding: Flint chip from one of the last planned shovel tests. The flint originated in France.

found from our shovel testing, we opened broad coverage excavations. Together, this has revealed a substantial Abenaki/Pennacook Indigenous occupation site with an interesting mix of activities and artifacts. This place is remarkable, but not because it was unique. There were likely many significant places Indigenous peoples lived, planted fields, and harvested abundant resources. What is remarkable is that we found it, because few precontact sites have been found in this ecosystem due to relatively limited archaeological work and ongoing postcontact site destruction by land use change, modern

Figure 2.3. Finding: Paul and Denise Pouliot, the Sag8mo (Head Male Speaker/Grand Chief) and Sag8moskwa (Head Female Speaker) of the Cowasuck Band of the Pennacook-Abenaki People blessing the opening of GBAS fieldwork.

development, and as we will see at the end of the book, increasing impacts from climate change. These things mean it is possible that few other sites like this will be found, making what this site tells us that much more important.[38]

It is also remarkable because we were surveying that field to find English colonial buildings, but GBAS's Indigenous collaborators, Paul and Denise Pouliot, the Sag8mo (Head Male Speaker/Grand Chief) and the Sag8moskwa (Head Female Speaker) of the Cowasuck Band of the Pennacook-Abenaki People, told us before we started that we should expect to find an Indigenous site in that meadow. Even though collaboration with these regional Indigenous leaders and knowledge keepers had been ongoing and built into GBAS from the start, when they told us this, I was skeptical. When we found the very kind of site they had told us we should expect in this meadow, I realized that as much as I thought I was a collaborative archaeologist, I still had work to do to check my internal biases as a Western-trained social scientist about where knowledge comes from and what constitutes our research frames. Today, the leaders of the Cowasuck Band and I copresent on this site, both to share its amazing story but also to show others how scientific/academic research must, and can, grow and become something more inclusive and more meaningful. Moreover, no fieldwork occurs in this meadow before opening blessing ceremonies are conducted (fig. 2.3).

A LOCAL DEEP TIME INDIGENOUS PLACE

The picture of this site emerging from our work is that this was a place of growing crops, harvesting seasonally available wild foods, processing and cooking these foods, sharing meals, ceremony, and reinforcing community. A suite of eight accelerator mass spectrometry (AMS) radiocarbon dates shows that the site was established as early as AD 1254 and occupied continuously through 1680.[39] Together, the radiocarbon dates demonstrate that Abenaki/Pennacook peoples lived in this place for centuries before contact and that it remained occupied through the threshold change of colonial encounter. Here, in this meadow along the Oyster River, they lived through what it meant to become New World people.

We know from postholes found in our excavations—stains left behind by wood posts placed in the ground—that different structures designed for a variety of activities were erected in this place. In addition to postholes, other larger soil stains and concentrations of cultural artifacts tell us there were cooking hearths, food-processing pits, and tool-making workplaces distributed across the site here. Figure 2.4 shows remnants of one hearth we found left behind from life at this site.

In these hearths and other features, inhabitants processed and cooked

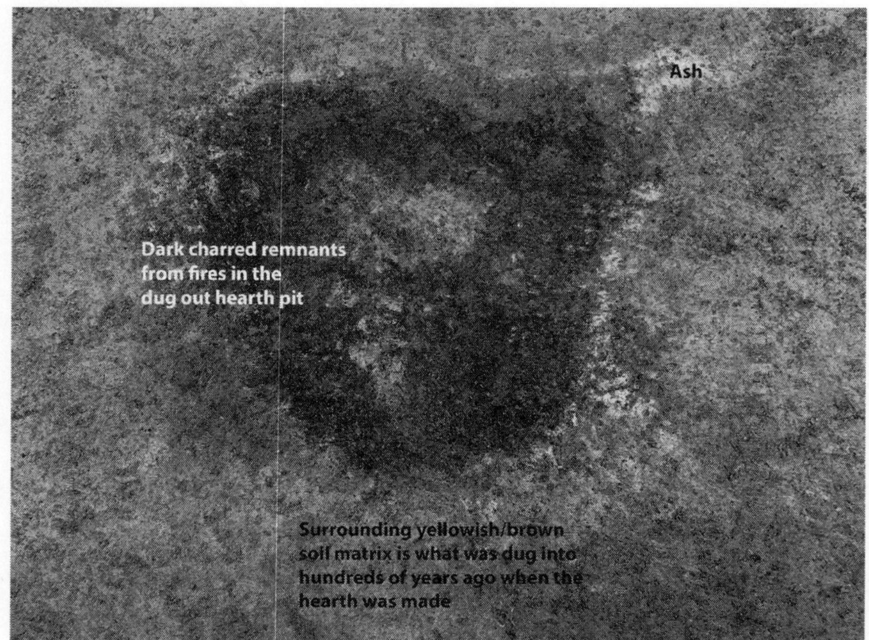

Figure 2.4. Fragment: Looking down at a plan view of a hearth uncovered at the site (this may have had some kind of trifold structure above it for roasting/processing food.) These kinds of nonmovable remnants of past life are what archaeologists call features (this was Feature 4 during GBAS digs here). This feature is about three feet side to side.

Indigenous domesticated maize (*Zea mays*), beans (*Phaseolus vulgaris*), and squash (*Cucurbita* sp.).[40] These crops are the three sisters, the hallmark of precontact Indigenous horticulture across North America.[41] The site's radiocarbon dates include dates from carbonized beans and squash and features containing maize, demonstrating ancestral Abenaki/Pennacook peoples living here practiced maize-bean-squash intercropping starting circa AD 1250, well before colonial contact. Where crops could be grown in the Northeast, this style of horticulture became widely practiced after AD 1300.[42] The radiocarbon dates from this village site align well with this time frame. The evidence of domesticated crops demonstrates that beans, maize, and squash were clearly part of the diet of Abenaki/Pennacook peoples living in the Great Bay Estuary during the later part of the Woodland period.

While domesticated crops were present, we found them alongside a rich array of wild, locally available plants that were significant in traditional foodways and medicinal practices. These included acorns (*Quercus* sp.) and hickory nuts (*Carya* sp.). These nuts offer an important source of protein, carbohydrates, healthy fats, and vitamins. A diverse mix of fleshy fruit seeds was also recovered, including barberry (*Berberis* sp.), raspberry (*Rubus* sp.), strawberry (*Fragaria* sp.), huckleberry (*Gaylussica* sp.), groundcherry (*Physalis* sp.), and blueberry (*Vaccinium* sp.). These could have been consumed fresh or dried and stored. We also found sumac (*Rhus* sp.), which could be eaten but has a wide range of medicinal uses, especially related to stomach pain, and was used across the homelands known as "our land," N'dakinna, in medicinal practices. Together, this shows local Abenaki/Pennacook peoples integrated horticultural products into long-established subsistence traditions that aligned with the natural rhythms of this ecosystem and its wild resources.

Additionally, Abenaki/Pennacook peoples living here hunted and harvested a robust suite of animal resources, both terrestrial and marine, available in the estuarine ecosystem. Moose, oyster, fish, and turtle remains were recovered from many places spanning the extent of the site. In addition to discarded animal parts, some of the hearths we found produced greasy soil, likely produced from fat lipids seeping into them during the processing of fatty meats. The Great Bay Estuary/P8bagok's natural precontact fish resource base included several fatty fish, such as salmon and herring, whose processing for consumption as well as longer-term storage could have left such greasy soils. Bear is another possibility as communities across the region have long traditions of rendering bear fat into grease, which makes it a highly storable source of calories.[43] Storing calories was critical for navigating lean times that were part of the region's seasonal fluctuations. Future analysis is necessary.

What we have recovered here offers important insights into what the baseline ecosystem was in this estuarine ecosystem before the shock of colonialism. The plant and animal remains show that the baseline was a high level of both terrestrial- and water-based biodiversity. The presence of so many different edible wild plant and tree foods indicates the Abenaki/Pennacook peoples living here occupied, and more likely actively fostered, a landscape conducive to such resource richness (potentially through controlled fires, tree coppicing, stand management, etc.). The animal resources are also rich and varied, showing the kind of biodiversity that can be present in this ecosystem when the rhythms of seasonal resource abundances are followed. English colonialism introduced extraction patterns that disregarded the seasonal rhythms of resources and emphasized economic gain, trends that continued, and escalated, over subsequent centuries. Today, the biodiversity of this estuary is severely degraded. For instance, oysters cannot self-propagate in this estuary today, including on the Oyster River itself.[44]

Figure 2.5. Fragment: Looking down at a plan view of a large burnt feature with fire-cracked rock radiocarbon dated to the threshold period of colonial encounter (AD 1488–1650) that produced the arrowhead fragment seen in figure 2.1. This feature is not fully exposed and continues into the next unit, but the core black burnt area exposed here is about three and a half feet long and two feet wide.

Figure 2.6. Fragment: Wild terrestrial and water-based animal foods: *A*, cut turtle shell; *B*, oyster shell; and C, cut moose bone, recovered on site from a feature dating through colonial encounter (radiocarbon dated to AD 1488–1650, see the feature in fig. 2.5). (Photographs by Ron St. Jean. Courtesy of GBAS.)

We know that Abenaki/Pennacook peoples continued to seasonally harvest diverse local wild foods through the threshold time of early contact from our excavation of another nonmovable find from the site, a particularly complex large burnt soil stain left at the site that dated to AD 1488–1650 (fig. 2.5). Whether this was exclusively a hearth or from some other kind of activity, we know it was used in food preparation, cooking, and consumption due to the presence of the large fire-cracked rock in the middle of the black burnt heart of this feature (fig. 2.5). Fire-cracked rock is rock that was heated and cracked by deliberate exposure to fire. Typically, it relates to food preparation as rocks were components of hearths and earth ovens and sometimes heated to boil water. The soil it is associated with contained domesticated crops and wild plant foods. It also had pieces of cut moose bone, cut turtle shell, and split discarded oyster shell (fig. 2.6).

These animal remains are from locally available wildlife acquired through land-based hunting and water-based harvesting. The broken arrowhead of English flint that opens this chapter was recovered in this hearth/food-processing remanent feature, perhaps intended for use in land-based hunting (see fig. 2.1). That these fragments were cut and split indicates that they were processed near and/or in this feature. The moose bone was cut with a metal tool, indicating that Abenaki/Pennacook peoples selectively used a variety of newly acquired European material goods, from flint to metal.

BECOMING, IN A STONE TOOL

Our hominin ancestors started making simple stone tools perhaps three million years ago.[45] Stone is durable, so it is a logical material for making tools that perform well. Some stone materials can take a sharp edge, and making the stone flake in the right way takes considerable skill. Stone tools are made by knapping, and it takes even more skill to knap tools for different purposes. Typically, a knapper starts with a chunk of stone (called a core) and reduces it by striking it with a hammerstone. Once reduced, the knapper pressure-flakes the core with a bone/wood/antler tool, taking off small chips (called flakes) of stone until the tool obtains its desired shape. Bifacial tools are made by knappers who shape both sides (bifaces) of the stone. Bifacial reduction is a sophisticated form of stone tool production. Common types of bifacial stone tools include projectile points (e.g., spears and arrowheads), drills, knives, and scrapers. Our opening fragment was on its way to being an arrowhead when it broke (see fig. 2.1). You can see evidence of pressure flaking on the bottom edges where the knapper probably tried to make side notches for the arrowhead.

Stone was the primary tool material in North America for millennia. Indigenous peoples were skilled knappers. Not all kinds of stone are suitable for knapping however. Stone must flake when struck, not crumble and break apart, and it has to take and hold a sharp edge. Cryptocrystalline stone, so fine-grained that its structure is barely discernable, is ideal for producing bifacial flaked stone tools.[46] Cherts are common cryptocrystalline sedimentary rocks with high silica (glassy) content. Varieties include jasper, chalcedony, agate, porcelanite, novaculite, and flint.[47] Beds and nodules of chert can be found around the world. Flint is a variety of chert found in chalk or marley limestone. It holds a particularly sharp edge when worked. Flint is found in many places across the globe and was always a widely preferred raw material for making stone tools.

Relatively little chert or any of its varieties can be found in New Hampshire. What is available comes from specific sources (e.g., Mount Jasper) with distinct visual appearance and chemical makeup.[48] For millennia Indigenous peoples in New England had limited options for acquiring high-quality stone tool raw material, and they actively sought out sources of fine-grained stone.[49] They traveled, sometimes very long distances, to quarries where cherts could be obtained and/or actively traded to obtain materials to make tools used in day-to-day activities. These chert sources can also be identified (e.g., Munsungon chert from northern Maine).[50] Because local sources are extremely limited in and around Great Bay/P8bagok, and regionally available cherts can be readily identified by their visual appearance, when we dug up this broken arrowhead (see fig. 2.1), GBAS team members knew immediately the flint that it was made of was exotic material.

The mottled gray-and-white flint of this fragment appears to be from sources near harbors in southern England.[51] Early colonial ships leaving England carried ballast in their holds to keep them low and stable in the water.

Ship ballast generally consisted of enough stone rubble placed in ship holds that, when added to weight of the cargo, the ship would be well balanced and handle well.[52] Upon arriving at their destinations, English ships would offload their cargo and take on shipments of bulk commodities. In seventeenth-century New England, this meant barreled fish and lumber. Ship's ballast would be adjusted according to how the ship rode in the water. Heavier return cargo meant that ballast would be offloaded.

For this reason, heaps of ballast stone from the seventeenth through the nineteenth century can readily be found near North America harbors.[53] Much discarded ballast is flint from the southern shores of England, widely available near ports of departure. This is commonly referred to as English flint. English ship ballast stones are common in the coastal entryways into the Great Bay region, found commonly by divers in New Castle harbor and also forming part of the historical collections in Portsmouth's Strawbery Banke Museum. In fact, there was so much of this ballast stone available by circa 1630 that colonists used it as building material.[54] During colonial encounter, people negotiated unprecedented relationships with not just new people, but a host of foreign material things that ranged from fancy trade goods to mundane, discarded objects, such as English flint ballast. Our arrowhead made from English flint demonstrates that Indigenous interest in foreign European materials was variable, creative, and innovative.

Where English colonists saw waste, Native peoples saw opportunity. The English flint dumped on the shores of this ecosystem was incredibly high-quality knappable material. To obtain equally good stone required travel and/or trade over long distances. When such valuable material was brought to their shores, the opportunity was taken. This seventeenth-century Abenaki/Pennacook crafter translated the cultural divide they faced in colonial encounter in a personal way by transforming foreign flint into a traditional Indigenous tool relied on for thousands of years. Becoming a New World person meant using introduced goods in a way that produced meaningful associations that enhanced their culture, well-being, and identity formation within the third space dynamics created by colonial encounter but that also showed that they were grounded in their ancestral homeland known to them as N'dakinna.

Near the spot where the English flint broken arrowhead was recovered, the GBAS team found another important object, a lead musket ball (fig. 2.7).[55] Again, a wide range of European goods were introduced to Native peoples during colonial encounter. Cloth, glass beads, kettles, and other metal tools were key North American trade items.[56] Guns were also highly prized. Around AD 1580, the snaphance gun, which used a flintlock mechanism to fire a projectile, was invented in Europe.[57] After this invention, flint became desired across Europe for gun manufacturing. Flintlock mechanisms were widely used in muskets, rifles, and pistols into the nineteenth century in some places.[58] Gunflints and other gun parts are among the most common artifacts recovered at early colonial sites in North America.[59]

This musket ball indicates that the site's Abenaki/Pennacook occupants had access to European guns. Yet they did not abandon bows and arrows, their traditional weaponry. Instead, they made room for both technologies, for being many things at once, something that seems an essential part of the process of becoming New World people. They transformed English flint ballast found on their shores into something traditional—an arrowhead—an object used skillfully for millennia to provision and sustain themselves and their communities. Even as they made something foreign into something traditional and useful, they also explored one of the most evocative novel technologies of the time—firearms.

Another fragment made of English flint was recovered at this site (fig. 2.8). This object came from another uncovered hearth that was likewise radiocarbon dated to crossing over the threshold of colonial encounter, circa AD 1474–1638. This fragment is made of English flint, but it appears to be of lower quality than the arrowhead material because it was from closer to the outside of the stone. It has part of the cortex, the outside covering of stone, on its top edge. The person who worked this stone had access to a raw chunk of the material with the cortex on, as would be expected for a ballast waste stone on these shores being picked up and worked.[60]

Its shape, unlike that of the broken arrowhead that starts this chapter, suggests that the knapper was not making a traditional stone tool, but rather, they were making a gunflint, using traditional techniques to do so.[61] Bifacial thinning flakes were taken off its front, and its edges were percussion flaked, which are traditional Indigenous toolmaking techniques. Gunflints manufactured in Europe did not employ bifacial production techniques until later.

Figure 2.7. Fragment: Lead musket ball recovered near the broken English flint arrowhead (shown in fig. 2.1). (Photograph by Ron St. Jean. Courtesy of GBAS.)

Figure 2.8. Fragment: Bifacially worked English flint being shaped into a gunflint, from a hearth radiocarbon dated to AD 1474–1638.

Gunflints made out of European flint using traditional Indigenous technology have been documented across North America during contact period.[62] This is what this fragment appears to be; the Abenaki/Pennacook residents of this site used traditional knapping techniques to make a new tool, a gunflint, using a newly locally available material, English ballast flint.

This tells us something really important, and that is that the decision to make an arrowhead out of English flint was not made in ignorance of the use of flint in guns. At the same time and place, gunflints and arrowheads were knapped out of the very same newly introduced raw material. This emphasizes Indigenous peoples' choices were not linear, unilateral, or foreordained. Instead, Abenaki/Pennacook peoples living here actively made decisions about foreign things and peoples. They were able to accommodate foreign objects in their world view, extending *manit* to these objects so that they could relate to them and incorporate them into their daily lives. In doing so, they generated situations and objects that existed for the first time in the world.

The fragments we have met in this chapter together reveal flexibility in accommodating the foreign, while at the same time retaining the shared identity of what it meant to be in and from the homelands they shared as N'dakinna. The introduction of colonial objects is not significant because it created some kind of sudden change; instead, what is compelling is the ways the foreign was culturally refined and put to use. Perhaps accommodating the foreign without giving up foundational cultural identity is the core of becoming a New World person. Indigenous peoples of seventeenth-century Great Bay/P8bagok were being drawn evermore into colonial encounter, but even in this difficult space where settler colonists were rapidly infringing on the place to which they had long belonged, they were still capable of making innovative choices.

Figure 3.1. Fragment: The broken end of an Indigenous ground stone tool recovered from the collapsed central chimney of the Burnham garrison, a seventeenth-century English colonial site on the Oyster River.

3

FRAGMENTS FROM BECOMING (THE ENGLISH PERSPECTIVE)

An Indigenous ground stone tool was recovered in GBAS's excavation of the Burnham garrison, an early colonial English homestead (fig. 3.1). For hundreds of years, Abenaki/Pennacook peoples had occupied a meadow on the west side of a small creek flowing into the Oyster River, a village explored in the last chapter. In the 1600s, English colonists entered this Native space and built the dwelling house that produced this fragment on the east side of that creek. Each place can be seen from the other.

Like the fragment of English flint (see fig. 2.1), the ground stone tool fragment in figure 3.1 reflects changes in the Great Bay Estuary/P8bagok during the threshold time of early colonial encounter as cultural boundaries became porous. English colonists dispersing along Great Bay/P8bagok were becoming their own version of New World people. Having parallel fragments from the same closely connected landscape allows us to appreciate the shared aspects as well as the distinctions between English and Indigenous experiences in the third space of colonial encounter.

What is a ground stone tool? In addition to knapped stone tools made of high-quality raw materials such as chert and flint, Indigenous peoples made ground stone tools for various uses out of large, dense rocks. Coarse-structured stones such as granite, basalt, and similar igneous rock and cobbles found in rivers and streams could be laboriously shaped by using one stone to repeatedly abrade, peck, grind, and polish another stone into a desired shape.[1] Ground stone tools were often used for ponderous work. Processing ground stone tools, such as mortars and pestles or manos and metates, pulverized seeds, nuts, and other plant crops to make finer-textured meal or flour (animal products, pigments, clay, and temper were finely ground as well). Other ground stone tools include hoes for clearing land and tending gardens, axes for felling trees, adzes and gouges for making dugout canoes, and weights for fishing nets.[2] Occasionally, tools were highly polished, which tends to indicate ceremonial significance. Some specific polished ground stone tool forms for ceremony were also made, including stone pipes and bannerstones.[3] Across the Northeast, ground stone tools were made from the Archaic period onward.[4]

Our fragment is likely the broken end of an ungrooved ground stone axe. It tapers on the bottom and shows some battering from use. Tools like it would have been hafted to wood handles and used for chopping and woodworking.[5] Note that it was polished: some shine from polishing remains on the bottom edges (see fig. 3.1). GBAS recovered this broken axe during excavations inside the colonial dwelling. Because it was recovered in the remains of the chimney, we know that this Indigenous tool had been intentionally incorporated into this English colonial home.

Looking back from our contemporary vantage point, the outcome of colonialism seems clear—after all, we call the region New England today. We know that it was the English who ultimately gained structural power, power that directs the flow of energy and the allocation of social labor.[6] The capacity to transform Great Bay Estuary/P8bagok's natural resource base into commodities and gain profit from these exports, which we explore in chapter 1, is an example of the structural power colonists came to hold. But this fragment, and others presented in this chapter, tell an important parallel story that shows on the ground, in the lived condition of colonialism, things were murkier and more nuanced.

SEVENTEENTH-CENTURY ENGLISH DISPERSAL INTO GREAT BAY/P8BAGOK'S WATERWAYS

How did this Indigenous tool fragment end up in the central chimney of an English colonial house, and what does that tell us about the English lived experience of becoming New World people? Before we look at the evidence that we found at the Burnham site, we need to look at seventeenth-century colonial expansion along the rivers of the Great Bay Estuary/P8bagok to understand this fragment and the specific context and broader insights it offers.

We already know that colonial settlement in the Great Bay Estuary, what early English colonists typically called the Piscataqua region, began in earnest in the early 1620s. Employees of the Laconia Company, organized by the merchant adventurers John Mason and Ferdinando Gorges, were among the earliest colonial settlers in this region. Cod fishing was a good way for early colonialists to pay back their investors, and, as we have seen, fishing enterprises were an early economic focus. Other colonists diversified their pursuits to include trading, intensified farming, and lumbering. Great Bay/P8bagok's waterways provided resources, transport, and power, features essential to all early colonial activities. The spread of English colonial settlement into the estuary over the 1600s was dendritic, pushing farther and farther up and along the ecosystem's waterways, something that is evident in Scott's 1667 map of the region (see fig. 1.2).

This spread was fed by early colonial concepts of property. Owning, inheriting, buying, selling, and trading property and deeds to property are familiar terms that we use today when we talk about land. We find it perfectly normal to talk about land as real estate—where it is, who owns it, what it is worth. However, these seemingly ubiquitous ideas of land ownership are a direct legacy of European global colonialism. The loss of Native lands to colonists through acts of territorial dispossession was a key feature of colonialism. Territorial dispossession could not have happened without the construction and naturalization of particular cultural concepts. Among the most powerful was the concept of land as property: land could be owned, conveyed to others, and expropriated.[7]

Turning land into property was aided by the creation of another concept: colonial political legitimacy and legality.[8] Colonists made laws governing people and property. They staked out property lines, created deeds, imposed rules governing land inheritance, negotiated ownership, taxed landowners, adjudicated property disputes, and so on. Today, the concept of property underscores the global economy. Yet it was crafted from a particular ideology for a particular end. There are other ways of approaching land. As discussed, in the homelands Indigenous groups referred to as N'dakinna, reciprocal relationships between the land and people developed over deep time. The land was an animate presence, a vital part of "all my relations." This shared and close sense of land has been largely obfuscated by the concept of land as individual property inscribed during colonialism.

The physical and conceptual dispossession of Indigenous lands was wholly effective and thorough: Indigenous peoples in what is today the United States have lost 99 percent of the land they historically occupied.[9] Conceptualizing land as property has always benefited some and excluded and marginalized others. Today, property ownership is still tied directly to wealth and reflects disparities in wealth. People of color own staggeringly less property than white people in the United States. Lack of land hinders the accumulation and transfer of intergenerational wealth.[10] This has colonial roots.

One of the earliest English settlements up in the estuary, as seen in chapter 1, was the Hiltons' cod fishing station on Dover Neck/Point in the 1620s. Cod fishing did not come with heavy demands for land; it only needed enough for the fish flakes that dried the cod. By 1631, little land had been developed on Dover Neck, and the Hiltons sold their patent to other English investors. These investors gave colonists coming to this settlement relatively small twenty-acre grants of land. These land allocations created a compact community on Dover Point.[11] Compact communities were not, however, the norm across seventeenth-century Great Bay Estuary/P8bagok.

Other colonial activities were associated with increased demands for land. Farms required pasturage for domestic animals and a woodlot to provide fuel for cooking and winter warmth and for building material. Land owned by first-generation settlers was often split up among the male heirs. Yet, as families grew larger and larger and engaged in more trade and barter, they required more land. Additionally, cows, sheep, and oxen required more pasture, and larger homes and businesses required more wood. Timber harvesting for the lumber industry, which we have seen grew quickly over the region, demanded extensive landholdings. As the need for farmland, pasture, and timber harvest grew, the footprint of the English colonial settlement expanded up the tributaries of the estuary. Land grants of forty, sixty, one hundred, two hundred, even five hundred acres were common along rivers as English settlements sprawled across the landscape.[12]

THE LINEAGE OF AN OYSTER RIVER ENGLISH COLONIAL HOMESTEAD

Ambrose Gibbons, employed by John Mason, was among the first to foray upriver from coastal settlements in search of new economic opportunities. In 1631, he built a great house and trading post on the Newichawannock, the Abenaki name for what is today known as the Salmon Falls River. Its several falls are located in what is known today as South Berwick.[13] Gibbons had likely explored the Newichawannock previously and established some kind of relationship with the local Indigenous leader S8gamo (Sagamore) Rowles, who lived in a village on the river called Quamphegan. Presumably, such a relationship would have allowed Gibbons to acquire the land and establish his trading post here. There was no signed deal for this, but, later, Sagamore Rowles did sign formal land deals with other English colonists.[14]

In 1629, Mason and Gorges had split the holdings of the Laconia Company in two, with Mason receiving the southern portion, his erstwhile colony called New Hampshire. After establishing his trading post, Gibbons sent commodities to Mason in England obtained from Mason's employees or acquired through trade with other colonists and Abenaki peoples. One common commodity was animal pelts, but both Gibbons and Mason expressed frustration in the meager profits from this venture.[15] We know that Gibbons acquired a "modell of a saw-mill" from England in 1631.[16] Three years later, with the help of eight Danes and indentured carpenters whom Mason sent over from England, Gibbons oversaw the building of a sawmill and stamping mill on the upper falls of the Great Works River, an offshoot of the heretofore undammed Salmon Falls River ecosystem.

Mason died in 1635. Soon after, Gibbons complained that some of Mason's indentured carpenters were taking (stealing) company possessions.[17] Others, however, acquired land legally. They stayed, acquired more land, and built homesteads and trading posts.[18] By 1700, some of these families had become rich.[19] After operating the mill and overseeing developments along the Salmon Falls River, growing discontent with life in Salmon Falls/South Berwick after Mason's death led Gibbons to leave in the late 1630s.

According to records, Gibbons owned land on the Oyster River before December 3, 1640.[20] Oyster River is another major Great Bay/P8bagok tributary. The earliest English colonists into Oyster River were, like Gibbons, colonists frustrated with their options in more compact and established settlements south in Massachusetts Bay or even those closer to home in Dover, Portsmouth, and Salmon Falls/South Berwick. English colonists could acquire large land grants here, and their homesteads were widely spread out along the banks of the Oyster River. One of Oyster River's early colonists, Valentine Hill, amassed several large tracts of land in many places along the Oyster River. In 1643 he acquired land at the head of tide of the Oyster River and obtained permission to build the first mill on this river in 1649. Some of the laborers who helped build this mill were Scottish prisoners who were captured at the battle of Dunbar in 1650 and sent as indentured servants to the Massachusetts Bay Colony.[21] This rural colonial settlement became known as Oyster River Plantation, formally part of Dover (fig. 3.2).

Most of the settlements constituting the Oyster River Plantation developed downstream from the head of tide along the north and south sides of the Oyster River, which was the communication, transportation, and commercial highway out to the bay, to Dover Point and other nearby villages, to Piscataqua River ports, to the Atlantic Ocean and, ultimately, to England (see fig. 3.2). When Gibbons died in 1656, he was living in the Oyster River Plantation on two hundred acres he owned on the south side of the Oyster River

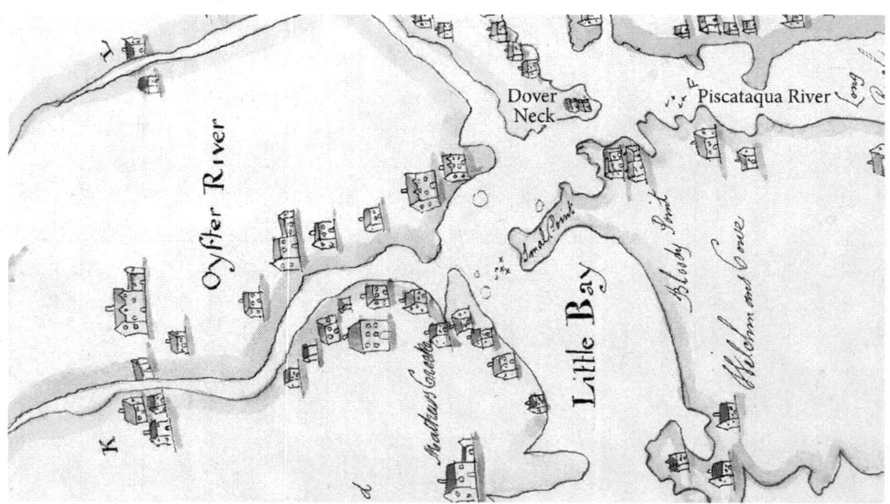

Figure 3.2. Fragment: A zoom in of the Scott map (see fig. 1.2) showing colonial era rendering of the Oyster River Planation. The map is oriented north. Some mentioned geographic features have been added. (Map courtesy of the Maine State Archives, Baxter Rare Maps Collection.)

about one mile downriver from the head of tide.[22] His land ran along the river. It included the large meadow where we found the Abenaki/Pennacook village featured in the previous chapter, a forested upland, and a creek flowing into the Oyster River known variously as Burnham Creek and Horsehide Creek.

Gibbons had a daughter. Given that English colonial law prohibited women from inheriting land, he left his real estate to his grandson, Samuel Sherborne. The estate was handled by his son-in-law, Henry Sherborne, who lived in Portsmouth. Sherborne had no interest in land on Oyster River, so he sold to Robert Burnham in 1657:

> one dwelling house with the Out houses appertaining thereto with all the Land which the said Ambrose Gibbons dyed posses:sed of, & did of right appertain unto him by the Grant of the Town of Dover lying in Oyster river aforsd between ye brook upon the lands of William Pitman formerly William Robards towards the Southeast and a certain Creek towards the West, abutting upon the said River called Oyster river to wards the ~~South~~ East; & so runneth up into ye Woods to wards the South to the quantity of about two hundred acres answerable to the Grant of the Sd Town of Dover aforesd, which the said Ambrose Gibbons died possessed of, tho it be not within the line next before expressed with all right

> [comonage] and priviledges & appurtenances unto the said houses & lands belongeth to HAVE AND TO HOLD the houses lands & meadows mentioned as aforesaid with the said right privileges & appertenances.[23]

Burnham had come from England with two brothers in 1635. He was the youngest, still a teenager. His voyage to New England was complicated. To start, he and his brothers traveled hundreds of miles across England from Norfolk, in the east, to the western port of Bristol. Bristol's harbor had long been a hub of Atlantic marine trade. As global trade increased starting in the mid-1500s, Bristol started to boom. By the seventeenth century, Bristol was a major departure point for passenger ships headed to the New World and key port in the emerging West Indies trade system. Some Bristol residents became very wealthy from this shipping industry, including via involvement in the transatlantic slave trade.[24] This busy port town was a dangerous place in the seventeenth century, as piracy abounded.[25]

The Burnham brothers overcame these dangers and took passage for New England on the *Angel Gabriel*. During its voyage, this large, heavily laden ship encountered, in late August 1635, one of the worst hurricanes in New England history, known as the Great Colonial Hurricane.[26] The *Angel Gabriel* sought refuge from the storm in Pemaquid Bay, in Ferdinando Gorges's Province of Mayne (Maine). There, it wrecked and sank. Although many passengers made it to land, several left onboard the vessel were lost along with its cargo. After the storm passed, surviving passengers were taken to Boston in smaller vessels manned by local settlers. In the 1600s, people attributed "tempests" to God's providence.

After his harrowing Atlantic voyage, Robert Burnham moved around the Massachusetts Bay Colony. He came to Oyster River around 1654 and worked as a carpenter, a valuable occupation on the frontier. He purchased Gibbons's two hundred acres in 1657 for one hundred pounds.[27] Land was plentiful, but labor was in demand. In 1670, a bill introduced, but not passed in Massachusetts's General Court, aimed to regulate the fees charged for skilled and unskilled labor in the colony. It gives us an idea of what workers could earn at the time.[28] As a carpenter working 6 days a week, 52 weeks a year (312 days) at the given rate of 33.3 cents per day, Burnham would have earned no more than $104 in a year's time. In this seventeenth-century colonial frontier, there was little hard currency. Economic transactions were based on the exchange of goods and services in barter and trade, rather than cash money. It was not uncommon for early colonial residents of the Great Bay Estuary to pay taxes in bushels of corn. By working hard, Burnham could have saved the purchase price for the property during his three years in the Oyster River settlement.

A GARRISON ON A STEEP CRAGGY HILL?

After his 1657 purchase, Burnham laid out a house lot in 1661 and built his home thereafter. This first Burnham dwelling house has long been recorded as a "garrison." GBAS, following convention, has referred to this archaeological site as the Burnham garrison. The term garrison conjures up images of military structures. Yet, during most of the 1600s, calling a house a garrison did not mean that it had fortification features. The largest houses in a plantation were often distinguished as garrisons, places where neighbors knew to gather if danger was imminent. As discussed in chapter 1, this estuary was one of the last English settled spaces in the seventeenth century before vast lands that were Indigenous power-scapes met New France, its capital French Quebec. As we learn more about in chapter 6, many Native peoples living in these northern spaces had alliances with the French. Tensions were often high between New France and New England, and this estuary was impacted by these politics. When tensions were high and the Massachusetts Bay perceived imminent threats from French/Indigenous forces, Boston would send a few soldiers and "garrison" them at larger houses.

Figure 3.3. Fragment: Historic photograph of a typical seventeenth-century colonial homestead called a garrison in the Great Bay Estuary/P8bagok frontier. This is the Damm garrison built circa 1675 and on display today at the Woodman Institute. (Photograph courtesy of the Dover Public Library.)

Figure 3.3 is a historic photograph that shows the kind of seventeenth-century homestead that was called a garrison. This is a typical seventeenth-century regional style, but it is unique in having the timber structure preserved. This garrison was moved to the Woodman Institute in Dover, New Hampshire, in the early 1900s and is still on display there today.[29] The region's early colonial houses were simple structures like this, built on stone foundations with timber siding. A central stone and brick chimney serviced fireplaces used for heating and cooking. No defensive structural features appear. As violence in southern New England spread north during the late 1670s and escalated around Great Bay/P8bagok toward the close of the century and into the 1700s, garrisons with actual defensive features like lookouts and palisades (defensive wooden fences) were increasingly built. Some settlements reorganized and built forts.[30]

Notions of these later fortified garrisons are engrained in the region today. Dover's nickname is Garrison City. Schools, restaurants, and breweries with garrison in their names can be found in towns all around the Great Bay Estuary/P8bagok.[31] There are also several garrison revival style houses, circa 1930s–80s, typically two-story buildings with a second-story overhang aiming to recall early colonial lookouts. New England has a long tradition and continued interest in publicly celebrating early colonial history. Ideas of fortified garrisons support a widespread view of colonial history in which settlers overcame great obstacles, especially violence from Native peoples, to forge an early American identity based on enterprise and political liberty.[32] Simple timber houses do not do much for that narrative, but fortified garrisons testify to stalwart "Yankee" stock.[33]

In New England, interest in the early American past and fascination with local colonial era heritage, such as garrisons, surged after the Revolutionary War. Formal institutions were founded for preserving and interpreting the past, frequently in ways that justified and rationalized the growth of the new nation.[34] The earliest was the Massachusetts Historical Society, established in 1791, embodying postrevolutionary antiquarianism in New England. Efforts to document early colonial history spread outward from this base and continued throughout the 1800s. This trend came to many established towns around the Great Bay Estuary/P8bagok where different groups and institutions continued these historical cultural efforts. Fortifications and garrisons were promoted as a mainstay of the early New England colonial experience in a valorized colonial past that persists today.[35] And because of this interest, efforts were made to document where early colonial garrisons and other colonial infrastructure had been.

One of the most remarkable local efforts to document colonial occupation in the Great Bay Estuary was undertaken by Mary Thompson with her *Landmarks of Ancient Dover, New Hampshire* (1892).[36] The location of the Burnham garrison is described as on "a steep craggy hill," which is emphasized as evidence of its role as a garrison. She notes, "It would seem that no one, except for safety, would ever have built a house in so inaccessible a place, certainly not a mere dwelling-house."[37] This "hill" is the large, distinctive rock formation, set back about three-quarters of a mile from the south bank of the Oyster River. Looking west from the top of this outcrop gives a clear view of the large meadow on the other side of the creek where GBAS found the Abenaki/Pennacook deep-time occupation site. Looking north, one can see the Oyster River.

When Gibbons came into Oyster River in the 1630s, Abenaki/Pennacook peoples lived in a village in the meadow across the creek from this rock outcrop. Gibbons had interacted with Abenaki (and likely other Indigenous groups) at his trading post on Salmon Falls. Thus, he was familiar with their presence and their deep knowledge of the landscape and its resources. What if, when Gibbons came to Oyster River, he chose to settle where he did because of the Native presence, not despite it? The Abenaki/Pennacook village was not a side story to colonial occupation of this landscape. Instead, it is important to consider a scenario in which it drove colonial decision-making. Gibbons would have known Abenaki/Pennacook peoples lived here, grew crops here, harvested wild foods here. This would have shown him that he, too, could secure resources from that land, farm it, and survive on it. He could not viably build his house on Indigenous space: on crop fields or important wild harvesting grounds, like marshes and shellfish beds. The large rocky landform across the creek offered a spot clearly removed from the place Abenaki/Pennacook peoples had lived for centuries, while ensuring proximity to critical resources and river transport.

The promontory's high visibility offered value to colonists settling in unfamiliar terrain. It helped one view and be viewed by neighbors. Many things besides interpersonal violence could harm family and neighbors, for instance, unpredictable weather, wild animals, fires, and accidents. Moreover, this prominent landform is unlike anything else in the vicinity. It could have easily been a landmark orienting anyone dwelling in, or moving through, this landscape for meeting, trade, and exchange. From this perspective, the very elements that made this "steep craggy hill" inaccessible can instead be appreciated for heightening its accessibility and visibility. Gibbons could have settled there to advertise his presence, not hide it, and Burnham could have followed suit, taking advantage of these same benefits.

FINDING: SURVEYING AND EXCAVATING THE BURNHAM "GARRISON"

Working with historic maps, records, and deeds, GBAS identified the original two-hundred-acre property along the Oyster River that Burnham bought from Gibbons's estate. We then secured permission from the current landowner to explore this land. In Thompson's nineteenth-century account of the Burnham garrison, she describes two foundations as still visible on the surface of the rock outcrop—"the cellar with its stone wall is still perfect, as well as a smaller cellar, entirely sperate, which no doubt was for ammunition and other dry storage."[38] Describing the smaller cellar hole as an ammunition storage structure again shows how notions of threat, violence, and fortification were layered into accounts of this site.

When our GBAS team walked over this land and rock outcrop in 2018, we found the two cellars described in this century-old record. We, too, saw one large cellar with its stonework in nice shape and a second, smaller cellar. In an area that has seen significant development, the preservation of these cellars is a testament to the care the current landowner has taken of this site. Such an intact colonial site also made for a virtually unique archaeological research opportunity.

As archaeologists, we did not assume that the historical description of the large cellar as the house and the small cellar as ammunition storage was correct. Instead, we investigated. We established a site grid and conducted more than one hundred shovel test surveys every five meters across the entire rock outcrop landform (as described in chapter 1).On completion, we noted what kind of artifacts we found and where. This made it clear that the large, intact cellar hole was not a house but a barn. Very few artifacts were found there; mostly we uncovered large nails and parts of metal oxen shoes. In contrast, we found dense remains from everyday life around the smaller cellar, things one would associate with a house, including broken ceramic pots and dishes, utensils, food remains, buttons, shoe buckles, combs, jewelry, smoking pipes, broken glass, and bricks (fig. 3.4 and fig. 3.5).

Interestingly, we also hit similar residential artifacts in high density in an area just west of the small visible cellar hole, but these were in a spot with no visible habitation signs on the surface (for example, a cellar hole, stone foundation). We let artifact densities guide our excavations, not what we saw on the surface. Thus, we situated our first round of excavation units in two places, the area with no visible structures but dense artifacts and the small visible cellar hole.

When we opened units in the area with no visible surface structures, our excavations kept producing dense artifacts but nothing that explained why

Figure 3.4. Finding: Smal cellar hole visible during GBAS's initial field survey for the Burnham garrison.

these things were there. We were perplexed. During the last week of that summer's field season, we caught a break. At about sixty centimeters deep in one of our excavation units, we hit a buried stone foundation. We did not have time that season to fully examine our find, but at the start of the next season, a big group of volunteers was assigned to work in that location. By the end of those excavations, it was clear that we had uncovered a buried stone house foundation (fig. 3.6). This wall turned degrees as the foundation continued into and along the bedrock, making the bedrock part of the foundation.

Historical records and accounts offer different notions of where Gibbons's house was on the property Burnham bought, although the deed is clear that it was on the property. Some accounts suggest that Burnham expanded Gibbons's existing house. Others suggest that Gibbons's house was closer to the Oyster River near a marsh and that Burnham built his "garrison" separately, placing it on the "steep craggy hill" for defense.[39] At the base of the entryway foundation, we found ceramic sherds from a broken delftware dish. Delftware was tin-glazed earthenware made in the Netherlands starting in the early seventeenth century (colonial ceramics are explored further in chapter 5). This tells us that our buried stone foundation was likely built in the early part of the seventeenth century. We interpret this foundation as being from

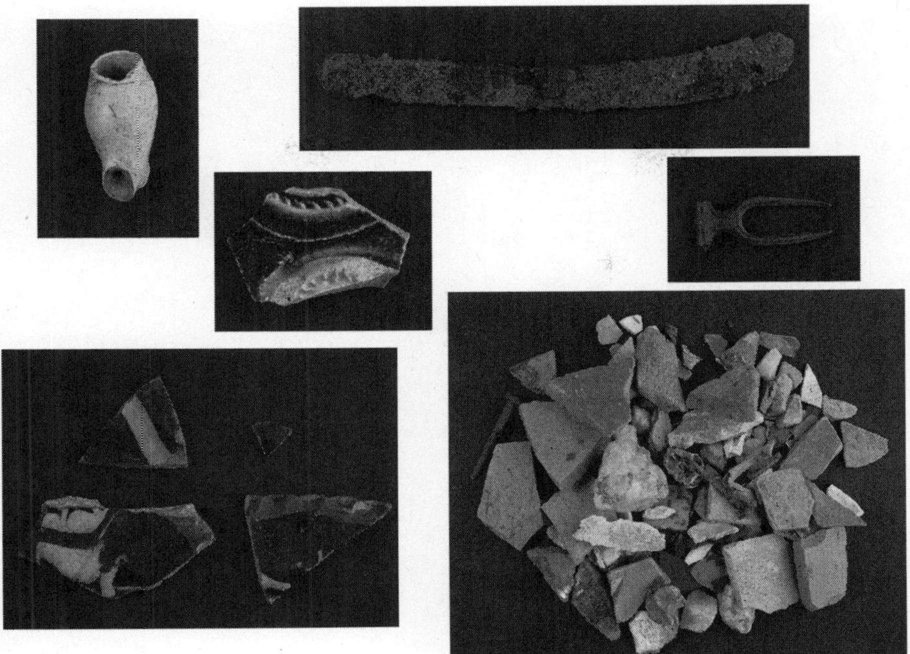

Figure 3.5. Finding: Burnham "garrison" site shovel test finds that indicated proximity to a residential structure, including a broken pipe, a discarded knife blade, ceramic sherds from two European-origin trade wares, a brass shoe buckle, and a pile of more mundane discarded materials including bits of brick, ceramic sherds from plain redware jars, small pieces of animal bones, broken window glass, and more. (Photographs by Ron St. Jean. Courtesy of GBAS.)

Figure 3.6. Finding: Pictures of A, our GBAS team working early in the excavations and B, the end of excavations at what turned out to be a buried early seventeenth-century foundation built along bedrock. The small cellar hole was added kitty corner to this foundation, with a chimney built in the center.

Figure 3.7. Finding: Clay-backed base for central chimney. The broken ground stone axe, shown in figure 3.1, was recovered in this secure context.

Gibbons's house, incorporated into Burnham's house as rooms were added over time. It runs along the bedrock and connects to the small visible cellar hole at a central chimney and oven structure.

Thus, we quickly determined that the structure associated with the smaller visible cellar hole had not been a storage cellar, as some historic accounts contend. Our shovel tests had turned up a range of everyday residential debris, and signs of habitation continued to appear in our grid excavations. This was another room built around the central chimney in Burnham's house, which was a typical layout for early colonial dwellings constructed in the region (as shown in fig. 3.3). Our excavations uncovered the collapsed remains of the central chimney. Clay had been packed onto the bedrock to make a level platform and provide a sturdy base for the stone and brick chimney (fig. 3.7). Brick from the chimney was found tumbled to the side. Brick was the dominant artifact found in these excavations, but one sunny day, a longtime GBAS volunteer jumped up from her unit holding the fragment that is described at the start of this chapter. This fragment was decidedly not a brick. It was not a colonial-produced artifact at all but rather part of a Native-made ground stone axe.

FRAGMENTS FROM A NON-GARRISONED COLONIAL EXPERIENCE

Based on GBAS's findings, framing this colonial site in defensive terms misses the more nuanced and dynamic realities of the lived colonial experience here. I want to walk us through a new interpretation, one where Burnham did not build a "garrison" at all. Instead, he built a homestead that expanded Gibbons's earlier dwelling. Incorporating the structure his predecessor left behind saved on construction work and also gave him an advantageous location and valuable connections with Abenaki/Pennacook neighbors that helped colonial survival in the rural setting of seventeenth-century Oyster River.

It is significant that we found the broken ground stone axe in excavations of the chimney remains in the smaller visible stone cellar structure (see fig. 3.7). When archaeologists find artifacts in disturbed settings, we cannot be certain with what to associate them. In contrast, this broken piece of a ground stone axe has a secure context: it was intentionally brought into this English colonial house.[40] The axe was placed at the center of activity on its most central and prominent structural feature—the chimney. It would have been regularly seen by people living in this house and by anyone visiting them.

At the start of this chapter, I note that the edges of this axe were polished. Polishing is time intensive and unnecessary for a utilitarian axe that chopped wood or felled trees. Polishing suggests that the axe in this house was designed for special purposes. Polished ground stone tools are common in trade and/or ceremonial activity (these often go together). It is likely, therefore, that the Burnhams acquired this axe through some kind of purposeful and structured process of interaction, like organized trade, with its Native makers. Because they valued it highly, this colonial family placed this Indigenous object in the center of their home.

You might wonder why, if they valued it so much, was it broken? It broke after the house was abandoned. Burnham gave his house to his son Jeremiah in 1684. When Jeremiah died in 1718, his sons inherited the land, divided the property, and built new houses closer to their greatly expanded farming operations.[41] Historical records indicate that timbers from the original house were taken down after this, but the chimney stood decades longer. Around 1760, Burnham's great-great-grandson (also named Robert Burnham) harvested the best bricks from the chimney. It seems that, during this process, unwanted parts of the chimney were pushed off the clay platform, and/or what remained of the abandoned chimney's structural integrity was undermined. Our excavation found a collapsed mix of chimney stone and bricks tumbling off the clay platform: many bricks were broken (see fig. 3.7). The axe may have been broken after the original seventeenth-century structure was demolished by these salvage operations.

Other evidence from our excavations of this chimney debris offers further compelling support for Indigenous presence in this early English colonial house. This ground stone axe sat on the central chimney where Native foods were cooked and consumed. As we excavated the chimney remains, we collected all excavated portions of the clay platform for floatation, then floated fifty liters of clay soil. The only plant food remains found in this chimney were Indigenous domesticated crops of maize (*Zea mays*), beans (*Phaseolus vulgaris*), and squash (*Cucurbita* sp.). These very same crops had long been grown by the communities living in the meadow across the stream from this site. The English could only have come into contact with these foods through interaction with Indigenous communities. It seems judicious to conclude the Burnhams obtained these foods, and perhaps learned how to grow them, from their Abenaki/Pennacook neighbors.

Remains of animal foods at the site are also telling. There are bones from domesticated animals, including sheep and pigs, that the English colonists brought with them to New England. Preliminary faunal analysis of the site collection has shown that several lambs were killed. While lamb was often consumed in England during festivals and celebrations, particularly at Easter, the number of juvenile sheep bones is beyond what can be explained by occasional celebratory feasts; rather, it indicates an atypical slaughtering pattern. Killing juveniles reduces the herd's overall breeding potential, as younger animals have little or no time to reproduce. This may suggest that, at times, the Burnhams experienced food scarcity and killed young sheep for food, something that countered longer-term productivity.

Intermixed in the remains at the site are several wild animals. These include moose, deer, rabbit, wild turkey, seal, Atlantic cod, shellfish, and frog. The Burnhams clearly utilized wild food resources. Moose would have been wholly unfamiliar to the English, coming as they did from a more temperate island climate. Hunting moose is a winter activity and processing carcasses is challenging work. As English colonists, the Burnhams likely acquired moose meat from their Abenaki/Pennacook neighbors in trade and/or learned how to hunt and process moose from them. These Indigenous communities were intimately familiar with moose hunting because they lived in the lands of this large mammal, studied its behavior, learned how to hunt it and efficiently process its meat, and shared this knowledge intergenerationally. Newly arrived English colonists could not just automatically successfully hunt moose.[42]

In addition to indicating some of the complexities of becoming New World people, these foods, like those from the Abenaki/Pennacook site, further show what the Great Bay Estuary ecosystem was like before the shock of colonialism and subsequent years of postcolonial degradation. Moose are a forest-dwelling species and do especially well in forests with a mix of old and young stands of trees. Old stands provide shade and young stands provide forage. Because moose cannot survive in deforested landscapes, the deforestation started by, and accelerated after, colonial encounter made the area inhospitable to moose. By the 1800s few moose were recorded in all of New Hampshire. Moose returned to the state only after ecologists began focused efforts on forest restoration and management in the twentieth century. Today, moose remain in northern zones where there are especially large protected forests.[43] Finding moose at this seventeenth-century site tells us that the healthy local ecosystem included mixed forests harvested and likely maintained by Abenaki/Pennacook peoples before and during contact.

Our excavations also produced Atlantic cod bones and otoliths (biomineralized ear stones in fish that record aspects of the animal's life and environment).[44] Isotopic analysis can reveal the salinity and temperature of the waters the fish lived in over its lifetime. We conducted a preliminary analysis of the barium (Ba) to calcium (Ca) ratios (Ba/Ca) of one cod otolith recovered in GBAS's chimney excavations (fig. 3.8). This ratio yields a faithful proxy for water salinity, as the Ba/Ca is higher in otoliths from waters with higher salinity.

Each peak on the graph corresponds to a yearly cycle in the fish's life: this fish was around eight years old when it was caught and eaten at Burnham's house (see fig. 3.8). Over its life, this cod spent lots of time in waters with lower salinity, such as an estuarine mix of seawater and fresh water. Because

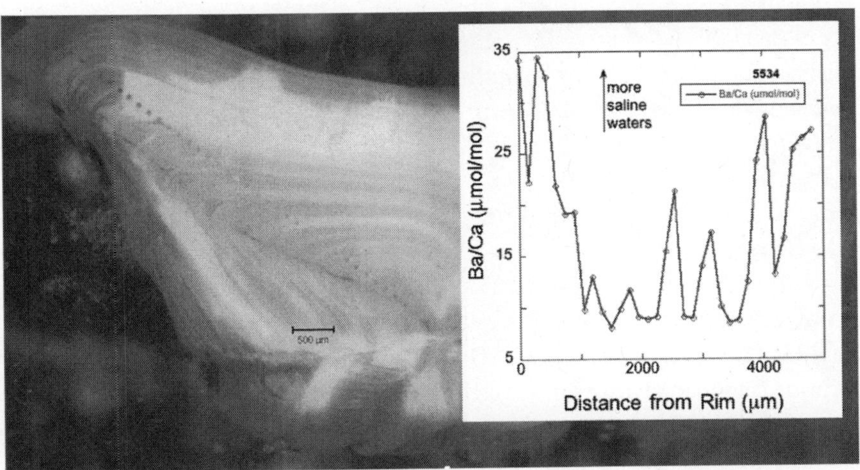

Figure 3.8. Fragment: Cod otolith recovered in the excavated central chimney feature. The results of the barium/calcium isotopic analysis shown here indicate a very different life cycle profile for cod in the seventeenth century. These fish enjoyed a much longer lifespan in coastal and estuarine waters. (Analysis and output results by Julie Bryce, professor, earth sciences, University of New Hampshire.)

of severe overfishing, Atlantic cod are rare anywhere in the Gulf of Maine today. Most commercial fishing for Atlantic cod takes place offshore in deep ocean waters. In contrast, this seventeenth-century cod spent much of its life in near-shore waters. Cod lived much longer, grew much larger, were much more abundant, and lived closer to shore in the early colonial period before regional ecosystems had been radically degraded. Even the age of this fish speaks to a healthier ecosystem. In commercial cod fishing today, most cod that are caught are juveniles one to two years old. Older female fish are better breeders because they produce more eggs of better quality. Increased reproductive capacity creates larger populations. Therefore, the cod the Burnhams ate lived a relatively long life in shallow, estuarine waters, probably in the Great Bay Estuary, before it was caught and eaten. Almost every aspect of cod populations has been radically altered since then.

From the fragments we have recovered in our work at this site, we see that the process of becoming New World people did not mean early English colonists garrisoned themselves on a "steep and craggy hill" living an English life in this foreign land. In fact, they thrived by doing quite the opposite. They heeded Indigenous presence and made it central to their homes and lives. The Burnhams traded and exchanged with their Abenaki/Pennacook neighbors, but connections went further and deeper. They learned from them how to live in a place unlike England, with a harsher, more unpredictable climate. They learned how to grow Indigenous foods and hunt and process wild animals to supplement food from animals and plants brought from England.

Jeremiah Burnham, who inherited the property from his father, Robert, died in 1718. In his probate inventory was a canoe.[45] Canoes were long used to traverse the region's waterways. Traveling on the Great Bay/P8bagok's tidal water is not a straightforward proposition. People who are unaware of the tide can easily get stranded at low tide or swept out to sea on a strong outgoing tide. This canoe was not an Englishman's boat. Jeremiah likely acquired it through trade and would have learned how to safely navigate the Great Bay/P8bagok's waterways from his Indigenous neighbors. This is evidence of trade, but also of learning, exchanging ideas and knowledge and cultural modes of behavior.

This site has long been misinterpreted. Because there are historic records of the English experience during the colonial period and because there have been dedicated efforts to document the Euro-colonial experience, it is easy to take such records at face value and to orient interpretations of events and developments in colonists' terms. At GBAS, we fell into this ourselves. We came to this particular landscape to find, survey for, and excavate the Burnham garrison, only to find the Abenaki/Pennacook village site featured in the previous chapter as we looked for colonial out structures. Our orientation was from the Burnham site out, not the other way around. It is clear now that this approach was driven by historical bias, not the order or significance of events and presences.

Our findings show clear limitations in the perspective that violence was the driving factor in the early colonial experience. This perspective masks much more complex, nuanced processes at work in this third space. As late as 1684 when Robert Burnham left his property to Jerimiah, he did not call his home a garrison but deeded to his son "all my houses."[46] Here, for these English colonists, becoming a New World person did not involve entrenched hostility to the non-English world outside the perimeter; rather, it meant making room for non-English foods, things, ideas, and peoples. Just like their Abenaki/Pennacook neighbors, they moved into and through the third space of colonial encounter and made creative adaptations and accommodations of differences as they did. Colonial inscription of these lands as wholly New England was powerful and ultimately successful. However, some of those living through this period of change looked outward as much as inward to sustain themselves in their daily lives.

Figure 4.1. Fragment: A posthole in a builder's trench found in GBAS's excavations of a 1654 local meetinghouse on Dover Neck; this post was from activity thirteen years later, part of a palisade (a wooden defensive fence) added in 1667 when the Massachusetts General Court mandated the fortification of the meetinghouse.

4

FRAGMENTS FROM "DISORDERLY ELEMENTS"

In a home, dirt can imply disorder, but in an archaeological dig, this is not the case. The dirt itself has a story to tell. The dirt shown in figure 4.1 is from a builder's trench dug by colonists living on the Great Bay Estuary/P8bagok. The darker soil denotes the position of a post from the palisade erected in 1667 on an embankment surrounding Dover's meetinghouse. As will be seen, these soil stains are fragments that reveal tensions between colonists living in the Great Bay Estuary/P8bagok and the Puritan government of the Massachusetts Bay Colony. An ecological frontier where fresh water and salt water meet, this estuary was also a frontier of colonial settlement where political and religious differences between English Puritans and English Royalists mixed like oil and water. Great Bay colonists living on Boston's periphery were as independent, unpredictable, and difficult for the Massachusetts Bay Colony to control as the strong, turbulent tidal currents of the estuary.

As discussed, economic motives, not religious ones, animated colonial life around the Great Bay. Religious outcasts escaping Puritan persecution settled here in relative safety. Throughout the early decades of colonialism in this frontier, connections to Puritan Massachusetts Bay were weak and half-hearted. So was any sense of organized government functioning on the ground in this erstwhile colony. Chapter 1's *The Province of Mayne* showed how the highly organized and more powerful Massachusetts Bay Colony eyed this resource-rich region. Worn down by the lack of leadership inside the erstwhile colony or from England and embroiled in political turmoil as Parliament assumed governance in the 1640s and on the verge of the conflicts that would come to be known as the English Civil War, New Hampshire's independent colonists, seeing no other path forward, finally capitulated to Puritan Massachusetts's governance. This governance sought to quell the "disorderly elements which prevailed in the settlements."[1] But resistance remained strong. These soil stains reveal that "disorderly elements" still prevailed in the Great Bay Estuary/P8bagok in 1667 after Boston ordered the locals to fortify their meetinghouse (fig. 4.1). In this chapter, I explore the trajectory of this fragment and introduce others that attest to the lived reality of this area's disorderly elements.

A PRECARIOUS COMBINATION

By the 1630s, a heterogenous mix of English colonial communities dotted Mason's portion of the Great Bay Estuary/P8bagok. There were some clustered settlements, such as Strawbery Banke (Portsmouth) at the mouth of the Piscataqua River and Exeter on the Squamscott River. However, across much of this landscape, as well as in Gorges's patent with the estuary in it to the north and east, colonial presence was more scattered and rural, as we have seen along the Oyster River.[2] Upper New Hampshire Plantation, or Dover Plantation, occupied a broad swath of the estuary's inland shores. Dover Neck was this plantation's center point. With little proprietary oversight in this northern colonial frontier setting, each community developed its own character. Little united neighbors but a shared sense of independence. Events in England, including the death of original English patent holder John Mason in 1635, made the legitimacy and stability of what was already a loosely structured emergent colonial frontier society ever more precarious.

The colonial settlement at Dover underwent a dizzying array of leadership claims, changes, and general structural turmoil over the course of the 1630s. Again, the Hiltons had the original colonial holdings on Dover Neck, but they had never developed this place much. Fishing and trade were the primary foci, with permanence and growth secondary concerns. This started to change in 1633 when Capt. Thomas Wiggins arrived with thirty settlers as an agent of the Bristol Company, which had bought the Hilton's original patent to Dover Neck (the exact negotiations for which are not well-known but seem to have begun in 1630).[3] Captain Wiggins was the authority who granted twenty acres of land to each of the settlers with him, and they set up the small, compact English colonial community on Dover Neck.[4]

A devout Puritan, Captain Wiggins erected a small wooden meetinghouse on Dover Neck near the first Hilton trading post and brought Rev. William Leverich to minister to the settlers' spiritual needs.[5] Reverend Leverich's first sermon at this meetinghouse on October 30, 1633, constituted the beginning of Dover's First Parish.[6] For much of the colonial era, town and parish were one and the same; the First Church did not become a parish distinct from the town of Dover until 1762.[7]

Reverend Leverich left less than two years later, in large part because many of the Dover settlers in his First Parish congregation were not devoutly Puritan. His successor, the Rev. George Burdett who came to preach two years later, followed the Church of England and was a strident Royalist.[8] By all accounts, he found "the discipline of the [Puritan] church too straight for his loose conscience."[9] He inserted himself in civil government as well as in religious life to undermine Captain Wiggins and return civil control of the Upper Plantation to his Royalist political faction. In this role, he urged then king of England, Charles I, to secure the plantation for loyal settlers and keep it separate from the Massachusetts Bay Puritan colony looming on its southern border.[10] But Burdett's call was not heeded, both because it came at a time when King Charles I's reign was falling into disarray back in England as parliament was increasingly questioning Royal authority, and as Burdett himself found his tenure in Dover cut short. While initially popular with Dover's less zealous settlers, the minister was found to be a scandalous adulterer. He spent time in prison and eventually returned to preach in England.

Soon after, Capt. John Underhill came to Dover. While brief, his tenure brought significant developments to Dover that rippled across the northern erstwhile colonies. An experienced soldier in England as well as a Puritan, Captain Underhill came with John Winthrop to Boston in 1630 to organize colonial defenses. He was fifty-seventh on the list of members of the First Church of Boston.[11] A fierce military proponent of Boston and foe of Indigenous communities, he is best known for leading a contingent of militia during the Pequot War in 1637, in the brutal assault on a Mystic River (Connecticut) village where some four to seven hundred Pequot were killed.

Captain Underhill had circulated in the highest circles of the Massachusetts Bay Colony for years when things took a turn; he came to follow Ann Hutchinson's religious teachings, which orthodox Puritans considered blasphemous.[12] After she and her followers were banished, her brother-in-law, the Rev. John Wheelwright, took his congregation north to the Great Bay Estuary and founded Exeter, New Hampshire (one of the larger area settlements drawn on the Scott map, fig. 1.2). Captain Underhill was part of this banishment and went to England. He returned to New England just a year later and settled in Dover. He brought with him another schismatic minister, the Rev. Hanserd Knollys, who followed the new Baptist teachings. Captain Underhill was appointed commander of the Dover and Exeter militias, and Reverend Knollys organized the church in 1638.[13] Unlike many former ministers, Knollys did not seek civic authority. He was a pious Christian scholar who focused on his pastoral duties.

Two years into Knollys's time as reverend, in 1640, Rev. Thomas Larkham, a wealthy Puritan minister new to Massachusetts, came to settle in Dover. This timing corresponded with a hallmark moment in the building tensions in England, as parliament assumed governance in 1640 and refused to do King Charles I's bidding, this coming to be known as the Long Parliament, which, again, hindered effective governance for the next twenty years and set the stage for conflicts that came to be known as the English Civil War. Political shifts played out in this colonial frontier landscape. Larkham objected to Reverend Knollys's Baptist doctrines and was eager to control both church and civic life. Although Knollys had a following among the area's settlers, disruptive elements saw an opportunity in Larkham's arrival.[14] Puritan adherents and land grabbers ran Knollys out of town, and Larkham assumed religious and civic control, but he faced much discontent as his rise to power had been divisive.[15]

By 1640, Dover colonists were far from a unified group, but they did have one thing in common, they were change weary. Captain Underhill took advantage of this weariness. He convinced Dover's leaders that the best hope for stability was in joining the Massachusetts Bay Colony. And so, a group of forty-one leading area residents entered into "The Combination for Government by ye people at Piscataq," the Dover Combination, on October 20, 1640.[16] On August 9, 1641, Upper (Dover) Plantation became the Upper Province of the Massachusetts Bay Colony.

Controversy is layered in the Dover Combination. The combination itself starts with a disclaimer: "Whereas, sundry Mischeifes and inconveniences have befaln us, and more and greater may in regard of want of Civill Government, his Gratious Ma'tie having hitherto setled no Order for us to our knowledge."[17] The Massachusetts Bay Colony certainly seemed to be a last resort, turned to only after the majesty, the king of England, himself failed to settle things. Some signatories even wrote "Protest" next to their names.

Within months of signing, a majority of the signers (twenty-five) wrote to the governor of Massachusetts declaring that Captain Underhill had used sundry tactics to get signatures for the combination. He "hath went from house to house, and for his own ends, by flattery and threatining, gotten some hands to note of their willingness to submit themselves under your government."[18] Given that Underhill had been banished from Massachusetts Bay, Dover residents might have expected a sympathetic ear in the Massachusetts governor. However, political and economic hegemony took precedence. Underhill and Boston had been backdoor dealing during much of his time in Dover. Underhill returned to Boston less than a year after Dover was secured for Massachusetts Bay and was restored to the Puritan church.[19]

TURBULENT LOCAL CURRENTS UNDER MASSACHUSETTS BAY COLONY RULE

While the Massachusetts Bay Colony sought to assert control over what they saw as an unruly area, from the outset they recognized, at least to some degree, the nature of the Great Bay region's loosely organized towns/settlements and independently oriented residents. Built into the combination were special exemptions that gave the Upper Plantation more local control over its own economic and political affairs than towns to the south, which were closer to Boston, enjoyed.[20] Townsmen could transact their own town meetings, grant land within town borders, and no man could be taken into the colony militia without local town consent.[21]

Joining with Massachusetts Bay did settle some issues that had been locally troublesome for decades. Particularly problematic were the aforementioned ministers who conflated their religious authority with political, civic, and economic ambitions. After agreeing to the combination, one of the things Dover residents requested was a reliable minister. Reverend Larkham was replaced by Rev. Daniel Maud, a Puritan minister and school master who served faithfully until his death in 1655.

Other aspects of the arrangement remained turbulent however. Dover residents were constantly brought to court for breaking Massachusetts Bay laws, especially mandatory church attendance.[22] Violators were routinely fined and "admonished" by Boston courts. By 1646, Dover was petitioning the General Court for increased jurisdiction so that accused residents would not have to appear in Boston for minor violations.[23] Massachusetts Bay made more concessions. One major concession was installing a Dover court with local magistrates. Another was allowing Dover men who were not members of the Puritan church to vote in elections.[24]

Boston relied on loyal Puritans living locally to lead their community and keep up support of Puritan rule. But this was no easy task along the colonial frontier, the living border between order and disorder, at once dangerous and charming, harsh and rewarding, the only guarantee being it was always unpredictable.[25] Local inhabitants kept close tabs on their Boston-backed local leaders and how their interests were represented in the General Court. Residents routinely passed voting instructions for leaders warning them not to do anything "impugning our privileges in Boston."[26]

Richard Waldron was one of the most influential Massachusetts Bay leaders in Dover.[27] In 1642, he built a large mill at the lower falls of the Cochecho River, one of the Great Bay Estuary's seven main tributaries. This was the first colonial push inland from the hub of the original colonial settlement on Dover Neck/Point. As Waldron became wealthier, his mill employed more people, and the settlement around his mill and homestead grew (today, this is "downtown" Dover). As a wealthy Puritan, Waldron served in various local political roles over twenty-five years, including representing Dover for seven years in the General Court. Despite his long tenure and stature in the community, even he was routinely given voting instruction by Dover residents. In border life, loyalty was ever shifting.

Waldron figured prominently in many significant events in the early colonial history of the Great Bay Estuary/P8bagok. Long heralded as a local hero, his misdeeds, including his persecution of Quakers, a religion Puritans saw as heretical, and betrayal of his once Abenaki/Pennacook allies and their subsequent retribution, are too often obfuscated by glorifying narratives. Waldron and his place in history are actively being reconsidered. Currently, his story is being decolonized, or reindigenized, by local Abenaki/Pennacook leaders.[28] Waldron is not the focus of this chapter, but he is emblematic of the differences between colonialist and decolonial historical narratives. He appears in this chapter because he was the Puritan-backed leader who agreed to construction of the meetinghouse on Dover Neck where GBAS excavations found the intriguing soil stain that opens the chapter (see fig. 4.1).

A NEW MEETINGHOUSE FOR DOVER

Across colonial New England, meetinghouses were the principal public buildings. Puritan esthetics influenced their concept and form. Since there was no separation of church and state, colonial meetinghouses were Puritan houses of worship, courthouses, and town civic centers. They were often the largest built structures in early colonial towns. Typically square and/or rectilinear in form with three doors, one for the minister, and two on the sides separating men and women, these simple dignified structures proliferated across New England.[29]

By the 1650s, the English colonial population had increased in the Great Bay Estuary. Since church attendance was mandatory under Puritan law, Dover Neck's wooden meetinghouse—built by Wiggins twenty years earlier—had become too small. On August 8, 1652, Waldron agreed to the construction of a new meetinghouse on an elevated landform on Dover Neck colloquially called Nutter's Hill, less than 1 kilometer (0.6 mile) northeast of the first meetinghouse. This location was on the first major thoroughfare up the Dover Neck peninsula connecting the earliest colonial settlement with the one inland on the Cochecho River. This thoroughfare is Dover Point Road today.[30] Early colonial records specified the material form of the meetinghouse: "Mr. Richard Walderne doth bind himself to erect a meeting house on the hill near Elder Nutter's; the dementions of said house is to be forty-foot longe, twenty six foot wide, sixteen foot stud, with six windows, two doors, and to plancke all the walls; with glass and nails for it; and to be finished betwixt theis and April next, come twelve months, whc will be in the year 1654."[31]

The structure was not quite finished in 1654. Four years later, town residents voted that the meetinghouse be underpinned, catted, and sealed with boards and that a pulpit and seats be made. This meant that its foundation was to be propped up or strengthened, the interior finishing work completed, and a pulpit and pews installed. These repairs and additions took two years, as shown in Historic Dover Records in June 1660. A tax of one hundred pounds was levied to fund these capital improvements.[32] Five years later, Waldron had town officials build a steeple on the meetinghouse to house a bell he had brought from England. The ringing bell would have been an audible reminder for local colonial residents of Massachusetts Bay's Puritan rule over the region and its strident ideal of the unity of church and state.[33] Boston imposed additional orders soon after.

IMPOSING ORDER(S)

In 1667 the Massachusetts General Court ordered the meetinghouse to be fortified: "Buld the forte about the meetinghouse on Dover Neck, one hundred foot square with two Sconces of sixteen foot square, and all the timber to be twelve inches thick and the wall to be eight foot high, with sills and Braces."[34] The legislators wanted Dover's residents to construct a one-hundred-foot square embankment and ditch earthen structure with two circular watchtowers (sixteen feet in diameter). A wood palisade (a stockade fence) eight feet high was to be built, braced, and silled on top of the embankment.

At that time, increasingly hostile relationships between aggressively expansionist English colonizers and Indigenous peoples seeking to maintain their sovereignty and homelands plagued southern New England. Less than a decade later, King Phillip's War would break out in southern New England (1675) with consequences that would eventually reverberate northward to the colonial frontiers.[35] But, in 1667, colonists living along the Great Bay Estuary/P8bagok did not consider fortifying their meetinghouse a compelling need.

Dover residents pushed back against this mandate, which came with significant material and labor costs. Waldron was instructed to tell Massachusetts "not to engage the town by compulsion to build fortifications."[36] The General Court responded that officials would be fined and taken to court if they did not fortify their meetinghouse.[37]

Back in Europe, centuries of conflict between France and England meant fortifications were familiar constructions to English people, and those English venturing to colonize new places routinely erected large, fixed material fortifications as they spread across the globe.[38] In seventeenth-century North America, English colonists were familiar with fortifications.[39] Across early English colonial settlements in North America, forts were often the first structures built.[40] The ditch-embankment, watchtower (bastions), and palisade combination to be erected around Dover's meetinghouse was a common style of fortification along the English Atlantic seaboard of North America.[41] English inhabitants living in Dover in 1667 would have been familiar, both generally and specifically, with the design laid out in Massachusetts Bay's order.

The 1654 meetinghouse was used until a new one was built farther inland in 1713 at Cochecho (where Dover's town center is today). The 1654 meetinghouse itself fell into disrepair and was cleared away just before the American Revolutionary War.[42] The site remains today as an undeveloped grass lot. A low stone wall and iron fence, installed by the Daughters of the American Revolution (DAR) in 1908, mark the site boundaries.[43] The site has a large flat area with nothing standing in it but a large pine tree. This large flat area is surrounded on all sides by undulations in the earth that form a square enclosure flanked by two circles, the apparent remnants of earthen embankments (and an associated outside ditch) built to support a wooden fortification structure and flanking watchtowers. Going by visible surface appearances, it looks as though local colonists fulfilled the 1667 order from Boston to fortify their meetinghouse.

At GBAS, we wanted to know whether this was the whole story. Visible surface embankments alone are not sufficient to tell us how the meetinghouse and its added fortification were actually constructed, repaired, and used over time. GBAS designed a field-testing program to explore these material processes at this colonial-era civic and ceremonial center.

FINDING: APPROACHING A PRESERVED FORTIFIED COLONIAL MEETINGHOUSE SITE

Archaeological fieldwork is destructive. Digging up a site destroys it. This puts us, as archaeologists, in a weird spot, where our passion for learning the hidden stories of the past, and sharing them widely, crash into the reality that we destroy the past as we do our work. I try to remember the great responsibility that this puts on me as archaeologist; being a professional means following a strong set of ethics.[44] This responsibility is amplified when we are working on a site where preservation is secure, which is the case with this 1654 First Parish meetinghouse site. This site is on the National Register of Historic Places and maintained by the First Parish Church of Dover, which stipulates in its ownership deed that the lot cannot be sold.[45]

A critical first step in doing any archaeological fieldwork, but especially work at a preserved site, is to establish a compelling purpose for the work, including the interests of key stakeholders, such as a site's current owner, descendent communities, town leaders, and more. In this case, the First Parish Church of Dover invited GBAS to do archaeological fieldwork at this site, a connection facilitated by GBAS's community historian, Diane Fiske, who is also the historian for the church. Their historical committee had long wanted to know how this early meetinghouse, critical to the church's history, was built and used. Before developing any fieldwork plans, we went with First Parish Church leaders on a site visit to both the location of the first meetinghouse built in 1633 and the existing site of the 1654 meetinghouse.

As seen in figure 4.2, the 1633 meetinghouse, erected close to the original colonial settlement on Dover Neck, has been destroyed by a highway. The 1654 meetinghouse site is on what is known today as Dover Point Road, which in the 1600s was the overland trail from the colonial settlements on Dover Neck inland to Cochecho, where Waldron had set up his mill. This road is very busy and the area quite built-up, but the meetinghouse lot is undeveloped thanks to the church's continued protection of this important heritage site (see fig. 4.2).

After establishing both a compelling purpose and stakeholder support, GBAS developed fieldwork plans. As we did, we kept this site's protected status at the fore of our decision-making. Before doing any digging, we turned to the nondestructive tool of ground-penetrating radar (GPR). GPR is an active geophysical sensing technique that uses wide-band electromagnetic pulses to produce high-resolution subsurface images.[46] As illustrated in figure 4.3, the undulations of earthen fortification embankments run in due directions (north, south, east, and west) forming a square enclosure; circular watchtower embankments flank the square on its southeast and northwest corners.[47] Our team established a site datum that allowed us to create a grid across the site so that GPR could be done in systematic transects and any results could be connected back to the exact spot on our grid. Peter Leach of Geophysical Survey Systems, Inc., shown in figure 4.4, ran a GPR survey at

Figure 4.2. Finding: An aerial photograph of Dover Neck showing the location where the 1633 meetinghouse once stood (destroyed by the highway) and today's 1654 First Parish meetinghouse lot. (From Howey and DeLucia, "Spectacles of Settler Colonial Memory," fig. 5. CC BY-4.0.)

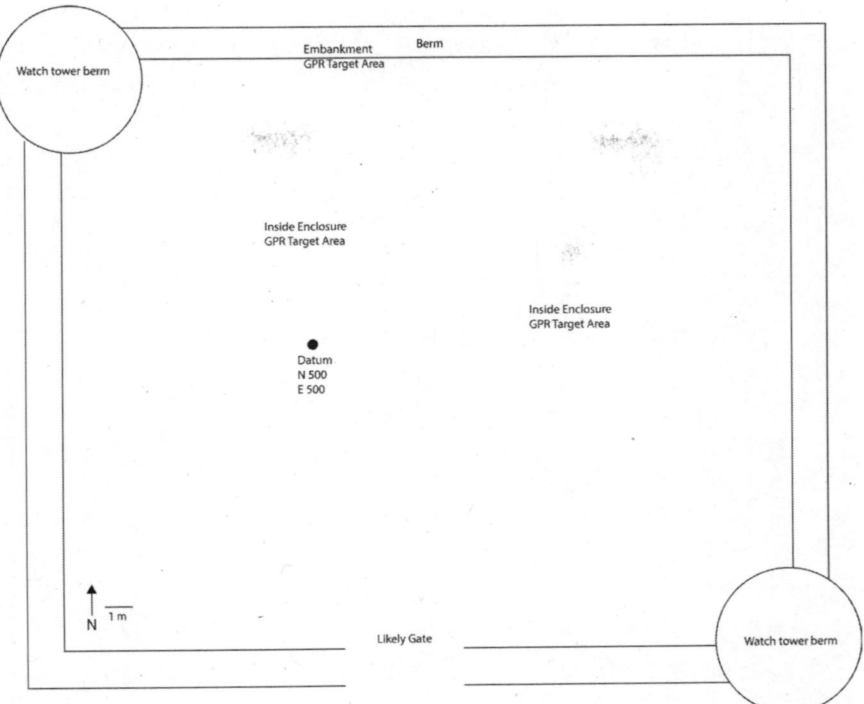

Figure 4.3. Finding: Illustration of today's visible embankments at the site, GBAS's site datum, and the location of field-tested ground-penetrating radar (GPR) targets.

1-meter (3.2-feet) transects to a depth of 2.5 meters (8.2 feet). He scanned the area enclosed by extant earthen berms and across the berms themselves, including the two watchtower berms.

While GPR is having a major impact on how archaeology is practiced, including opening doors for more minimally invasive work and site preservation, it is important to keep in mind that GPR does not find archaeological features and artifacts. Outputs from GPR surveys show anomalies in the ground, and these have to be "ground-truthed" through excavation to determine whether they are archaeological, and if so, what they actually are. As the GPR survey results show (fig. 4.5), the most dominant subsurface anomaly at this 1654 meetinghouse site is not archaeological at all, but, rather, the root system of the large pine tree in the middle of the grass lot (the dendritic white spreading feature in center of fig. 4.5).

Figure 4.4. Finding: Peter Leach of GSSI, a company specializing in ground-penetrating radar, on site running nondestructive ground-penetrating radar (GPR) and teaching a UNH student working on GBAS how the collection process works.

Working with these GPR results, Leach informed our GBAS team that there were three high-priority areas with possible evidence of structural remnants, two within the enclosure and one on the embankment. These three locations are indicated on the site illustration (see fig. 4.3). GBAS did not do any

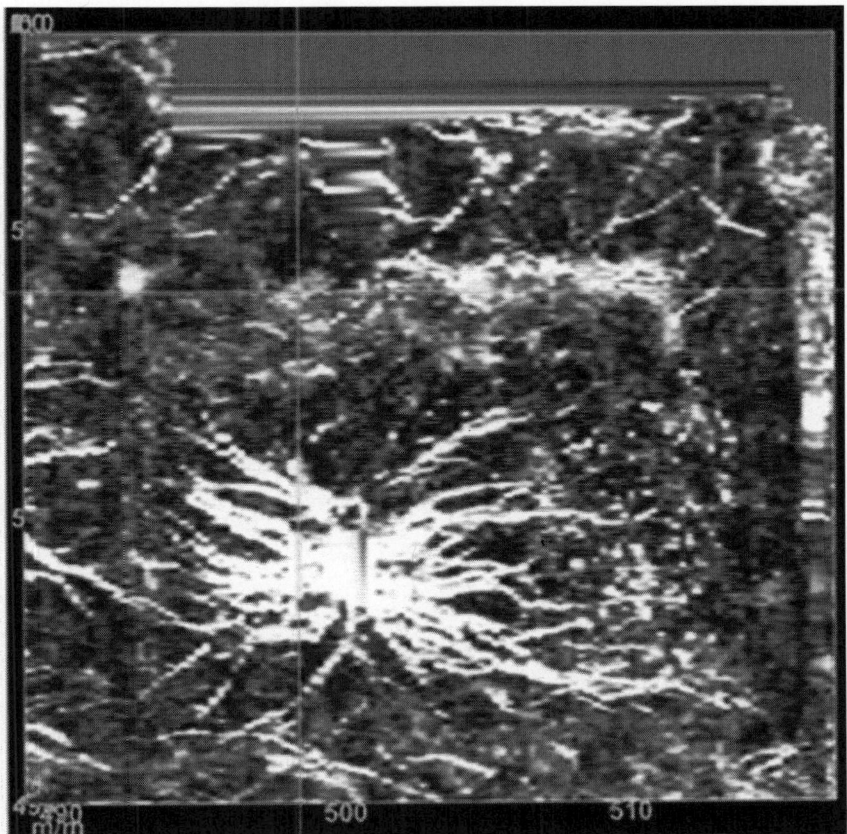

Figure 4.5. Finding: Image of ground-penetrating radar (GPR) results showing various subsurface anomalies at the 1654 meetinghouse site. The dendritic white spreading feature in the center of the photo is the root system of the large pine tree in the middle of the site lot today.

additional exploratory survey, such as shovel testing, which would have disturbed the site below ground. Instead, we performed test excavations on the three GPR-identified targets. Two of these targets—the one on the embankment and the northwesterly target in the enclosure—held colonial-era structural remnants, which I discuss below. The third, southwesterly target in the enclosure, proved to be a twentieth-century structure that damaged the site.[48]

A majority of colonial-era fortifications across the eastern United States have been destroyed through centuries of development and expansion. Hence, this preserved fortified meetinghouse site is quite unique. However, visiting

Figure 4.6. Finding: Today's wooden sign on Dover Point Road marking the 1654 First Parish meetinghouse site. (From Howey and DeLucia, "Spectacles of Settler Colonial Memory," fig. 7. CC BY-4.0.)

the site today, you would not know it. Dover Point Road is very busy. Zipping along in a car, you would have to be on a keen, purposeful lookout for this site, which is marked only by a small hand-painted wooden sign (fig. 4.6).

While all GBAS work has been community engaged, we thought that it was especially important to make our fieldwork at the 1654 First Parish meetinghouse site accessible to the public, given that this site is on the National Register and, thus, recognized as a place of value for our shared cultural heritage as a nation. Although downplaying the site's significance, the understated marker adds to its protection. We realized that working here along this busy road would draw new attention to this site. GBAS knew sharing how important the site is and emphasizing the need for its continued preservation would be critical to protecting it from unwanted, potentially destructive attention. During each excavation season, with permission from the First Parish Church, we welcomed the media. We opened our excavations to drop-in visitors and volunteers, which included many members of the First Parish Church, the majority of whom knew the church owned this site but not much else beyond that basic fact. Today, these volunteers continue to be important community advocates for protecting this site and its important heritage. In addition, we hosted an Open Archaeology Weekend each October after the summer excavation season was over. That way, people who work during the week could come visit, and GBAS team members could give focused, dedicated site and excavation tours without the distraction of an active summer field season.

POSTHOLE WOES: SHODDY CONSTRUCTION AS CONTESTATION

Our GBAS team opened a one-meter-wide excavation trench where GPR had indicated the presence of possible structural remnants on the embankment. This testing trench ran from the interior back end of the embankment, over the top of the embankment, down its exterior side, and then into the ditch outside of the embankment.[49] These excavations show that the colonists used a straightforward method of making the embankment: they dug up earth and threw it onto the adjacent ground surface, leaving a berm next to a ditch. They repeated this process, making the square enclosure and circular watchtower berms. Colonists did not bring in soil from elsewhere to build and shape the embankments.

Toward the back end of the embankment facing the interior of the enclosure is where we found the builder's trench and posthole shown at the start of the chapter (see fig. 4.1). Figure 4.7 is an annotated version of figure 4.1 for better visualization of this fragment. The builder's trench ran east–west along the interior back end of the embankment. We can tell from our excavations that the trench was built after the embankment was made because it cut down through soil that had been piled up to form the embankment, then cut through the existing ground surface below the embankment (see fig. 4.7). This tells us something about the order of construction. Locals

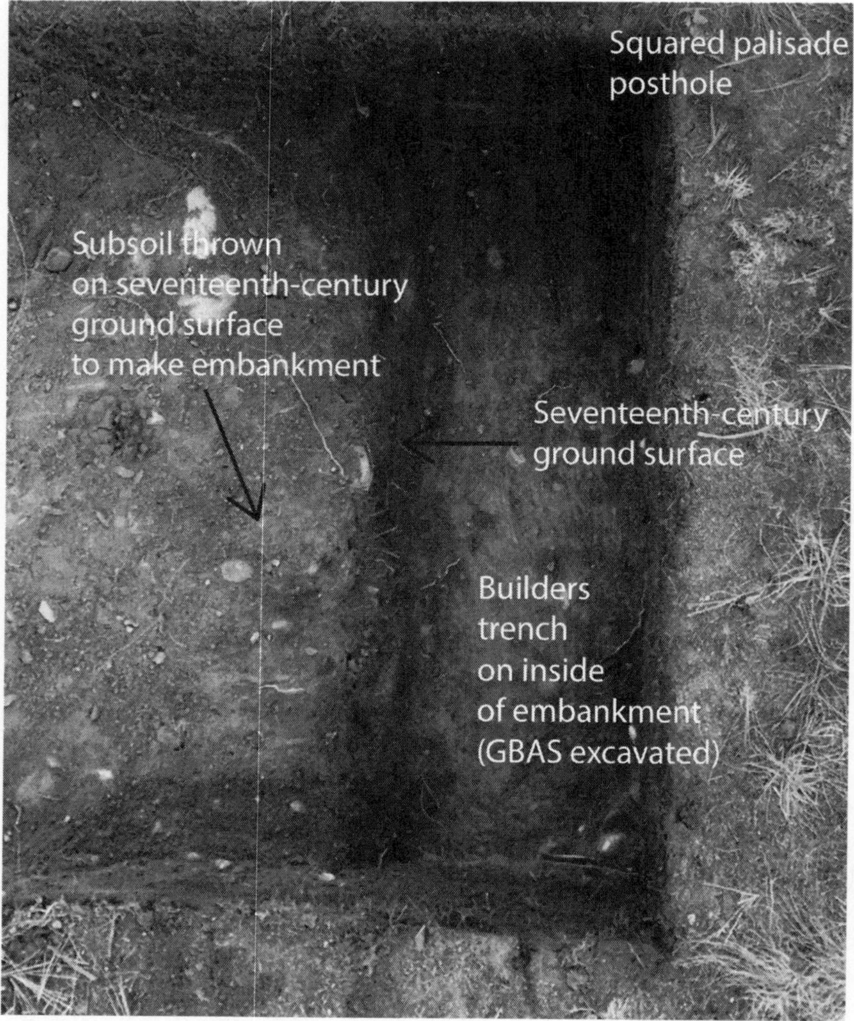

Figure 4.7. Fragment: An annotated version of the fragment in figure 4.2. The notations show soil details of the excavated builder's trench and the squared posthole from the palisade built after the 1667 imposed order for the meetinghouse to be fortified.

made the embankment, then they cut a builder's trench to erect the palisade, again a wooden defensive fence/stockade, atop the berm. The squared palisade posthole was placed in this trench. Complying with Boston's order for "all the timber to be twelve inches thick," the squared posthole we found is about twelve inches wide (see fig. 4.7).

We excavated through the builder's trench to learn how far down the palisade posthole extended. To our surprise, it was rather shallow. It was sunk not far below the ground surface that existed at the time of construction in 1667 (see fig. 4.7). Palisades were common features in colonial fortifications in eastern North America because timber was a readily available construction material. For a broadly comparative perspective on early English colonial palisades, palisades in Jamestown were found to be sunk four feet in the ground.[50] This is a rather striking discrepancy.

Of course, one may expect variation across diverse English colonies, and so this makes this a somewhat weak comparison. It is important, then, to put the construction processes we found on this embankment in a local comparative context. Such a context for comparison comes from our excavations inside the enclosure just five meters (fifteen feet) away from this post. As noted, we opened excavations in one area on the embankment and two areas inside the enclosure the GPR results pointed out as targets (see fig. 4.3). In our excavations at the more northwesterly GPR inside enclosure target, about five meters from the embankment testing trench, we found colonial-era structural remains, including another posthole, this one most likely from the 1654 meetinghouse itself.

The only image presently known to depict Dover Neck's fortified second meetinghouse was published in George Wadleigh's (1913) Notable Events in the History of Dover, New Hampshire: From the First Settlement in 1623 to 1865. Its label reads "The Old Meeting House on Dover Neck," but no artist credit is given (fig. 4.8). The woodcut shows the entrance through the fortification on the eastern palisade wall; the doors to the meetinghouse would fall then in this depiction on the north-facing long wall of the rectangular meetinghouse. For whoever made this woodcut in the early 1900s, depicting the entrance through the fort as facing east makes sense given colonists aligned many of their structures (and graves) to face east toward Jerusalem in accord with Christian theology.[51]

However, our walkover and GPR survey of the site both indicate the gate/entrance through the fortification embankment was on the south, not the east, wall of the embankment.[52] When the position of the gate is corrected, the meetinghouse would be located due north of the southern gate and its doors would face east toward Jerusalem. Given the meetinghouse was built

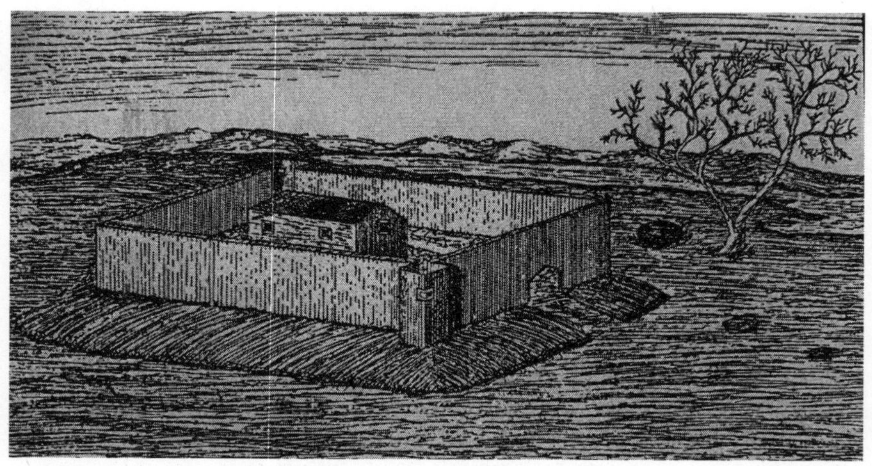

Figure 4.8. Fragment: The only known depiction of the 1654 meetinghouse. (From the front pages of George Wadleigh's Notable Events in the History of Dover, New Hampshire.)

before the fortification, it makes sense that it was oriented with doors facing east, not the later added fortification. Instead, the fortification's entrance was located behind the meetinghouse to accommodate this preexisting structure's sacred orientation. And flowing from this positioning logic, here is where one of GBAS's test excavations found remnants from a colonial-era wooden structure we interpret as being from the 1654 meetinghouse.

The 1654 meetinghouse was built on Nutter's Hill along the trail that, during colonial times, was becoming a land route from the Piscataqua River up Dover Neck to Cochecho and today is the busy road next to the site. Nutter's Hill is a glacial outwash feature composed of distinctively sandy, excessively drained soil with a sandy gravelly substrate.[53] Our excavations around the meetinghouse found a thin layer of packed clay, which had to have been brought in because the soil at the site has no clay in it. Just down the hill is the Bellamy River, another of the Great Bay Estuary's seven main tributaries. Early colonists knew the Bellamy River was rich in clay as they made bricks from Bellamy clay during this time.[54] Our excavations suggest that clay was brought in to create a smooth base over the sandy soil for constructing the meetinghouse, possibly even to serve as its temporary floor. Unlike the embankment, the ground surface for the meetinghouse was amplified and purposefully prepared.

Cutting through this clay surface were postholes, most likely from the construction of the 1654 meetinghouse. Taking our responsibility for limited excavations at this protected site seriously, we only cross-sectioned one post, but this fragment was telling (fig. 4.9). This post was sunk over a foot and half into the clay-prepared ground surface. It was also bolstered with a distinctive layer of stones placed purposefully around the post edge for additional support (see fig. 4.9). This posthole from the 1654 meetinghouse shows that local Dover-area colonial English residents knew how to design, organize, and construct sturdy timber structures with real posts. No documentation indicates any repairs performed on this meetinghouse after 1658, and our archaeological fieldwork found no evidence of additional repair. This meetinghouse was a sturdy structure.

Dover's colonial inhabitants who "fortified" their meetinghouse nine years later, however, did so under duress. They had contested the General Court's orders. When their protest was denied, they did just enough to appear to

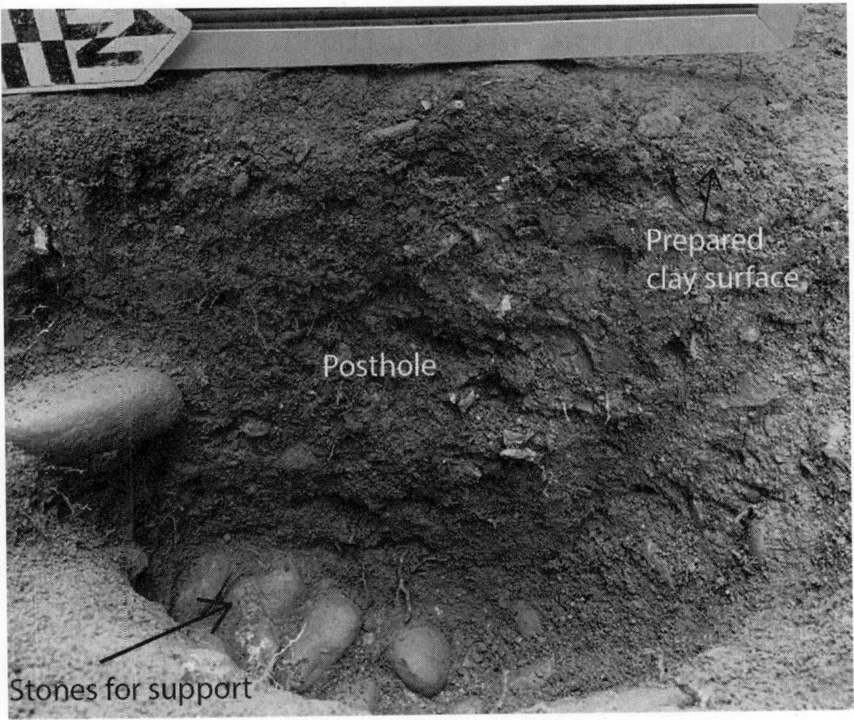

Figure 4.9. Fragment: A posthole from the construction of the 1654 meetinghouse itself. It is lined with stones for support. This sturdy construction contrasts with the post found from the 1667 ordered palisade (see fig. 4.7).

comply with the orders when inspectors came from Massachusetts Bay to check on the work. They met the aesthetics of the orders. Local residents knew that clay would improve construction site conditions: they had brought it in for the meetinghouse but did nothing of the kind for the ditch-and-berm embankment. Yet, an outside observer would not notice this shortcut. For the meetinghouse, they sunk posts deep into the ground and bolstered them with stones. In 1667, they built the palisade of timber cut to twelve inches, as stipulated by Massachusetts Bay. This could be seen from the outside. But the post was sunk just below the surface of the ground without support from stones, unlike the meetinghouse post erected just a decade earlier.

The fragment in this chapter attests to the dynamic persistence of disorderly elements on this colonial frontier. People living on the Great Bay Estuary/P8bagok experienced different social, ecological, economic, and political landscapes than Massachusetts Bay inhabitants. To Puritan officials, the region's residents seemed disorderly, but disorder was actually a coherent adaptation to the lived realities of frontier life. In 1667 these realities did not include fortifying the meetinghouse. Shoddy construction was a tool of protest to undermine Puritan Boston's outside political impositions.

WEIGHING IN

By 1654, meetinghouses were an established part of English colonial settlement in New England that served in many capacities in civic and religious life. Colonists living in the Great Bay Estuary/P8bagok were often bad or indifferent Puritans, but in seventeenth-century New England, meetinghouses held salience as hubs of interaction. Near the excavation area, where we found the meetinghouse floor and posts, we recovered fragments that demonstrate how the Dover meetinghouse supported economic activity paramount to

Figure 4.10. Fragment: A lead weight lined with kaolin clay recovered near the meetinghouse inside the enclosure. It weighs one troy ounce. (Photograph by Ron St. Jean. Courtesy of GBAS.)

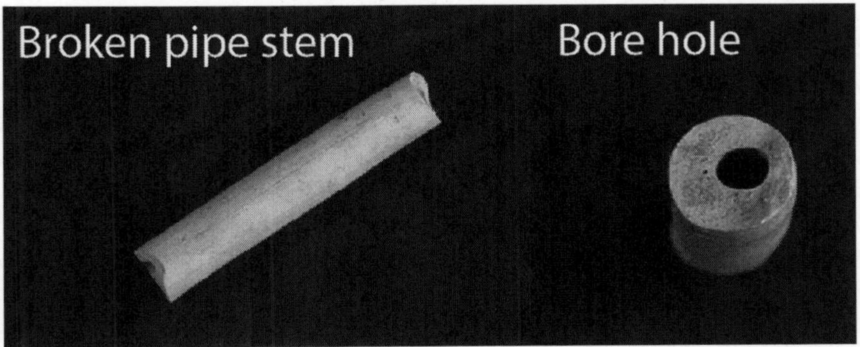

Figure 4.11. Fragment: A kaolin pipe stem recovered in same context as the troy weight. Measuring the diameter of the bore hole shows that this pipe dates to circa 1650–80. (Photograph by Ron St. Jean. Courtesy of GBAS.)

colonial settlements in this frontier region. Early colonialism was marked by complicated interplays of religion, politics, and economics. This helps explain why, even in this independent region, local colonists still built a meetinghouse with careful attention.

One of the most striking fragments is a small, well-crafted object made of lead and coated in a thin layer of white kaolin clay (fig. 4.10). This object weighs 31.1 grams, which makes it one troy ounce (oz t). Troy weight is based on twelve troy ounces to a pound. Some believe troy measurement has its origins in ancient Rome. It was certainly in place in medieval Europe by the ninth/tenth century, likely deriving its name from merchant trade in Troyes, France. King Henry II brought the troy system to England in the twelfth century.[55] Five hundred years later, the troy system was used in England to measure the weight of precious metals, gunpowder, medicines, and other rarities.[56] We interpret this fragment as a trade weight.

As European powers rapidly expanded around the globe, colonies and emerging market systems operated in a chaos of varied monetary units, measuring systems, and bills of credit. There was marked variation across emergent colonies.[57] Standardization did not come until later. Currency use, measurement systems, commerce values, barter practices, and other trade and exchange practices varied from place to place, but troy weight would have been one system familiar to English colonists living in seventeenth-century New England.[58]

This troy ounce trade weight is coated in kaolin clay, the same clay used to make pipes in England, a major export in high demand in the colonies.[59] And a broken pipe stem tells us that this trade weight was associated with a particular period of meetinghouse use. In the same excavation unit, at the same depth as this trade weight—thus in the same context—we recovered a broken piece of a kaolin pipe stem (fig. 4.11). The bore hole on this pipe stem piece measures 7/64 diameter. Because the clay pipe industry is relatively well documented, archaeologists can date pipes by measuring the diameter of their bore holes.[60] This pipe dates to circa 1650–80, overlapping with the meetinghouse construction, use, and "fortification." By extension, we infer that the trade weight is contemporary or overlaps in time.

This tells us that Dover colonists bought, sold, and/or traded goods using a familiar English measurement system at their local meetinghouse. Trade would have been a critical activity for colonists living in the Great Bay Estuary. A desire for economic independence and gain motivated many to live in this northern frontier, which, while rich in natural resources, came with harsh winters and hardships of remote living. We do not know precisely what was being measured and traded at this meetinghouse site, but there are suggestive indications. Near where this trade weight was recovered, we found a few small fragments of French gun flint. As we saw in chapter 3, French gunflint at English colonial sites is suggestive of Native presence. Again, the troy weight system was used at the time to measure gunpowder, and it actually continues to be used for this purpose today. Finding the gun flint near this trade weight might indicate that gunpowder was traded at the Dover meetinghouse.

The pipe stem date range covers the time before and after the 1667 "fortification" orders, so we cannot know for certain whether trade occurred before or after the stockade went up. If after, it would mean that, even after local English residents were forced to fortify their meetinghouse against Indigenous peoples (and their French allies), they let them inside to trade in gunpowder. If it occurred before the site was ordered to be fortified, it still emphasizes how Boston and the Great Bay (dis)ordered their worlds in radically different ways, especially when it came to gauging risks from Native peoples. Boston demanded a fortified frontier, whereas those actually living in the frontier, the colonial inhabitants of the region, may well have been profiting from trading weapons with Abenaki/Pennacook and perhaps other regional Indigenous peoples, right next to their meetinghouse.

This 1654 meetinghouse was a hub of interaction that drew together the area's dispersed colonists, creating the chance for interaction and exchange with a wider group of people than could be found in everyday activities. Puritans mandated coming to the meetinghouse, but they could not stop Great Bay frontier colonists from using that mandate for their own means and ends.

The plain simplicity of meetinghouses repeated across New England was intentional, aimed at making these hubs of a Puritan-led colonial identity formation. But, during the seventeenth century out in this colonial frontier, Dover's 1654 First Parish meetinghouse and imposed "fortification" became a site of colonial identity contestation.

Figure 5.1. Fragment: A red-clay tobacco pipe stem recovered from excavations at the Field-Bickford site, a seventeenth-century English colonial site in the Great Bay Estuary/P8bagok. (Photograph by Ron St. Jean. Courtesy of GBAS.)

5

FRAGMENTS FROM SHIFTING REALITIES

Clay tobacco pipe fragments are some of the most common artifacts found on colonial-era sites in the Americas and Caribbean, the lands where tobacco originated and was first cultivated (fig. 5.1). Tobacco use has ancient roots among Indigenous communities across the Americas and was often, and continues to be, part of religious practices and ceremonies.[1] Encountered during some of the earliest European contacts in the "New World," tobacco and Indigenous smoking pipes had been brought back to Europe by the 1500s. But transforming tobacco into a commodity and smoking into an industry took a convergence of global practices. During the late sixteenth and early seventeenth centuries, white, hard-paste Chinese porcelain ceramics came to Europe across sea routes traveled by Portuguese and Dutch merchants.[2] The key ingredient in porcelain is kaolin clay. Although available in many places around the world, kaolin had only been used to make ceramics in China. When European potters saw porcelain, they recognized the value of the fine white clay and started mining kaolin nearby for their own use.[3]

The arrival of Indigenous tobacco and smoking pipes and Chinese porcelain ceramics in Europe was the global convergence that led to the creation of white kaolin clay pipes. As smoking grew popular, England became a leader in mass-producing white kaolin clay pipes, using a mold to form the signature long stem and belly-shaped bowl (fig. 5.2).[4] These pipes came to be called

Figure 5.2. Fragment: A typical seventeenth-century kaolin pipe bowl (found at the same site as the red-clay pipe in fig. 5.1). (Photograph by Ron St. Jean. Courtesy of GBAS.)

white-ball clay pipes because clay miners in England lumped white clay into balls for shipment to production facilities. These pipes became a major English export to New World colonies, where they were used by colonists of all ages and also traded with Indigenous peoples.[5]

Kaolin pipes have been widely studied by historic archaeologists and, as seen in chapter 4, serve as valuable chronological site dating tools. Other types of clay pipes are found at colonial-era sites as well: locally made red earthenware tobacco pipes have been found at sites in North and South America and the Caribbean.[6] In North America, locally manufactured tobacco pipes are commonly found at early English colonial sites in Virginia and Maryland near the Chesapeake Bay. These red clay pipes are called Colono tobacco pipes, and they show a wide diversity of form and decoration.[7] It appears that in the Chesapeake, Indigenous peoples, enslaved Africans, and English colonists all produced red clay pipes locally and expressed group identities in varied pipe forms and decorative elements.[8]

Red clay pipe fragments have also been recovered in New England, including at northern colonial frontier coastal sites.[9] Found less frequently than in the Chesapeake, New England's colonial red clay pipes also show much less variation than those in the Chesapeake. They have little or no decoration and were made in a belly-bowl form using the English-mold approach or a manufacturing process that mimics it.[10] New England's red clay pipes have not been the subject of much research, but what has been done suggests that, unlike these other examples, here they were primarily English colonial products manufactured by English colonists locally in several places across New England.[11]

New England's red clay pipes serve as a kind of index to the complex shifting realities in colonial-era New England: this is why a fragment of one opens this chapter (see fig. 5.1). In New England, settler colonists remained bound materially and ideologically to England in many ways, despite internal differences like those explored in chapter 4. Colonists wanted finished goods from Europe and worked to acquire them.[12] As the British imperial project expanded over the seventeenth century, England increasingly sought to control all trade and imports and exports from its colonies via a series of Navigation Acts. The three thousand miles separating New England from England meant that, while colonists still desired European goods, they generally made do with limited amounts of them. As constricting English trade controls began to bite, living day to day in new ways inevitably had a transformative cultural impact.

In geographic extent and area, New England is vastly larger than England, but during colonial times its entire English population was much smaller than the population of England. By 1700, New England is estimated to have had around ninety thousand European inhabitants, and Boston, its largest city, held around fifteen thousand people. In comparison, London alone had a population of over half a million.[13] Of necessity, these very different demographics made colonial settlements more self-sufficient and particularly sensitive to local social and ecological conditions. In more urban centers like Boston and across rural frontiers like the Great Bay Estuary/P8bagok, generations turned over, marriages formed new kinship networks, settlers adapted to local ecosystems and conditions, and colonial communities evolved. Part of this evolution saw colonists start to produce local versions of items that were expensive to import from England or just hard to find. This included utilitarian goods and wares and more desirable luxury items.[14]

This red clay pipe stem, recovered at a colonial English site at the mouth of the Oyster River and Little Bay, known as the Field-Bickford site,[15] shows how these trends played out on the ground in this frontier (see fig. 5.1). Although made in New England, this pipe emulated an imported English finished good (see fig. 5.2). It is at once English, and not English, at once global and local. This chapter explores how settler colonialists in the Great Bay region navigated changing global trade networks. Bonds to Europe persisted, but their focus shifted from Europe to the new realities and relationships that were developing as they lived in this place.

COLONIAL POTTERY: GLOBAL AND LOCAL PROCESSES

I want to draw our attention to another category of artifacts made of clay that are also ubiquitous at colonial sites in New England: ceramic sherds from broken pottery vessels. A wide range of ceramic vessels, from plates to jars to teacups to tankards, were an integral part of colonial life and foodways. Pottery was used to store, prepare, serve, and consume food and drink on all occasions from the most mundane to the highly celebratory. Pottery can be divided based on firing temperatures. Earthenwares are fired at the lowest temperature, 900 to 1050°C, and tend to be porous. Stonewares are fired at 1200–1300°C and become harder bodied. Porcelains are hard white-bodied ceramics produced from kaolin (like English clay pipes) that can be fired at over 1300°C.[16]

Pottery making was a long-established domestic craft tradition in Europe. Local potters made a range of vessel forms using vernacular decorations and techniques that reflected their regional affiliations and traditions.[17] Earthenware was most widespread but stoneware, produced in the Rhine region of Germany beginning in the last decades of the thirteenth century, held a significant place in precolonial European domestic-scale pottery production.[18] During the expansion of European colonialism, pottery production was transformed into a global market-based endeavor.

Chinese porcelain was already thousands of years old when its introduction into European markets spurred significant developments in pottery production, including, as we just saw, the development of the ceramic pipe industry.[19] Blue-and-white Chinese porcelain, a hallmark of the Ming Dynasty, became wildly popular after 1602, when the Dutch captured the *Concepcion*, an enormous Portuguese trading ship loaded with ceramics, and sold their booty in the Netherlands.[20] In the 1600s, blue-and-white porcelain became an item of high demand in growing global colonial markets as well. To meet rising demand, Chinese potters started producing blue-and-white porcelain for European and colonial markets that were decorated to suit European aesthetics.[21]

Trying to imitate Chinese porcelain, European potters began to make tin-glazed earthenware for the same European and colonial markets. The Dutch city of Delft was highly successful at this in the early 1600s.[22] By around 1615, English entrepreneurs had imported potters from the Netherlands to develop a robust delftware industry of their own that produced a wide variety of ceramic shapes and decorations.[23] Over the course of the seventeenth century, potteries producing delftware and other earthenwares proliferated in England: between 1660 and 1700 alone, the number of English pottery workers doubled.[24] Pottery was such an important industry that, in 1672, King Charles

II forbade the importation of foreign ceramics to England and its colonies.[25] The only two exceptions were for porcelain and for Rhineland stonewares.[26]

By the seventeenth century, Rhenish stoneware production had shifted to Westerwald. Salt glazing had been added to the manufacturing process. Two major varieties of Rhenish stoneware circulated in seventeenth-century markets. One was coated in a brown slip that was specked from salt glazing. The face of a bearded old man became such a prevalent motif that brown-slipped stoneware jugs were given their own name—*Bartmannskrug*, or "Bartmann jug," which was also called Bellarmine.[27] The other variety featuring a cobalt blue glaze and elaborate sprig decorations is known as Westerwald. As the seventeenth century progressed, floral designs with medallion motifs increasingly decorated Westerwald stoneware, and, during the last two decades, a deep black-and-purple manganese glaze occasionally appeared. England's pottery industry started manufacturing its own salt-glazed stoneware in the late seventeenth century. As English stoneware production expanded over the course of the eighteenth century, Rhenish wares became less common in English markets.

The English government controlled colonial imports to make their colonists "buy British." Over the seventeenth and into the eighteenth century, New England's markets were ever more dominated by English ceramics, with the exception of those foreign ceramics approved by the king, Rhenish stoneware and Chinese porcelain. With a wide variety of pottery types produced in England, New England colonists had many types of pottery to choose from, and they developed preferences for certain pottery styles. Fine English-made earthenwares along with imported porcelains and Rhenish stonewares were particularly fashionable but expensive.[28] It was not until English entrepreneurs, such as Josiah Wedgwood, perfected a refined cream-colored English earthenware in the late 1700s that ceramics became both more standardized and affordable. By the end of the 1700s, creamwares and pearlwares came to dominate the New England market and displaced the previously popular, more varied, ceramic styles of the seventeenth century.[29] Understanding this ceramics timeline helps date and explain the distribution of ceramics at colonial New England sites.

FINDING: RECOVERING, PROCESSING, CURATING, AND ANALYZING GBAS'S ARTIFACTS

So far in the book, the archaeological finding sections focus on fieldwork, but surveying and excavating sites are only two parts of the process of archaeology. This section shares a bit about the less well-known, some may say less glamorous, side of archaeological research: lab work. A rule of thumb in archaeology is that for every hour in the field, there are four hours of associated lab work to clean, process, catalog, curate, and analyze recovered artifacts and associated field samples. As discussed in chapter 4, professional archaeologists must follow a strong set of ethics, and this includes taking proper responsibility for cultural artifacts and other materials recovered and collected during fieldwork.

Figure 5.3. Finding: GBAS team members screening for artifacts during a dig (Diane Fiske, GBAS's community historian, is in the front).

At GBAS, we find artifacts by screening 100 percent of our excavated soil through a quarter-inch mesh screen. We pour dirt through the screens and gently shake the screen sifters so that the dirt falls to the ground, leaving objects contained in the dirt in the screen. Then we examine these to collect any possible cultural artifacts (fig. 5.3).[30] As we collect artifacts, we put them in a "Lot" bag with an identification number. Any excavation component we undertake—be it a shovel test, a 1 × 1 meter excavation unit, a feature cross-section excavation, or a soil sample—is assigned its own individual Lot number. As we dig, each stratigraphic layer within a given Lot is assigned its own bag. This way, artifacts from a given excavation unit are contained in the same Lot and bags within the Lot separate them by depth and level.

Lot information is recorded in the Lot book. It is also recorded on excavation unit and level forms and written on artifact bags with Sharpies (fig. 5.4). Additionally, within each bag, we place a bag tag with the same information. So much duplicate record keeping is built into our field recovery because knowing the context of each artifact is critical to our work. We must be able to associate an artifact with the exact place it was recovered at a site and what surrounded it. An artifact without this contextual information, which archaeologists refer to as provenience, may be interesting or pleasing to look at but is not analytically useful. Our primary interest in objects is their archaeological context as this allows us to analyze associations between artifacts, features, structures, landscapes, and so on and reconstruct past behavior. This differs from the art historical approach to archaeological objects, typical of museums that emphasize the rarity, aesthetics, and display value of objects over their context.[31]

At the end of each day, GBAS's fieldwork finds are taken to the archaeology lab at the University of New Hampshire. The first step in lab work is cleaning the artifacts. To keep track of context, we work Lot by Lot, cleaning each bag

Figure 5.4. Finding: A UNH student volunteer on GBAS holds up a "Lot" bag.

individually (fig. 5.5). Artifacts are washed and/or dry brushed depending on what is best for their material stability. Once cleaned, everything from the same Lot and bag is placed on a tray to dry. Once dry, the items are placed into clean bags with all information duplicated on bag tags and labels. Once the finds from a field season are washed and dried, we catalog the artifacts. To catalog, we separate each Lot bag into its component material categories (ceramics, bone, metal, stone, etc.), and we count, weigh, and take other relevant measurements on each category of material. We enter provenience information and these counts and measurements into a catalog database. Cataloged items are placed in archival-quality bags, with archival-quality labeling

Figure 5.5. Finding: GBAS field crew clean artifacts in the University of New Hampshire Archaeology Lab.

that retains field provenience. Collections are stored in archival quality boxes. Tedious, meticulous work is the backbone of archaeology.

After cataloging and curating a collection, lab work shifts to the analytical phase. Each type of material from an archaeological site requires analysis based on specialized knowledge and training. Sometimes this knowledge is available in the project team, and sometimes an outside expert has to be hired. GBAS hired an outside zooarchaeologist to analyze our faunal (animal) remains. The zooarchaeologist took all GBAS animal remains recovered in the field to their own lab where they identified and created output tables documenting species present, estimating the number of individuals of each species, determining animal age and sex, recording skeletal elements present (butchering patterns), and documenting bone modifications (e.g., burning, cutmarks). Likewise, GBAS hired an outside expert, a paleoethnobotanist, to analyze recovered botanical (plant) remains. The paleoethnobotanist created data records of plant species, part of plant, plant distribution, and plant seasonality. GBAS conducted its own analysis of two other major categories of archaeological artifacts: stone tools and ceramics. Ceramic sherds, broken parts of pottery vessels, are among the most ubiquitous artifacts found on archaeological sites worldwide. Ceramics have long been a subject of archaeological analysis and analytic approaches are well developed in the discipline.[32]

Colonial sites in New England also have a ubiquity of ceramics; excavations at colonial sites routinely produce thousands and thousands of ceramic sherds. Understanding what kind of vessels people were making, purchasing, using, and ultimately discarding provides insights into the broader social and economic setting and also on individual decisions and behaviors within this setting. GBAS analyzed ceramics sherds from collections from two colonial sites in the Great Bay Estuary: the Burnham site, excavated by GBAS and described in chapter 3, and the Field-Bickford site, which yielded the pipe fragment. This site is located where the mouth of the Oyster River joins Little Bay. Like the Burnham site, it was occupied by colonists who dispersed along the Oyster River sometime in the 1630s. While the main built structure of the Burnham homestead was taken down in the mid- to late 1700s, the Field-Bickford colonial structure is said to have stood until the early 1800s, when it was razed.[33] Because the sherds at these sites represent vessels used by people living in them, we started our ceramic analysis by conducting a minimum number of vessel (MNV) count, a standard approach in archaeological ceramic analyses. An MNV count estimates the minimum number of original vessels that could account for all the ceramic sherds found at a site.

To start our MNV count, we examined all the ceramic sherds in the collections of each site. Then, we sorted the sherds into four major ware categories:

porcelain, stoneware, earthenware (imported), and redware. "Redware" has many connotations in historical archaeology, but for our purposes here, it refers to red earthenware made by colonists in New England following English potting traditions using locally available clays, as the red clay pipe opening the chapter was made. Within each category, we first evaluated the location where the sherds had been found at the site. Ceramic sherds are created when a vessel breaks, so typically, sherds found very far apart at a site are not likely to be from the same vessel. After we made distance cut offs, we next examined the material, shape, and decoration (or lack thereof) of the sherds. Sherds are like three-dimensional puzzle pieces. In part, the shape of a sherd is determined by the shape of the vessel it came from, that is, whether it had been part of a plate, a bowl, a cup, a tankard, or a jar. Some sherds are so small or ambiguously shaped that vessel form cannot be determined. Sherds that can be identified are grouped by vessel type. Then we try to figure out what pieces go together. Were they made from the same kind of clay? Do they share the same decoration or glazing? What size vessel are they from?

By assessing the shared features of sherds, we worked to group them into an MNV from a site that would have produced those sherds.[34] The term minimum is important here as it emphasizes that our approach was conservative. We did not want to overestimate the number of pottery vessels. Our final MNV count was 447 from the Burnham site and 600 from the Field-Bickford site. We next coded a series of attributes for each MNV.[35] Given a site-use history that extended into the later part of the colonial era for Burnham, and into the 1800s for Field-Bickford, we excluded creamware and pearlware vessels from our analysis based on the ceramics history and chronology already discussed. This left an MNV of 460 from Field-Bickford and 385 from Burnham.

POTTERY TRENDS ON A FRONTIER

As shown in table 5.1, the distribution of the four ware categories is quite similar across these two colonial sites from this frontier landscape. Earthenwares include tin-enameled delftware (fig. 5.6) and other fine English-made earthenware, such as Staffordshire slipware (see fig. 5.6).[36] Stonewares include Rhenish Bellarmine and Westerwald (see fig. 5.6) as well as English white salt-glazed stoneware. These broadly similar ceramics distributions make sense given the site similarities: the dates are roughly the same, they are located on the same river tributary, and both were large, likely comparable colonial homesteads (both also long referred to as "garrisons" but as we have seen, not necessarily because they were fortified). In addition, the collections show that both sites shared a similar degree of affluence.

Table 5.1. Minimum number of vessels (MNV) distribution analysis of four broad ceramic ware types

	Field-Bickford	Burnham	Summed Both Sites
Porcelain	7.4% (34 MNV)	5.7% (22 MNV)	6.6% (56 MNV)
Stoneware	14.1% (65 MNV)	17.1% (66 MNV)	15.5% (131 MNV)
Earthenware (import)	19.1% (88 MNV)	19.2% (74 MNV)	19.2% (162 MNV
Redware	59.4% (273 MNV)	57.9% (223 MNV)	58.7% (496 MNV)

Note: Creamware and pearlware were excluded from earthenware.

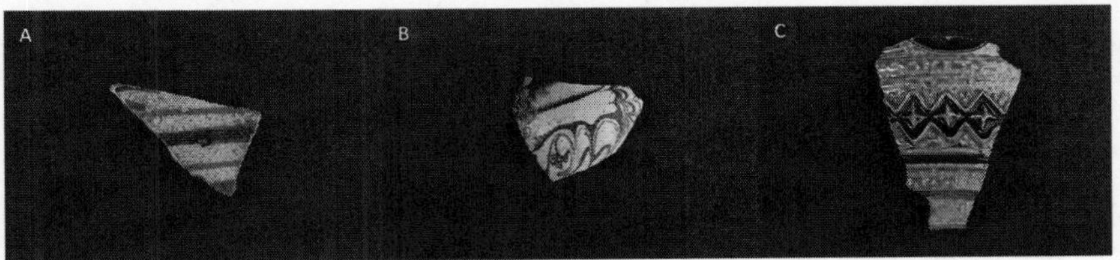

Figure 5.6. Fragments: Examples of seventeenth-century imported ceramics recovered from archaeological excavations of colonial sites on Oyster River: *A*, English delftware (Field-Bickford); *B*, Staffordshire slipware (Field-Bickford); *C*, Westerwald stoneware tankard (Burnham). (Photographs by Ron St. Jean. Courtesy of GBAS.)

Manufactured in New England, red earthenware, called "redware" here, is by far the most abundant ceramic type found on both sites. Research has shown that even New England colonists on the frontier could acquire European finished goods, so the abundance of redware here cannot be attributed to frontier isolation.[37] In fact, high redware abundance is common on excavations of colonial sites across New England, even in more populated centers.[38] Colonial-era red earthenware can be glazed or unglazed, but glaze makes pottery less porous, so different colors of lead glaze frequently appear on sherds. Both unglazed redware and glazed redware sherds were recovered across these colonial sites (fig. 5.7).

On the right side of the largest unglazed sherd, you can see a thumbprint, a physical trace left behind by the potter that speaks to artisanal aspects of colonial New England pottery making (see fig. 5.7). Potting, again, was becoming a large-scale, centralized market-oriented operation in England over

Figure 5.7. Fragments: Sherds from two redware vessels recovered in GBAS's excavations at the Burnham "garrison" site. *Top:* Unglazed redware storage vessel. Note the thumbprint on the right-hand side of the largest sherd. *Bottom:* Brown-glazed redware serving vessel. Yellow and red glazes were also common. The drilled hole was likely a failed attempt to prevent breakage. (Photographs by Ron St. Jean. Courtesy of GBAS.)

the course of the seventeenth and early eighteenth centuries, with laborious tasks divided among different craftspeople to speed up and standardize production. In the New England colonies, however, pottery production was initiated locally by colonists who needed vessels for regular, everyday activities. Even though England wanted to dominate colonial markets, England was far away. Imported vessels alone could not fill immediate needs as they arose. Moreover, English fine wares, Rhineland stoneware, and Chinese porcelain were expensive and could also be ill-suited to the quickly changing needs of colonial life.

Some colonial New Englanders came with knowledge of potting. Since the New England coast is covered in clay beds—placing the raw material necessary for pottery production quite literally underfoot—experienced potters started making pottery to meet immediate local demands, creating forms that appealed to local tastes. Virtually all New England vessels were made one at a time, thrown on pottery wheels. There is little evidence for the use of molds to mass-produce pottery or any kind of centralized production system.[39] Lacking centralization and industrial processing methods, colonial New England pottery production was limited to relatively coarse and porous earthenwares, and the composition of available coastal clays meant these were all redware (see fig. 5.7).

Bricks are also made of clay, and coastal clay deposits were routinely used for brickmaking across the region during and beyond the colonial era. Brickmaking and earthenware vessel production went hand in hand. Early seventeenth-century potteries in Boston and other Massachusetts Bay towns were associated with early brickyards.[40] It is highly likely that informal pottery making went on in many early colonial New England coastal settlements, with local potters filling local demands on an ad-hoc basis. Chronic labor shortages for fishing, farming, and timber harvest may have limited pottery production to slack times during the year, but little about early colonial New England pottery production is well-documented.[41]

By the late seventeenth century, pottery making in New England had grown into a more profitable activity, and it continued to expand over the next one hundred years.[42] In the Great Bay Estuary/P8bagok, rich marine clay deposits made brickmaking a notable enterprise.[43] While this coastal region's formally documented potteries do not appear until the 1720s, in places where redware potteries are better known, brickmaking and earthenware production went hand in hand. Thus, it is very likely that local redware production occurred before we have knowledge of it.[44] New England redware declined notably in the late 1700s when the virtual mass production of English creamwares made them readily available, inexpensive, and fashionable.[45] New England red earthenware production ebbed and flowed with British tides of mercantilism.[46]

PREFERENCES AND REALITIES

Global forces shaped pottery availability and style in overarching ways. By breaking down what vessel forms and types appear at these two sites, we gain insight into how early colonists living on this frontier used pottery. For each vessel identified from fragments in the MNV analysis, we tried to determine what kind of vessel it had been in its useful life and coded that information if we were reasonably confident in our determination. Serving vessels came in four forms: bowls, cups, plates, and tankards; the jar was the only form of storage vessel. We confidently determined vessel form for 230 of the 460 vessels from Field-Bickford in the MNV results. Given that the recovery context of the Burnham site produced more broken-up sherds, we could only confidently assign vessel form to 86 of its 385 resulting MNVs. Again, we sought to avoid overrepresentation by making conservative assessments.

Of the eighty-six identifiable vessel forms from Burnham, thirty-six were jars and fifty were serving vessel forms (bowls, cups, plates and tankards, taken together). Of these fifty serving vessels, forty were imported pottery (earthenware, porcelain, or stoneware) and ten were New England redware. For jars, however, the attribution was reversed: thirty-two were local redware and four were imported. It is tempting to speculate about why imported ceramics dominated the sample of serving vessels we found at this site, but these data are clearly limited, given that the vessel forms of only 22 percent of the MNVs were clearly recognizable. Comparing the Burnham results with those from the Field-Bickford site shows that the former probably does not present a full picture. Of the 230 identifiable Field-Bickford forms, 91 are jars and 139 are serving vessels. Serving vessels were almost evenly split between imports (70/139) and redware (69/139). Redware jars still dominated, but less so than in the Burnham data: 71 redware to 20 imports.

Small sample size introduces bias in data. If we could have identified more vessel forms in the Burnham collection, the striking imbalance between imported and redware serving vessels would likely have evened out to some degree. Similarities in distribution across the four broad ceramic types found at the two colonial sites mean that combining data from both samples will yield a more accurate ratio of import to redware vessels for Great Bay Estuary (fig. 5.8). Field-Bickford shows almost a 50/50 split between import and local serving vessels while Burnham's is closer to 80/20. For storage jars, Burnham shows a redware/import ratio of 90/10, while Field-Bickford's is closer to 75/25. After combining vessel forms from both sites, we find that 58.2 percent (110/189) of serving forms are imports, and 41.8 percent (79/189) are redware, whereas, for jars, 81.1percent are redware (103/127) and 18.9 percent are imported (24/127).

Again, it is tempting to construct an explanation from the Burnham data, where imports dominated serving vessels and redware dominated storage vessels. This is because strong results can fit in a tidy story. We could say that New England redware production mostly filled the day-to-day utilitarian needs of dairying and other storage, but when colonists consumed and/or shared food and drink, they preferred to use imported English market wares. That is, while local ceramics might have been functional, when colonists were seeing and being seen, they preferred to use ceramics imported from England: three thousand miles away, households in New England were still strictly adhering to English presentations. Yet, when ceramic fragment data from both colonial homesteads are taken together, we see that story, however tidy, is incomplete.

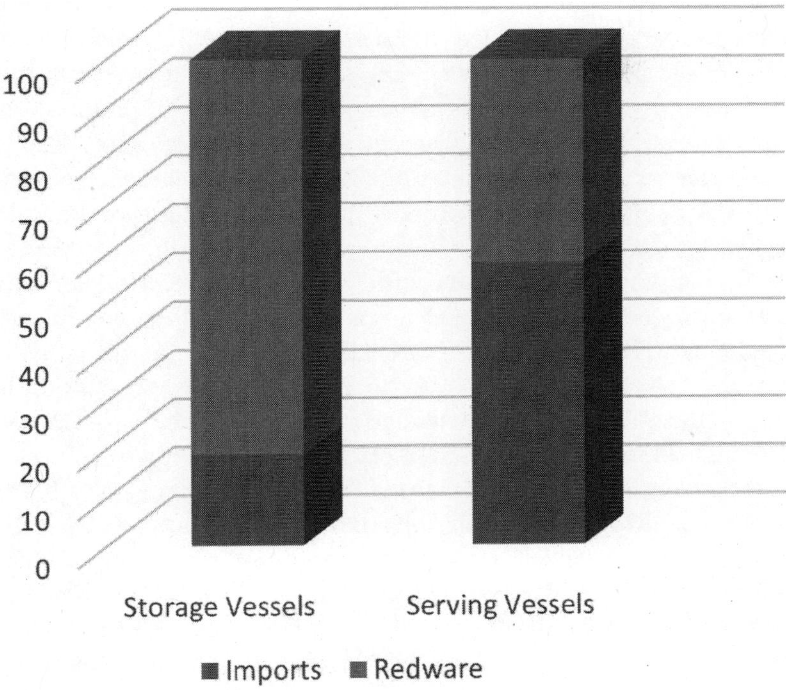

Figure 5.8. A graph of summed percentage of imports (all varieties) compared with redware across storage (jars) and serving vessels (plates, bowls, cups, and tankards) at the Burnham and Field-Bickford sites.

Combined evidence from both homesteads shows that colonists living along the Oyster River had access to, and acquired, imported English pottery vessels. As 58.2 percent of the serving vessels were imports, European forms were preferred for serving food and drink (see fig. 5.8). Likewise, most storage vessels were redware. Colonists relied on New England redware for storage functions and utilitarian activities, such as dairying and food preservation, Yet separation between categories was murkier than even colonial users may have realized.

We know that porcelain was in demand and a mark of status across Europe during the seventeenth and eighteenth centuries. It was popular in the colonies as well and also signaled wealth.[47] Porcelain cups, bowls, and plates were found at both sites (tankards are not made of porcelain). Looking at the summed MNV values from both sites, porcelain makes up 6.6 percent of the total assemblage but 17.2 percent of the plates, cups, and bowls. Porcelain is disproportionately represented in plates, cups, and bowls, vessels used to serve food and hot drinks, especially tea, to household guests. Tea was also an imported luxury good during the seventeenth and eighteenth centuries. Drinking tea was an important ritual act that reminded colonials of their English heritage and identity. Drinking tea was prestigious and often sociable, but tea was also scarce and expensive.[48] The beverage became more widely available by the mid-1700s as the Dutch East India Company expanded. We know how this story unfolds. The British Parliament passed a duty on tea in 1767 to benefit the English East India Company, which had assumed financial control of India after the end of the Seven Years' War (the French and Indian War in North America). Six years later, the Boston Tea Party signaled the beginning of the end of the English colonial era in New England.

Although an important segment of plates, cups, and bowls are porcelain, a greater proportion of tablewares are redware: 37.6 percent (fig. 5.9). If these three forms were broken down, one might assume that cups, vessels for serving prestigious tea, would deviate from the grouped vessel forms. But, in fact, the proportion of cups is even more skewed: 16 percent of cups are porcelain and 44 percent are redware (see fig. 5.9). So, although Oyster River colonists could roll out their "fine china," redware was more than twice as common in cups in their homes. Of course, fragments alone cannot tell us how, when, and for whom colonists living at these sites used these serving vessels. However, the ratios of redware to porcelain serving vessels make it likely that redware and porcelain circulated alongside each other at social events.

We see similar trends in tankards. Beer, ciders, and ales were drunk from tankards throughout the seventeenth and eighteenth centuries in homes, taverns, and inns across colonial America in widespread, sociable activity.[49] Our tankard sample is small, and conclusions are less robust, but trends are interesting nevertheless. Only twenty-four tankards could be confidently identified across both sites.[50] While stoneware accounts for only 15.5 percent of the total ceramics from both sites, six of the twenty-four tankards are stoneware. At 25 percent, stoneware is disproportionately represented in identifiable tankards (see fig. 5.9). These drinking vessels were common in Germany's Rhineland Westerwald, and all six of our sample's tankards are Westerwald. The Rhenish stoneware was a popular, high-status import good, especially during the seventeenth century before England ramped up its stoneware production (see fig. 5.6 for an example from the Burnham site). Although colonial families living in the Oyster River's frontier landscape had fancy

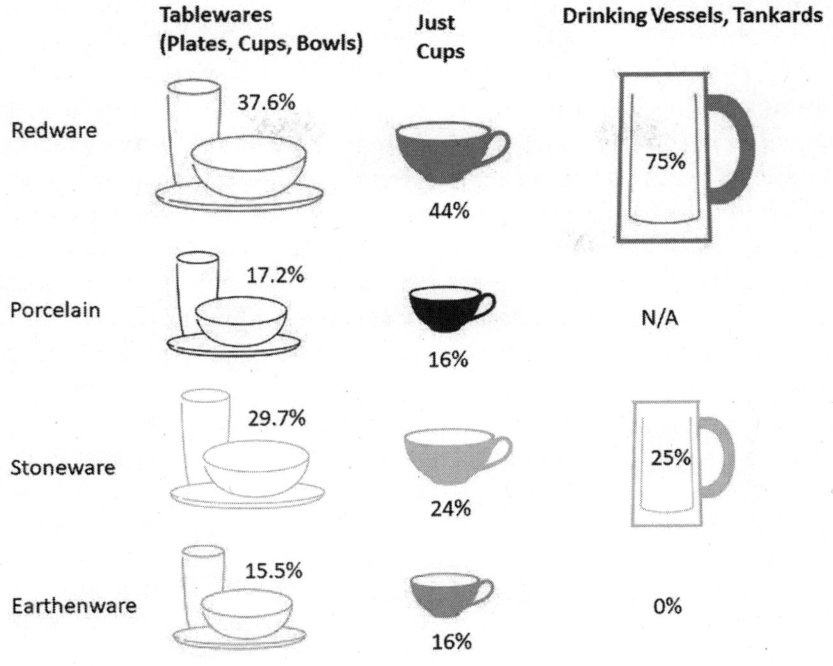

Figure 5.9. Tablewares and drinking vessels at the Burnham and Field-Bickford sites show the breakdown across broad ceramic types. Redware is dominant across all serving vessel categories.

imported Westerwald tankards on hand to serve beer, cider, and ale, three-quarters of tankards in their possession were redware (see fig. 5.9). When larger groups of people gathered, redware and Westerwald tankards must have been raised together in the same toast.

Although colonists living at these sites sought out porcelain teacups and stoneware tankards, supply chain realities meant that locally produced redware was increasingly available and accessible. And there was another intangible but no less real component: redware was more common and more familiar. Europe was far away in time and distance traveled and in psychological orientation for colonists living and raising families in a new, but increasingly familiar, place. Even as they acquired English goods and tried to maintain English identities and traditions, currents of change were tugging at them. They may have served tea in porcelain cups and drunk beer from Westerwald tankards, as their contemporaries, perhaps even their relatives in

England were doing, but our findings make clear that they also regularly used redware made in New England.

At first, redware may have been primarily utilitarian, but as potters became more skilled and redware more common, its relative status compared with that of English imports may have increased a bit. It is not uncommon to see hybrid material cultures emergence after contact or in colonial situations: two different cultures blend into one form.[51] This is not the case with redware vessels however. Redware was made in New England, but, like the New England redware pipe at the opening of this chapter, redware pottery emulated familiar English products and forms. Redware was not influenced by Indigenous ceramics, which were made of the same regional clay for millennia. Colonists followed English sensibilities of pottery production. Yet these products were decidedly local, not English finished imported vessels. I am not arguing that colonists living in New England's northern colonies, as here on the rural colonial frontier of the Oyster River, awoke one day and consciously decided that it would be okay to serve tea, beer, and meals on redware. Rather, acceptance came slowly, subconsciously: slippage happened as the local became more familiar in colonial residents' lives and the imported less relevant.

AN INVITATION TO A MEAL IN COLONIAL GREAT BAY ESTUARY/P8BAGOK

I conclude this chapter by inviting you to an imaginary meal at the Burnham "garrison" in the mid- to late 1600s. You enter a wooden house that is commodious for its time and place. But colonial structures were much smaller than houses today, so it feels rather cramped. In the central hearth, food cooks in simple metal pots. Candles and the central hearth offer the only light. A rustic wooden table is set. Your afternoon visit starts with tea served in imported Chinese porcelain cups and saucers. Then, your host pours you an ale in a fine Westerwald tankard but pours his ale in a redware tankard. You toast, clinking tankards.

Next comes the meal. As a guest, you are provided with metal silverware: maybe, you are given this seal-top spoon, an English import found in our excavations at the site (fig. 5.10). In England, spoons were preferred eating utensils for centuries, and they remained popular with English colonists for a long time.[52] The decorative baluster on this spoon appears to be from a mold used in England in the seventeenth century.[53]

Your meal is served on a redware plate. The meal is cod caught by your hosts at the mouth of the Oyster River, served with corn, beans, and squash (foods that GBAS recovered inside this English homestead, see chapter 3). Cod was one of the first commodities the English focused on in the region.

By the end of the seventeenth century, this wild marine species had been fished heavily by the English for decades. Lumber and grist mills and run-off from cleared land had polluted streams, rivers, and coastal waters. Therefore, cod was likely becoming scarce in the ecosystem. The corn, beans, and squash that you are served are the three sisters of Indigenous North American agriculture, obtained through trade or grown by your English hosts using knowledge learned from the Abenaki/Pennacook peoples who had lived on nearby land for centuries before the English had arrived (see chapter 2).

Stand back and take a mental snapshot. First, you drink imported Dutch tea from a Chinese cup, then you drink local beer from an imported German tankard, toasting your host who drinks from a local rendition of the same vessel form. You eat with a spoon imported from England or perhaps a treasured heirloom brought from England by the Burnhams. Your food is served on a New England–made redware plate: cod—harder and harder to catch in the estuary—is accompanied by domestic crops introduced to the English by Indigenous peoples whose foods, skills, and knowledge facilitated the colonists' survival in this surprising new land.

This meal is imaginary, but it is imagined from real fragments found at this English homestead, materials that inscribe the complex, shifting realities of living on a colonial frontier. The colonists living along the Oyster River and more broadly around the Great Bay Estuary/P8bagok were at once local and global, at once English and Other. This was a complicated space to occupy. The fragments we encounter in the previous chapters and again in this chapter attest to some of these complexities. In the next chapter, we explore how tensions between the local and the global took their toll and how the currents of change eventually came to include violence that still reverberates today.

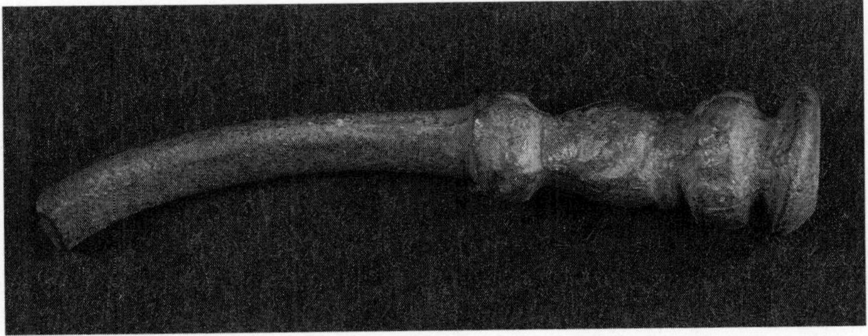

Figure 5.10. Fragment: A seventeenth-century seal-topped spoon recovered in the Burnham "garrison" site excavations. (Photographs by Ron St. Jean. Courtesy of GBAS.)

Figure 6.1. Fragment: New Hampshire Historical Marker about the Oyster River "Massacre" of 1694. Until recently, the marker could be seen at the head of tide of the Oyster River in Durham. It was removed after the state of New Hampshire selected it for revision and updating. (Photograph by Hantsheroes. CC BY-SA 3.0.)

6

FRAGMENTS FROM VIOLENCE

In exploring the archaeological elements of the seventeenth-century colonial frontier in P8bagok/Pascatway/Great Bay Estuary, we see how fragments left behind in this landscape diverge from what the prevailing historical narratives and understandings tell us, that violence is a common thread. We see that English colonists and Indigenous peoples in this place shared nuanced experiences and mutually beneficial interactions more often than has been generally portrayed. But, eventually, violence did come to this frontier, and how we grapple with it and remember it is important.

This chapter examines the infamous event in 1694, which the Oyster River "Massacre" Historical Marker (fig. 6.1) commemorates. I do not intend to write another history of this event.[1] Instead, I expand the context of a violent episode that radically altered the colonial project in this frontier landscape. Settler colonialism was successful in the Great Bay Estuary/P8bagok. The inevitability of this outcome can appear as a historical fact, foretold by events that led to our present state. I open with this historical marker because it helps us interrogate this sense of inevitability. It shows us the past is something that we help (re-)create in the present.[2]

The remembrance of historical violence takes place in the present.[3] Remembrance is an active curatorial process. Certain events, spaces, places, and perspectives are selected as worthy of commemoration. Others are marginalized and slowly slip out of memory. In New England, remembering colonialism largely involves commemorating incidents of violence, particularly Native violence against English colonists.[4] These narratives of violence seem powerfully self-evident despite the nonviolent relationships, webs of connections, and routine, even mundane, events that regularly linked colonists and Indigenous peoples from the earliest contacts but that were either never memorialized or have slipped out of memory. Such one-sided remembrances are maintained in contemporary memory and discourse.

Often, one-sided commemorations of violence appear as neutral descriptions of historical events on monuments and markers, such as the one shown in figure 6.1.[5] In New Hampshire, green signs with white text dot major and minor roadways to commemorate significant events, people, and places in state history. This sign was erected along New Hampshire Route 108 at the head of tides of the Oyster River in 1993 to mark the three hundredth anniversary of the Oyster River "Massacre" the next year. For almost thirty years it was an entry point into the area's seventeenth-century history. While the basic facts are correct, their selection and presentation are opaque and one-sided. A crucial question is unanswered: Why did this happen? Missing are the underlying geopolitical and socioecological relationships of this one episode, including the growing structural dominance of settler colonialism in New England over the seventeenth century and the ongoing territorial dispossession of Indigenous lands.

Yet the fact that the past is important enough to be remembered in the present gives us a chance to remedy such omissions and to develop shared pasts that can be foundations for shared futures. The state of New Hampshire is working on this very thing. Recognizing the problematic aspects of this Oyster River marker, the state recently removed it and convened a collaborative committee of regional Indigenous leaders, state employees, and scholars, including myself, to rewrite the message. None of us expect to capture the complexity of the era in a few hundred words, but we know that words matter. The words that stood for decades limited our understanding of what took place near that spot long ago and of what colonialism meant and how its legacies reverberate today.[6]

EXPANDING LIMITED ARCS

What are some limiting aspects of the arc of this episode as portrayed in this specific commemoration? Let us start with the word massacre. Massacre invokes images of one-sided, indiscriminate slaughter. Rev. John Pike was minister of Dover's First Parish Church, which served the Oyster River settlement at the time of the attack. Here is what he recorded in his diary about the event: "July 18. The Indians fell suddenly & unexpectedly upon Oyster

River about break of Day. Took 3 Garrisons (being deserted or not defended) killed and Carried away 94 persons. & burnt 13 houses—this was the fr act of hostility Committed by y after y peace Concluded at Pemmaqd" (spelling original).[7]

Pike's short, noneffusive description of this event does not stand out from other entries in his diary, a distinction one might expect for a massacre. While his entry makes it clear that this was a significant event for his Oyster River congregants, it does not imply that the event was exceptionally egregious in the context of the time. By living in this place at the time, Pike was immersed in the context of the raid. He had experienced the multifaceted nature of interactions (and clashes) between colonists, colonial powers, and Indigenous peoples. He knew loss and frustration went both ways and his entry reflected this context.

Historians only began describing this event as a massacre in the 1800s; thus, its dramatic memorialization occurred long after the actual event.[8] A group of mixed Abenaki warriors did kill English colonists on the Oyster River in July 1694, but this event was not isolated. It occurred within the frame of larger social and geopolitics of the time in a setting where raids by both sides were common.[9] An attack with a similar loss of life occurred thirty years later on the Kennebec River in Maine. There, English forces killed eighty Abenaki, mostly women and children, along with the Jesuit priest, Father Rasles, at the village of Norridgewock (August 23, 1724).[10] Unlike the Oyster River episode, nineteenth-century historians commemorated this as the Battle of Norridgewock. This difference in nomenclature is an example of how a dominant group can use the commemoration of historical violence as an exercise in structural power that enhances its long-term status.

Another limitation is the way the Oyster River marker highlights foreign involvement: a French soldier, de Villieu, is credited as having commanded the forces. This agrees with de Villieu's own account of his heroics to Frontenac, then the governor of New France, the territory colonized by France in North America that lay to the north and west of the New England colonies (again, its capital was Quebec, located north of New England's power center, Boston, which placed the erstwhile colonies of Maine and New Hampshire, and our boundary-spanning study area, the Great Bay Estuary/P8bagok, in a frontier position). Other contemporary records of the battle characterize de Villieu quite differently, as a self-promoting, frequently reprimanded career soldier in New France and also as a smuggler.[11] As the raiding party advanced toward Oyster River in late June 1694, he foolishly jeopardized its safety and received a bad beating for it—hardly the actions or treatment of a commander. In actuality, young chiefs and subchiefs from a mix of Abenaki bands, including Penobscot and Maliseet warriors, actually planned, scouted, and led the attack. The marker relays incongruous messages: on the one hand, Native peoples were extremely aggressive and hostile to the English; on the other hand, they were incompetent in organizing attacks and needed a French soldier to lead them.

The end of the sign's inscription highlights another limited perspective, the event is set in an Old World–European context of King William's War (1688/89 to 1697), the New World theater of the long-standing European conflict between Protestant England and Catholic France. Explaining the Oyster River event as part of a war makes it seem like this was part of a contained, coherent conflict with a clear beginning, a clear end, and with clear sides. This was not the case.[12] The sign fails to acknowledge New World circumstances that led to the conflict. Importantly, King William's War in New England was fought among New World peoples. Unlike European warfare's ponderous armies and choreographed battles fought near population centers, this war saw multifaceted raids, shifting allegiances, and varied clashes, some more coordinated than others, across the vast hinterlands of the northern colonies of New England and New France. Indigenous and colonial raiding parties followed similar tactics in a protracted conflict that died down and flared up again for years.

Well before King William's War, tensions were already high between New France and New England but also between the powerful Iroquois and the northern communities who shared in homelands they knew as N'dakinna and between New England colonial governments and sovereign Native groups.[13] Instead of contextualizing the Oyster River episode as a subset of European warfare, it is more prudent to look at it as part of a longer arc of Indigenous resistance to colonialism led by an uncontainable network of Indigenous leaders and families.[14]

TRACING THE ARC OF INDIGENOUS RESISTANCE

Relationships between Indigenous communities and English colonists in New England's more densely populated southern colonies turned tense early, with the Puritans starting the Pequot War less than a decade after their arrival. This conflict was marked by the devasting Pequot Massacre of 1637 (Battle of Mystic Fort) where some four to seven hundred Pequot were slaughtered by the Puritans.[15] Native peoples persisted in southern New England after these stinging defeats, engaging in creative resistance and diplomacy for decades, but pressures continued to mount. King Phillip's War (1675–78) emerged from this longer arc as Metacom, the Wampanoag sachem the English called Phillip, assembled a strong confederation of Indigenous communities to fight back against unrelenting English colonial incursions on their ways of life.[16] English colonialists were dealt heavy losses, but Indigenous communities ultimately bore more loss. Many Wampanoags, Narragansetts, and other southern communities sought refuge from the fighting with extended kin to the north.

Lake Winnipesaukee, the headwaters of the Merrimac River beyond the edge of English settlement, became an important locus in the region of refuge and resistance during and after King Phillip's War.[17] The Great Bay Estuary/P8bagok's waterways provided paths of connection to Lake Winnipesaukee, and this ecosystem became a place refugees moved to and through as southern New England destabilized. In 1675, the Massachusetts General Court passed a wartime bounty on scalps from Native peoples south of the Piscataqua River.[18] Perhaps not coincidentally, the first two documented raids on colonists in the Great Bay Estuary/P8bagok occurred in 1675. Along the Oyster River, colonial houses were burned and a few colonists killed.[19]

Massachusetts Bay Colony failed to grasp the realities of Indigenous peoples' extensive regional kin networks, and they also failed to understand the nature of colonial-Indigenous relationships on the northern frontier. As we saw with the issues around the fortification of Dover's meetinghouse, less than a decade before King Phillip's War (in 1667), local colonial leaders had no interest in taking aggressive stances against Indigenous peoples. As the violence of King Phillip's War reverberated north, it created ruptures in beneficial relationships between colonists and Native communities.[20] One critical rupture in the Great Bay Estuary/P8bagok occurred in 1676. Maj. Richard Waldron, introduced in chapter 4, who was the Massachusetts Bay Colony's backed leader in Dover, was ordered by Massachusetts General Court to capture Native warriors from southern New England who had raided English villages during King Phillip's War and had come north seeking protection with their extended kin, local Abenaki/Pennacook peoples.

Waldron had long-standing trade relationships with these local communities. He had no reason to alienate them. But he was also part of the Massachusetts political hierarchy. In an act of duplicity, he called local Abenaki/Pennacook peoples to gather for some kind of ceremonial gathering/feast.[21] Once there, all Native attendees, some four hundred or so, were surrounded by soldiers. When asked to lay down their weapons, the few among them with weapons did, yet the whole group was summarily captured by Waldron's soldiers.[22] A few were released but 350, including 250 women and children, were remanded to Boston. The event did not separate out local, peaceful, Abenaki/Pennacook peoples from southern New England fugitives, which is how dominant narratives have recorded this event. Instead, many were kept with the larger group of captives and likewise sent to Boston as prisoners. There, eight southern New England Indigenous leaders from King Phillip's War were executed, and the rest of the group was sold into slavery, likely to sugar plantations in Barbados.[23] This act of betrayal would be remembered.

Intermittent clashes continued in northern New England for the next decade and increased during King William's War and as the French began to encourage and subsidize hostilities against the English. One of the first coordinated attacks, in 1689, was on Waldron's mill and home site in Dover/Cochecho. Most commemorations and accounts of the Cochecho "massacre" emphasize the number of colonists killed and taken captive and Waldron's torture and demise, but they rarely acknowledge retribution as an important aspect of the attack.[24]

Accounts focus on the physical harm done to colonists, including Waldron, but the first thing targeted in this event was not personal/domestic at all; it was Waldron's mill, which was burned. We discussed earlier how mills usurped the natural functions of forests and rivers, taking fish, and transforming tidal waterfalls into great sources of settler colonial wealth. Mills were burned repeatedly during the raids of this time.[25] Livestock, another source of settler colonial wealth, were also targeted. Domesticated farm animals often ran wild, ravaging planting grounds and destroying wild plants that Indigenous peoples relied on in their seasonal rounds.[26] Destruction of colonial infrastructure was a consistent feature of Native-led raids in the northern colonies. Acknowledging the ecological devastation from the shock of colonialism as a factor that turned Indigenous communities against the English at the end of the seventeenth century helps reframe the violence of that time as Indigenous resistance to aspects of settler colonialism that stripped them of their ability to survive in their homelands.

By 1693, the English were more adept at fending off raids and at securing their settlements and infrastructure for their own ends.[27] The French-Native alliance was fraying under English advances. Native leaders led by Madockawando, a Penobscot, approached the English at their newly rebuilt stone fort at Pemaquid (Fort William Henry) asking for peace and reopened trade. The English convinced Madockawando and ten to twelve other leaders to sign a treaty that read more like a document of surrender than a joint agreement: including language having the sachems "hereby acknowledge our hearty subjection and obedience unto the Crown of England."[28] The English believed that they had broken Native alliances with the French and gained control of the vast northern and eastern Wabanaki lands. Accordingly, they imposed unfair trade conditions and provided no recourse to Indigenous communities who had expected reopened trade and exchange.

Once again, the English miscalculated networks of Native authority across the region. Hierarchical leadership was not a hallmark of Indigenous organization in the Northeast. Family groups and bands had their own male and, importantly, female leaders, this latter fact something often overlooked by the English.[29] Leaders who had not signed this treaty at Pemaquid were not obliged by it. New France, alarmed by this treaty that threatened their Native alliances, worked with dissatisfied leaders, including another Penobscot leader, Taxous, to continue pushing back on English colonists.[30] Additionally, the belligerent English interpretation of the terms of the treaty offended some of its original signers, who were becoming more and more resentful. This is where the seeds of the Oyster River raid were planted.

OYSTER RIVER, JULY 1694

Over the spring and early summer, a series of complex negotiations and coordinated moves by Indigenous leaders and French officials and miliary officers culminated in the large group of about 250 warriors circling Oyster River in mid-July 1694. The warriors came from many different bands, and the group included by-then disaffected Madockawando and Taxous. The party also had de Villieu and a few other French soldiers and Father Thury, a Jesuit priest.[31] In the days before the raid, Native scouts surveyed the area, made a detailed plan of the English settlements along the river, and developed the plan of attack. Bomazeen, a younger Kennebec leader, took on an important commanding role. Two divisions would approach the settlement along the river. Bomazeen would lead the division on the south bank of the river. Paquaharent, another Kennebec, would lead the one on the north bank. Madockawando, Taxous, and de Villieu would attack outlying settlements from the main river.[32]

The story of the attack has become canonical over the years. It goes like this. The raiders planned to spread out overnight, positioning themselves near English households up and down the river. The attack was to begin with a shot at dawn. However, the story goes, an unsuspecting English colonial resident left his house in the middle of the night and was shot dead. This gunshot alerted other Oyster River colonists to danger before the warriors were fully in position.[33] The attack commenced earlier than planned because of this unexpected development, but when it commenced, much damage was done. Bomazeen's division inflicted the most damage on the south bank of the river. Paquaharent's group along the north bank was somewhat less destructive. Many structures were burned, including perhaps five of the river's fifteen "garrisons" along with other houses. Around one hundred people were killed, and twenty or so were taken captive.[34] At the time of the attack,

Oyster River numbered around three hundred English colonial residents, so this was a sizeable loss.[35]

According to the canonical version of this event, the unexpected shooting of the colonist prevented the raiders from being fully in position for the attack and totally destroying the Oyster River settlement, which the historical narratives state was their original intention. I propose a critical examination of this statement. I ask us to consider this: What if the raid went mostly as planned? What if the targets whom they hit, those whom they spared, the destruction they inflicted, the moves they made, and the paths they took in and out of the Oyster River were planned and purposeful?

MATERIALITY AND SHIFTING PERSPECTIVES ON THE RAID

GBAS's findings include our extensive excavations at the Burnham "garrison," one of the English homesteads that was not attacked in the raid. If we take the commemorated story as reality, we must assume that it survived by dint of pure luck. Indeed, inherited traditions about the Burnham garrison support that notion. Traditions say that the yard gate (to presumably some kind of protective fencing) had been left open that night. The ten Native raiders sent to surprise the garrison had fallen asleep on the bank of the river near the house. A colonist at the garrison kept awake by a toothache heard the unplanned gunfire and immediately closed the gate and shouted to the neighbors. According to this story, the shout awakened the raiders who, seeing the closed gate, decided instead to attack a different house close by, the Pitman household.[36]

Let us examine this sequence of events in light of our excavations. One question is: Why would a hostile raiding party sleep near a heavily armed garrison? The answer to this question may be simple—they did not. As described in chapter 3, approaching the Burnham garrison site from a landscape perspective meant that GBAS established a grid and performed extensive shovel test surveys before excavating across the landform, down the hill, out to the creek, and eventually across the creek in the meadow. We found that the smaller depression visible at the hilltop site, which had been recorded in historic accounts as an ammunition storage facility, was actually part of the house. Our extensive excavations recovered many thousands of artifacts from the Burnham "garrison" site but not a single piece of ammunition or gun part. While we did not excavate every inch of the site, the material fragments we recovered clearly demonstrate that this site was not bristling with arms and ammunition.

How could closing a yard gate keep out a raging "massacre-ing" party? Again, I want to suggest the answer may be that it did not. In GBAS's sweeping and systematic exploration of the Burnham homestead landscape, we found no evidence of any kind of gate, palisade, or fortification around this site, either as post holes or as breaks in material distribution. We would expect to find a material signature from a wooden barrier and gate strong enough to stop attackers from getting through. But there is none.

When the raiding party suddenly awoke near the Burnham homestead, why did they not attack it anyway? Other "garrisons" were attacked despite the "warning shot." Why did this group target a neighboring house some distance away, giving people time to get defenses up, flee the raiding party, and rouse their neighbors? From a military perspective, this makes no sense. But it does make sense if you consider it in terms of relationships. What if the Burnham homestead was *never* a target in the Oyster River raid?

Many head-scratching aspects of these traditional narratives make more sense if we approach them from a different perspective. We know that Native scouts surveyed the Oyster River settlement in the days before the attack. English colonists who lived through the raid reported that, the night before the attack, "knocks were heard by night at certain doors and stones were thrown at garrisons." These actions were explained as efforts "to find out whether the houses and garrisons were defended and whether any watch were kept."[37] I want to suggest an alternate explanation: What if knocking on doors and throwing stones served a very different purpose? What if it was to offer some kind of warning to English colonists who had friendly relations with local Abenaki/Pennacook peoples to be on their guard? Of course, telling them a raid was coming would test the limits and the extent of loyalty of even the closest English-Indigenous relationship. So, if prompts to stay vigilant were not delivered in person, knocking on certain doors and throwing stones at certain dwellings may have been a way scouts subtly marked homesteads they wanted raiding parties to pass by.

We saw in chapter 3 that Burnham's dwelling contained notable amounts of Indigenous-derived objects and food. In chapter 2, we learned that the meadow west of Burnham's garrison was an Abenaki/Pennacook village that had been continuously occupied for hundreds of years before colonists arrived and overlapped with them for some years. There was a mutual relationship between Indigenous peoples and English colonists in this place. We will never know its exact nature, but objects found at both habitations suggest that it included beneficial exchange, respect, and trust. I contend that this relationship was at play on the night of July 18, 1694. The Burnham "garrison" was not "garrisoned" because its inhabitants did not fear outside attack. Raiding parties knew that it was safe to sleep near this English dwelling on the night before the raid. They also knew to pass it over in the attack, and so they did. All of Burnham's direct neighbors were attacked. Many other "garrisons" and dwelling houses on the river were attacked and burned. But they and some others were spared. It is hard to attribute salvation to sheer luck, to a toothache, and a (nonexistent) closed yard gate.

THE LANDSCAPE OF THE RAID

GBAS surveyed other sites across the landscape involved in this raid. One was located on the north side of the Oyster River near its mouth, where one of the colonial dwellings that was burned in the raid once stood.[38] Our survey found that there was an early colonial dwelling house, but, unfortunately, most of it and its associated cultural artifacts have washed out of the riverbank (I discuss the cause of this erosion in the conclusion of the book). However, we did find the edge of the dwelling house and recovered a few bricks from its central chimney. These bricks had been burned so extensively that they had "melted" (fig. 6.2).

Colonial-era brickmaking involved hand-molding locally procured clay and firing thousands of bricks together in seasonally built kilns that could reach about 1000°C, or 1850°F. Brickmaking was a common practice in colonial Great Bay.[39] In brickmaking, molded clay is fired at high temperatures.

Figure 6.2. Fragment: Examples of the melted brick recovered in GBAS's excavations at a colonial "garrison" site on the north side of the Oyster River that was burned during the 1694 raid.

Bricks that have "melted," as this brick had, were heated beyond their vitrification temperature until they lost their structural shape. Vitrification temperature varies based on the type of clay and the inclusions present in it but ranges from circa 1600 to 2200°C, that is, from circa 3000 to 4000°F.[40] These temperatures far exceed colonial-era kiln temperatures, indicating that these bricks were subject to a subsequent firing event that was deliberate and intense. Luck was not a driving factor in the attack in July 1694. The mixed Native forces leading the Oyster River raid could and did destroy some colonial structures and spared others.

The inherited narrative of the Oyster River raid ends this way: as the raiding party headed back up the Oyster River, on their way toward Lake Winnipesaukee and then farther north and east, they "assembled their captives in the meadow west of the Burnham garrison,"[41] a place we now know was the site of deep-time Indigenous occupation. The combatants knew that this meadow, in sight of the English "garrison," was as safe a place as they could find to regroup after the raid.[42] Yet safety alone is too expedient and English-centric to fully explain this decision.

We now know that this meadow had long been a place where Indigenous peoples lived, harvested wild resources, and grew crops to sustain themselves and their widespread kin networks across this estuarine ecosystem long before Europeans arrived. It was also an Indigenous place where residents became New World people, adapting to the arrival of foreigners, finding ways to interact with and persist in presence even as English colonists became more intent on permanent change, territorial dispossession, and structural dominance. The Abenaki/Pennacook village site in this meadow was no longer occupied in 1694. Intermittent violence rippling up from southern New England and across the northern frontier since the 1670s had induced many local Indigenous communities to move their villages away from English coastal settlements in favor of more interior places that were harder for the English to move to and through, such as Lake Winnipesaukee and even farther north and east toward Quebec.[43]

As we have explored at various points, Indigenous knowledge is often of and in the land. Places are sacred, they are knowledge repositories, they are teachers and they are relations.[44] This is powerfully true across the larger homeland Indigenous peoples understood as N'dakinna.[45] The warriors moving through Oyster River in 1694 knew that meadow was an Indigenous place. Elders perhaps knew this from firsthand experience and others via place-making traditions shared over generations. That they gathered together in this place was not an arbitrary decision, and it was not a historical happenstance. I propose that this was a purposeful decision, one that honored

Indigenous ways of knowing, that connected them to well-being and healing by being in a place steeped in all their relations, past and present.

IN THE WAKE

While the Oyster River raid was a real blow to the English, it was hardly terminal: the English colonial enterprise continued. King William's War ended a few years later with no obvious winner; the boundary between New France and New England was still set pretty much where it had begun, at the Kennebec River.[46] Hostilities between the European powers and their colonial governments were unresolved. In fact, Queen Anne's War broke out just five years later and lasted until 1713.[47] By the early 1700s, after many and varied conflicts, the nature of New England's once erstwhile northern colonies was changing. English colonial populations kept growing, early colonial settlements became larger and more established, other English settlements developed farther inland, Indigenous presence was drastically reduced, and armed conflicts moved farther and farther away to the northeast.

As the frontier retreated, English colonists were able to expand their landholdings.[48] In a process that occurred across the global colonial world, former Indigenous lands were transformed into cornerstones of intergenerational colonial wealth.[49] The ability to acquire land wealth and pass it on from generation to generation created a cascading waterfall of social impacts, including the rise of serious structural inequalities. Land wealth continues to be tied to deep social inequalities today.[50] The Oyster River raid sits at a threshold moment in a region undergoing much larger processes of global colonialism. Before the raid, we glimpsed a frontier landscape in which settler colonialism was not fully formed and what it would be was not completely determined. In its wake, English permanence had been secured, Indigenous lands dispossessed, and land transformed into a commodity tied to intergenerational colonial wealth.

These larger trends can be seen in the postraid history of the Burnham family. Robert Burnham's son, Jeremiah, lived at this "garrison" through the Oyster River raid when many of his neighbors lost their lives. By the early 1700s, he appears to have regrouped and prospered by acquiring several neighboring farms.[51] When he died in 1718, his substantial landholdings were divided among his four sons (he also had four daughters, but women could not inherit land).[52] His son John was executor of his estate.[53] Figure 6.3 shows that Burnham's estate paid Richard Wibird, a wealthy Portsmouth resident, to have his enslaved African dig Jeremiah's grave (fig. 6.3).

As noted, two interconnected parts of global colonialism and its dispossessions were land and labor.[54] Across New England, as English colonists

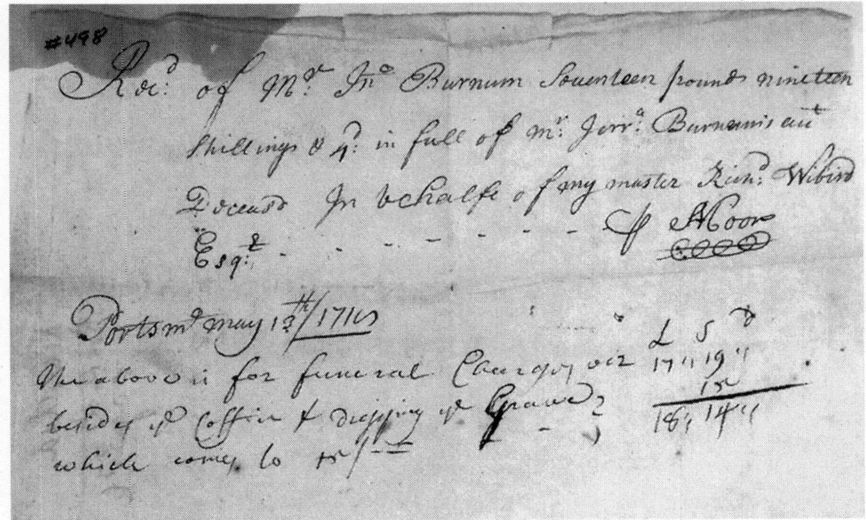

#498

Rec.d of Mr. Jno Burnum Seventeen pounds nineteen Shillings & 4d. in full of Mr. Jerr. Burnum's acct Deceased In behalfe of my master Richd Wibird Esq. - - - - - - ℘ Moor

Portsmo May 13th/1719

The above is for funeral Charges | £ s d | 17 19 4
besides ye Coffin & digging ye Grave | 15
which comes to | 18 14 4

Figure 6.3. Fragment: Record showing that Jeremiah Burnham's estate hired another local English colonist's enslaved African to dig Burnham's grave, an indication of rising colonial wealth. (From the Rockingham County Registry of Deeds: Administration of Jeremiah Burnham's Estate and Inventory, died 1718; RC Probate #498. Photograph by Diane Fiske. Courtesy of GBAS.)

acquired more land, more labor was required to extract profit from lumbering, farming, and pasturing.[55] A reality of colonial-era labor was that when free men could acquire property, they did so and would not work for anyone else. At first, New England's labor needs were typically supplied by the colonists themselves, their families (which often included large numbers of children), and their neighbors. Some forced labor was used during the seventeenth century, including captives from ongoing conflicts in England and occasional enslaved Indigenous servants.[56] One of the most notable groups forced to labor were indentured Scots captured during the English Civil War at the Battle of Dunbar in 1650, who were shipped to the colonies for seven years of servitude.[57] Their labor was critical to expanding lumbering in Massachusetts Bay as well as in the Great Bay Estuary/P8bagok.

As colonial landholdings expanded, these labor options were insufficient to meet labor needs. Increasingly, wealthy New Englanders turned to enslaved Africans. While chattel slavery did not reach the scale of plantation slavery in the Caribbean or the US South, it was still a real, and brutal, part of settler colonialism in New England.[58] Since colonists living in the Great Bay Estuary participated in the emerging global West Indies trade, this meant that they engaged in trade with economies ever more based on large-scale enslaved African labor.[59] There are accounts of enslaved Africans in the Piscataqua region as early as 1645, but for most of the seventeenth century, while enslavement was present, it was patchy. In the eighteenth century, labor based on enslaved Africans (or African descendants, predominantly from the Caribbean) grew substantially in coastal New Hampshire.[60] This growth coincides with reduced Indigenous presence and increased ability of colonists to expand landholdings.

More land required more labor. Those colonists who could purchase enslaved human labor could increase profits, acquire more land (which demanded more labor), and pass wealth on across generations. Jeremiah Burnham was not wealthy enough to enslave Africans, but, as we see, he was buried by one. His land, divided among his four sons, set them up for success to acquire more land individually, which they passed on to their sons.[61] By the third generational land transfer, Jeremiah Burnham's grandson, also Jeremiah Burnham, was wealthy enough to enslave Africans.[62]

In 1760, an entire enslaved family, consisting of two parents and seven children, lived on Burnham lands on a distinctive topographic jutting point into the Oyster River.[63] Some of these enslaved children were sold to other colonists, some stayed with the family, and others were given to Jeremiah's children. One son, Jubal, was given to Jeremiah's daughter Elizabeth to serve her until she married. After she married, Jubal went to another colonist and his sister Candace became Elizabeth's household servant. Accounts indicate that Candace was enslaved by Elizabeth for the rest of her life. Elizabeth Burnham was buried in a graveyard with her husband's family. Stories suggest that she arranged for her enslaved house servant Candace to be buried near her.

As part of GBAS, we surveyed several colonial cemeteries to document the presence and spatial distribution of uncarved gravestones in historic cemeteries. In New England, historic graveyards are common features, and many are well protected, visited, and studied.[64] While known for iconic standing carved headstones, these grave markers are only one piece of the region's mortuary landscape. Simple fieldstones were also used to mark colonial graves. Uncarved/marked fieldstones were widely used for early colonial English colonists' graves in frontier places like the Great Bay Estuary/P8bagok where there was no stone carver until the latter part of the 1600s/early 1700s. After carved headstones were an option, uncarved fieldstones continued to be used to mark the graves of children (in an era with high infant and child mortality rates) and those of low rank in colonial society, including enslaved Africans.

This chapter's closing fragment is one of the unmarked gravestones that GBAS encountered in our historic cemetery surveys (fig. 6.4). This fieldstone

Figure 6.4. Fragment: An unmarked gravestone in a colonial cemetery dating to the 1700s on Oyster River. Located near Elizabeth Burnham's carved gravestone, it potentially marks the grave of an enslaved African, Candace, who lived in forced service to her.

lies on the edge of a historic colonial cemetery along the Oyster River. It is located within a few feet of Elizabeth's carved headstone. Is this the gravestone of her enslaved house servant Candace? We cannot confirm it, but it is a compelling possibility. This fieldstone appears placed to the side, much like many hard realities of settler colonialism that we live with in some form today. These include the violent dispossession of Indigenous land and African labor, ecologically destructive economic practices, and the colonial aggregation of wealth. The way that this stone sits on the edge of a colonial space you might think it insignificant, unremembered, silent, but there is power in the materiality of this stone. Its presence speaks; it compels us to reflect on how it came to be, who it represents, and why we do not have vital knowledge of our shared history. May this fragment, and the many more like it embedded in place, help us acknowledge the things we need to bring in from the edges of our pasts and lead us to a more sustainable future.

CONCLUSION

Washing Away

As we worked on that extremely hot June day in 2021, our GBAS team could not shake off the collective feeling that something was wrong with the local weather. As I write the conclusion of this book in 2024, that feeling has strengthened to certainty. We are confronted almost daily with evidence that our relationship with the Earth is in dire need of repair. How to repair it is one of the most compelling questions of our time. At the planetary scale, this task is overwhelming. Humans cannot easily relate to changes so profound and widespread. Therefore, my aim in this book has been to help ground us in a shared past with the understanding that our current state is the product of numerous social, economic, and ecological ruptures that real people, people like us, situated in many places, times, and societies, lived through. Global crises play out on local scales.

I took us back to a rupture that is inextricably linked to the crises we are living through today: European global colonialism. This age of change may seem far removed from us, but today's natural and human environments were shaped by decisions made four or more centuries ago, early on in this radically transformative period. Environmental degradation due to changes in land and water usage is not a by-product of colonialism. Rather, "domesticating" the wild environment was colonialism's very aim. Resulting socioecological "shocks" and aftershocks remade the entire globe. Its collective legacy is still playing out. It is recorded in written archives, but it is also embedded in place. Understanding these transformative processes requires detailed research on the ground where these histories played out.

Accordingly, I focused on one New England colonial frontier, P8bagok/Pascatway/Great Bay Estuary, a unique estuarine ecosystem on the Atlantic Ocean in northeastern North America. New England figured prominently in the rise of European global colonialism and continues to be important in how we remember and celebrate our shared colonial past. In many ways still, colonial New England is understood as the canvas of early America.[1] However, our understandings of this period have been dominated by research on colonial New England's political power center: the Massachusetts Bay Colony and its capital, Boston. A northern New England colonial frontier landscape that predated Boston, the Great Bay Estuary/P8bagok holds overlooked stories of what it meant to live through the shock of colonialism. These stories hold the key to alternative interpretations of the past, alternative paths to the present.

In the book's chapters, I have shared how, working closely with Indigenous collaborators and local community members, GBAS has located, surveyed, mapped and excavated seventeenth- and early eighteenth-century residences (e.g., encampments, "garrisons," and homesteads), resource extraction sites (e.g., cultivated fields, sawmills, and dams), and shared civil and religious places (e.g., meeting places, meetinghouses, and cemeteries) across the Great Bay Estuary/P8bagok. Summer after summer, our GBAS team has worked in heat and rain, in fields full of mosquitoes, ticks, and poison ivy, going any- and everywhere we thought that we could find deep-time sites that might hold material evidence of what it meant to be someone—English colonist and Indigenous alike—living on the ground, in place, through the unfolding threshold changes of global colonialism. Taken together, the fragments we have found reveal stories of unexpected diversity and dynamism among the English colonists themselves, much more nuanced and multifaceted encounters and relationships with Indigenous peoples whose ancestors had thrived here for millennia, and lasting environmental legacies of colonial-era labor-intensive economic pursuits that inexorably degraded the local environment.

GOING BACK TO GO FORWARD

The Shock of Colonialism in New England has taken us back in time to take us forward. The ways we remember our shared colonial past, the stories we tell about it, the lessons we learn from it are active choices made in the present, not a set of inherited, unchangeable facts. Representations of New England colonial histories are politically forceful projects in which erasures and silences are not neutral. Such (mis)representations skew the social and cultural realities that are recognized, legitimized, and valued today and into the future.[2]

As we learn to think critically about representations of the past and turn to the material traces left by people who lived through colonialism, a pressing question arises: What things do we need to bring in from the edges of our past to lead us to a more sustainable and just future? I have tried to show that conducting systematic, collaborative archaeological research on the shock of colonialism presents an opportunity to layer memory and materiality in more inclusive ways. Stated simply, it gives us the chance to bring forward different and long-overlooked stories that can help ground us in the present and guide us to better futures. However, destructive socioecological processes that global colonialism unleashed centuries ago threaten to erase these stories before we get to them.

SEA LEVEL RISE AND CULTURAL HERITAGE RISK

Across the globe, climate change threatens cultural heritage. Of its varied impacts, sea level rise is critically pressing for cultural heritage sites because of the long relationship between humans and the ocean and its inland estuarine and river systems.[3] Numerous cultural heritage sites lie on the world's fragile coasts. Sea level rise is caused by two factors related to global warming: added water from melting ice sheets and glaciers and the expansion of seawater as it warms.[4] The global rate of sea level rise has escalated rapidly since it began being monitored in 1993. In the messy Anthropocene that we occupy today, sea level rise is now and will increasingly continue to literally wash away evidence of the varied trajectories that led us here and the important lives and stories that have been overlooked along the way.

This is playing out locally on New Hampshire's seacoast. In any coastal area, sea level rise is influenced by global patterns and also by regional processes and localized phenomena. Relative sea level rise is measured by tidal gauges that account for changes resulting from the vertical motion of the land and the sea surface. In coastal New Hampshire, tidal gauge data are collected in Portsmouth Harbor. Tidal data collected over decades show a relative rise in sea level. As this progresses in the future, the coastal flooding the region already experiences will only increase in frequency and severity. Extreme precipitation events, damaging storm surges, and astronomical tides are likely to submerge low-lying coastal land within the next fifty to one hundred years.[5]

Combining tidal gauge data with airborne light detection and ranging (LIDAR) topographic data enabled scientists to produce spatial models of sea level rise impacts for coastal New Hampshire, including the inland reaches of the Great Bay Estuary/P8bagok.[6] This model used two greenhouse gas emissions scenarios, intermediate and high, developed by the Intergovernmental Panel on Climate Change (IPCC). Estimates were made of the one-hundred-year still water and storm surge flood height in 2050 and 2100. Maps of coastal flooding for six relative sea level rise scenarios were created that indicate which areas are prone to flooding and to submersion.

These models were created with the primary purpose of helping municipal and state governments plan mitigation strategies for sea level rise impacts. However, I repurposed them to analyze the vulnerability of cultural heritage sites in coastal New Hampshire by overlaying locations of officially recorded historic and precontact coastal archaeological sites on each sea level rise scenario to see how many of them would be damaged or submerged by sea level rise. In every sea level rise model, known precontact and historic sites, including several on the National Register of Historic Places, will experience partial or complete destruction from increased coastal flooding.[7] The results of this analysis, illustrated in figure C.1, make clear that the cultural heritage of the Great Bay Estuary/P8bagok is very much at risk.

In fact, the risk is much higher than this analysis indicates. This landscape has not seen extensive archaeological research. There are major gaps in knowledge about its cultural heritage sites, and recorded sites are strongly biased toward Euro-American heritage. Often, standing architecture makes Euro-American sites easier to find. More effort has gone into locating, researching, and preserving them for their potential as attractions in the region's lucrative maritime heritage tourism industry.[8] Compared with historic Euro-American sites, Indigenous living sites and sacred places are quite poorly documented. The Abenaki/Pennacook village site that GBAS unexpectedly found (chapter 2) clearly indicates that significant Indigenous sites across this landscape are waiting to be found.[9] And this is true for early colonial sites as well; only one of the early English colonial sites that GBAS surveyed for, Dover's 1654 First Parish meetinghouse (chapter 4), was officially recorded before we started working on it. This indicates the magnitude of what we do not know.

Extrapolating from GBAS's survey find pattern, I suggest it is possible that upward of 75 percent of cultural heritage sites in this important ecological landscape are currently unrecorded. Many of these sites will likely wash away without us ever knowing about them. In our survey, we encountered sea level rise impacts at multiple sites. The most drastic was at the English colonial "garrison" site on the north side of the Oyster River where we found the melted bricks (presented in chapter 6). In figure C.2, the large stones that are eroding out of the bank onto the river's edge are from that

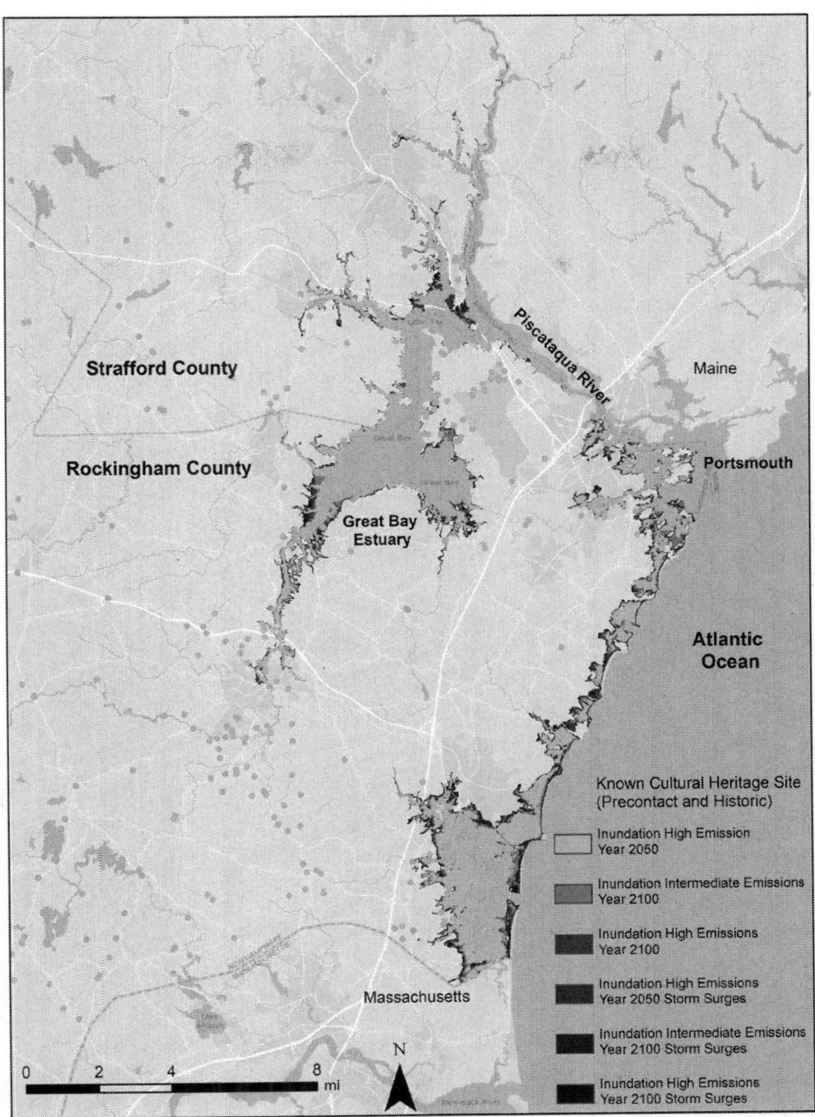

Figure C.1. Results of the cultural heritage risk analysis showing that, in each sea level rise scenario, known historic and precontact cultural heritage sites in New Hampshire's coastal zone will be damaged and/or destroyed. In the highest-impact scenario, 14 percent of recorded, known sites will be impacted, including a notable twelve sites on the National Register of Historic Places. (Base map from Esri. From Howey, "Harnessing Remote Sensing Derived Sea Level Rise Models to Assess Cultural Heritage Vulnerability," fig. 4. CC BY-4.0.)

seventeenth-century homestead; much of the site has already been washed out into the estuary. We know that this site was burned during the Oyster River "Massacre." Now that it has washed away, that is all we will ever know. We will not learn of other stories that came before that violent end. What was the tapestry of living (and dying) at this place during the radical threshold changes of early colonialism? How did the English colonists living here transform their land and surroundings? Did they too trade and interact with Indigenous communities? Did betrayals in these relationships lead this homestead to become a target in the raid? We will never know.

The seeds of sea level rise were planted in the age of European global colonialism. Rising waters continue the work of colonialism by slowly, but surely, taking away fragments that testify to a more dynamic and nuanced colonial past, threatening to silence these stories for good. We need to ask ourselves: What care and pain are we willing to take in gathering the broken pieces, literally and figuratively, inscribed in place as colonialism ripped lands and peoples apart?[10] What will we carry forward and what will we leave behind?

Figure C.2. Large stones from a seventeenth-century English "garrison" site washing away today into the Great Bay Estuary/P8bagok.

NOTES

Introduction

1. To meet and hear from GBAS team members and to see more visuals, please see GBAS's interactive story map searchable online, From the Fragments: The Places and Faces of the Great Bay Archaeological Survey (ArcGIS StoryMaps).

2. A quick Google search about record-breaking weather will bring up numerous articles from across the globe. This summer of records I am describing for New Hampshire was 2021, but the summer of 2022 and 2023 also set new records; record setting is becoming the norm rather than the exception.

3. For examples of such deteriorations, see Xianyao Chen et al., "The Increasing Rate of Global Mean Sea-Level Rise during 1993–2014," *Nature Climate Change* 7 (2017): 492–95; Jeremy B. C. Jackson et al., "Historical Overfishing and the Recent Collapse of Coastal Ecosystems," *Science* 293, no. 5530 (2001): 629–38; or explore NASA's Climate Change website that collects critical long-term observations of our changing planet.

4. Intergovernmental Panel on Climate Change (IPCC), *Climate Change 2021: The Physical Science Basis (6th Assessment Report of the Intergovernmental Panel on Climate Change).*

5. Emily Elhacham et al., "Global Human-Made Mass Exceeds All Living Biomass," *Nature* 588, no. 7838 (2020): 442–44.

6. Paul J. Crutzen, "Geology of Mankind," *Nature* 415, no. 6867 (2002): 23; Paul J. Crutzen and E. F. Stoermer, "The Anthropocene," *IGBP Newsletter* 41 (2000): 17.

7. Ian Angus, "Anthropocene: What's in a Name?," *Climate & Capitalism*, 2015.

8. Charles Lyell, *Principles of Geology, Being an Attempt to Explain the Former Changes of the Earth's Surface, by Reference to Causes Now in Operation*, vol. 3 (London: John Murray, 1833: Google Books).

9. Lyell, *Principles of Geology.*

10. For reviews, see Erle C. Ellis, *Anthropocene: A Very Short Introduction* (Oxford: Oxford University Press, 2018); Will Ruddiman et al., "Defining the Epoch We Live In," *Science* 348 (2015): 38–39; Bruce D. Smith and Melinda A. Zeder, "The Onset of the Anthropocene," *Anthropocene*, When Humans Dominated the Earth: Archeological Perspectives on the Anthropocene, 4 (2013): 8–13; Will Steffen et al., "The Trajectory of the Anthropocene: The Great Acceleration," *Anthropocene Review* 2, no. 1 (2015): 81–98.

11. In March 2024 the International Commission on Stratigraphy (ICS) voted to not declare the Anthropocene a geologic epoch due to those long-standing debates over a stratigraphic golden spike; this vote was hotly contested. A Google search will bring up multiple news articles about this heated vote and its fallout; I would point to the *New York Times* and *Nature News* for thorough and multipointed coverage.

12. Heidi Bostic and Meghan Howey, "To Address the Anthropocene, Engage the Liberal Arts," *Anthropocene* 18 (2017): 105.

13. See the editorial in *Nature* 627, 466 (2024) in response to the ICS vote, "Are We in the Anthropocene Yet?" For more on the conceptual utility of the Anthropocene see also Nancy Langston, *Climate Ghosts: Migratory Species in the Anthropocene* (Waltham, MA: Brandeis University Press, 2021).

14. Dipesh Chakrabarty, "The Climate of History: Four Theses," *Critical Inquiry* 35, no. 2 (2009): 215.

15. Plastic debris is the most abundant type of litter in the ocean. The Great Pacific Garbage Patch is a prime example of this pollution. Current estimates are that over ten million metric tons of plastic end up in the ocean a year. Learn more at Confronting Ocean Plastic Pollution at the Pew Charitable Trusts website.

16. Heather Davis and Zoe Todd, "On the Importance of a Date, or, Decolonizing the Anthropocene," *ACME: An International Journal for Critical Geographies* 16, no. 4 (2017): 761–80; Simon L. Lewis and Mark A. Maslin, "Defining the Anthropocene," *Nature* 519, no. 7542 (2015): 171–80.

17. Steve Mentz, *Break Up the Anthropocene* (Minneapolis: University of Minnesota Press, 2019).

18. Anna Lowenhaupt Tsing, Andrew S. Mathews, and Nils Bubandt, "Patchy Anthropocene: Landscape Structure, Multispecies History, and the Retooling of Anthropology: An Introduction to Supplement 20," *Current Anthropology* 60, no. S20 (2019): S186–97.

19. Eduardo S. Brondizio et al., "Re-Conceptualizing the Anthropocene: A Call for Collaboration," *Global Environmental Change* 39 (2016): 318–27.

20. Christophe Bonneuil and Jean-Baptiste Fressoz, *The Shock of the Anthropocene: The Earth, History and Us*, trans. David Fernbach (London: Verso, 2016).

21. Bonneuil and Fressoz, *Shock of the Anthropocene*; Kai Bosworth, "Feminist Geography in the Anthropocene: Sciences, Bodies, Futures," in *Routledge Handbook of Gender and Feminist Geographies*, ed. Anindita Datta et al. (London: Routledge, 2020); Brondizio et al., "Re-Conceptualizing the Anthropocene"; Noel Castree, "The Anthropocene and Geography I: The Back Story," *Geography Compass* 8, no. 7 (2014): 436–49; Noel Castree, "Framing, Deframing and Reframing the Anthropocene," *Ambio* 50, no. 10 (2021): 1788–92; Lewis and Maslin, "Defining the Anthropocene"; Simon L. Lewis and Mark A. Maslin, *The Human Planet: How We Created the Anthropocene* (New Haven, CT: Yale University Press, 2018); Dana Luciano, "The Inhuman Anthropocene," *Avidly* (blog), 2015; Anna Lowenhaupt Tsing, *The Mushroom at the End of the World* (Princeton, NJ: Princeton University Press, 2015).

22. Bruno Latour, *Facing Gaia: Eight Lectures on the New Climatic Regime*, trans. Catherine Porter (Cambridge: Polity Books, 2017).

23. Indeed, some have proposed early global colonialism as a candidate for the "golden spike" for the Anthropocene, most notably termed the "Orbis spike" at 1610 AD by Lewis and Maslin, "Defining the Anthropocene."

24. Mentz, *Break Up the Anthropocene*; Edward W Said, *Orientalism* (New York: Pantheon Books, 1978); Eric R. Wolf, *Europe and the People Without History* (Los Angeles: University of California Press, 1997).

25. Steve Mentz, *Shipwreck Modernity: Ecologies of Globalization, 1550–1719* (Minneapolis: University of Minnesota Press, 2015).

26. Kathryn Yusoff, *A Billion Black Anthropocenes or None* (Minneapolis: University of Minnesota Press, 2018), 32.

27. Kyle Powys Whyte, "Settler Colonialism, Ecology, and Environmental Injustice," *Environment and Society* 9, no. 1 (September 1, 2018): 125–44.

28. Kent G. Lightfoot et al., "European Colonialism and the Anthropocene: A View from the Pacific Coast of North America," *Anthropocene* 4 (2013): 101–15; Tsing, *Mushroom at the End of the World*.

29. John Hanson Mitchell, *The Paradise of All These Parts: A Natural History of Boston* (Boston: Beacon Press, 2009), 133.

30. Eyal Weizman, *The Conflict Shoreline: Colonization as Climate Change in the Negev Desert* (Göttingen: Steidl, 2015), 36.

31. I am drawing inspiration for the use of the term *shock* for colonialism impacts from various sources including Bonneuil and Fressoz, *Shock of the Anthropocene*; Davis and Todd, "On the Importance of a Date"; Robbie Ethridge and Sheri M. Shuck-Hall, eds., *Mapping the Mississippian Shatter Zone: The Colonial Indian Slave Trade and Regional Instability in the American South* (Lincoln: University of Nebraska Press, 2009); Christina Elizabeth Sharpe, *In the Wake: On Blackness and Being* (Durham, NC: Duke University Press, 2016); Michel-Rolph Trouillot, *Silencing the Past: Power and the Production of History* (Boston: Beacon Press, 1995).

32. The concept of historical legacies and wake is well developed in Sharpe, *In the Wake* (this specific phrasing from p. 9).

33. Trouillot, *Silencing the Past*, 15.

34. Lisa Brooks, "Turning the Looking Glass on King Philip's War: Locating American Literature in Native Space," *American Literary History* 25, no. 4 (2013): 734.

35. David C Smith et al., "Climate Fluctuation and Agricultural Change in Southern and Central New England, 1765–1880," *Maine History* 21 (1982), 179–200. William R. Baron, "Historical Climates of the Northeastern United States," in *Holocene Human Ecology in Northeastern North America*, ed. George P. Nicholas (Boston, MA: Springer US, 1988), 29–46.

36. This term "want and plenty" comes from William Cronon's important work that offered one of the first broad view explorations of how settler colonists transformed the landscape of New England: William Cronon, *Changes in the Land: Indians, Colonists, and the Ecology of New England*, rev. ed. (New York: Hill and Wang, 2003), 34.

37. Lisa Brooks, *Our Beloved Kin: A New History of King Philip's War* (New Haven, CT: Yale University Press, 2018), 11.

38. Lisa Brooks, *The Common Pot: The Recovery of Native Space in the Northeast* (Minneapolis: University of Minnesota Press, 2008); Brooks, *Our Beloved Kin*; Amy Den Ouden, *Beyond Conquest: Native Peoples and the Struggle for History in New England* (Lincoln: University of Nebraska Press, 2005); Jean M. O'Brien, *Firsting and Lasting: Writing Indians Out of Existence in New England* (Minneapolis: University of Minnesota Press, 2010); Christine M. DeLucia, *Memory Lands: King Philip's War and the Place of Violence in the Northeast* (New Haven, CT: Yale University Press, 2018); Thomas M. Wickman, *Snowshoe Country: An Environmental and Cultural History of Winter in the Early American Northeast* (Cambridge: Cambridge University Press, 2018).

39. Neal Salisbury, *The Indians of New England: A Critical Bibliography* (Bloomington: Indiana University Press,1982); Lisa Brooks and Cassandra Brooks, "The Reciprocity Principle and Traditional Ecological Knowledge: Understanding the Significance of Indigenous Protest on the Presumpscot River," *International Journal of Critical Indigenous Studies* 11 (2010): 1837–144.

40. A wide array of Indigenous communities lives in the Northeast. Contemporary state and international boundaries have contributed to sometimes arbitrary divisions among groups, and likewise, colonial and other governmental powers over time grouped together separate groups. This is to say that there are various ways one could list out the Native peoples of the region, and so this list is neither definitive nor meant to be exclusive, only to offer an informative introduction. This follows a recent Indigenous-engaged publication's ordering, see Siobhan Senier, ed., *Dawnland Voices: An Anthology of Indigenous Writing from New England* (Lincoln: University of Nebraska Press, 2014).

41. Brooks, "Turning the Looking Glass," 724.

42. Den Ouden, *Beyond Conquest*.

43. Cronon, *Changes in the Land;* Mitchell, *Paradise of All These Parts;* Wickman, *Snowshoe Country.*

44. W. Jeffrey Bolster, *The Mortal Sea: Fishing the Atlantic in the Age of Sail* (Cambridge, MA: Harvard University Press, 2012); Cronon, *Changes in the Land;* Sung Bae Jeon, Pontus Olofsson, and Curtis E. Woodcock, "Land Use Change in New England: A Reversal of the Forest Transition," *Journal of Land Use Science* 9, no. 1 (2014): 105–30; Jonathan R. Thompson et al., "Four Centuries of Change in Northeastern United States Forests," *PLOS ONE* 8, no. 9 (2013): e72540; Jonathan R. Thompson et al., "Forest Loss in New England: A Projection of Recent Trends," *PLOS ONE* 12, no. 12 (2017): e0189636; Gordon G. Whitney, *From Coastal Wilderness to Fruited Plain: A History of Environmental Change in Temperate North America from 1500 to the Present* (Cambridge: Cambridge University Press, 1996).

45. Jill Lepore, *The Name of War: King Philip's War and the Origins of American Identity* (New York: Vintage Books, 1998); Colin G. Calloway, *The American Revolution in Indian Country: Crisis and Diversity in Native American Communities* (Cambridge: Cambridge University Press, 1995).

46. Ned Blackhawk, *The Rediscovery of America: Native Peoples and the Unmaking of U.S. History* (New Haven, CT: Yale University Press, 2023), 49.

47. O'Brien, *Firsting and Lasting.*

48. O'Brien termed and elaborated on this process in *Firsting and Lasting;* see also DeLucia, *Memory Lands.*

49. Michel-Rolph Trouillot, *Global Transformations: Anthropology and the Modern World* (New York: Palgrave Macmillan, 2004), 12.

50. This broader concept is explored in detail in Michel-Rolph Trouillot's *Silencing the Past.*

51. Christine M. DeLucia, "The Memory Frontier: Geographies of Violence and Regeneration in Colonial New England and the Native Northeast after King Philip's War. (Garrisoned Piscataqua Pp. 484–618)," PhD diss., Yale University, 2012, 487.

52. Brooks, *Our Beloved Kin*, 215; DeLucia, "Memory Frontier," 487; Learn more also at the website of the Indigenous New Hampshire Collaborative Collective (INHCC).

53. This draws on the idea of New World people as presented in Jennifer Reid, *Myth, Symbol and Colonial Encounter: British and Mi'kmaq in Acadia, 1700–1867* (Ottawa: University of Ottawa Press, 1995).

54. Emerson W. Baker and Nina Maurer, *Forgotten Frontier: Untold Stories of the Piscataqua* (exhibit catalog) (South Berwick, ME: Old Berwick Historical Society, 2018); W. Jeffrey Bolster, ed., *Cross-Grained and Wily Waters: A Guide to the Piscataqua Maritime Region* (Portsmouth, NH: Gundalow, 2002).

55. This *8* in *P8bagok* was something Jesuit linguists used during early contact to represent a nasalized, unrounded 'o' they heard in Abenaki. In the Abenaki language the "**i**" is the strong "**e**" sound: **8** = Ô or ô = nasal long "**o**" sound. So *P8bagok* is

pronounced P-ohn-ba-gock. Learn more on Abenaki language at the website of the Indigenous New Hampshire Collaborative Collective (INHCC).

56. Learn more at National Oceanic and Atmospheric Administration (NOAA)'s National Estuarine Research Reserve System website.

57. Patrick Kirch, "Archaeology and Global Change: The Holocene Record," *Arer* 30 (2005): 409.

58. Mentz, *Break Up the Anthropocene.*

59. Cindy Milstein, ed., *Rebellious Mourning: The Collective Work of Grief* (Chico, CA: AK Press, 2017).

Chapter 1

1. Matthew H. Edney and Mary Sponberg Pedley, eds., *The History of Cartography*, vol. 4: *Cartography in the European Enlightenment* (Chicago: University of Chicago Press, 2020).

2. Benjamin Schmidt, "Mapping an Empire: Cartographic and Colonial Rivalry in Seventeenth-Century Dutch and English North America," *William and Mary Quarterly* 54, no. 3 (1997): 552.

3. W. Jeffrey Bolster, *The Mortal Sea: Fishing the Atlantic in the Age of Sail* (Cambridge, MA: Harvard University Press, 2012), 17.

4. This map was probably based on earlier maps, most likely, Samuel de Champlain's map of 1612 and John Smith's chart of 1616. Arguably the most accurate North American cartographer in the early 1600s, Champlain personally surveyed the coastlines and drew his own maps and charts, gleaning information about the interior from Native informants. Smith also surveyed the coast, and some English mariners used his well-known chart for navigation, but his party ventured only a short way inland.

5. Mark Kurlansky, *Cod: A Biography of the Fish That Changed the World* (New York: Penguin Books, 1998).

6. Heritage Newfoundland and Labrador, "The International Fishery of the 16th Century," 1997.

7. Poul Holm et al., "The North Atlantic Fish Revolution (ca. AD 1500)," *Quaternary Research* 108 (2022): 92–106; Ruth Holmes Whitehead, *Nova Scotia: The Protohistoric Period 1500–1630* (Halifax: Nova Scotia Museum, 1993), Curatorial Report #75.

8. Whitehead, *Nova Scotia*, 9.

9. Samuel Foster Haven, *History of Grants under the Great Council for New England, a Lecture of a Course by Members of the Massachusetts Historical Society* (Boston: Press of John Wilson and Son, 1869; Internet Archive), 6.

10. Holm et al., "North Atlantic Fish Revolution." The Basque were known also for whaling these waters.

11. Samuel de Champlain, *The Voyages and Explorations of Samuel de Champlain, 1604–1616*, 2 vols., trans. C. Pomery Otis (Boston: Prince Society, 1878; Canadiana).

12. Colleen Thompson, *State of the Gulf of Maine Report: The Gulf of Maine in Context* (Nova Scotia: Gulf of Maine Council on the Marine Environment, 2010).

13. Bruce J. Bourque and Ruth Holmes Whitehead, "Tarrentines and the Introduction of European Trade Goods in the Gulf of Maine," *Ethnohistory* 32, no. 4 (1985): 327–41; Neal Salisbury, "The Indians' Old World: Native Americans and the Coming of Europeans," *William and Mary Quarterly* 3 (1996): 435–58.

14. Charles Orser, *An Archaeology of the English Atlantic World, 1600–1700* (Cambridge: Cambridge University Press, 2018).

15. W. Jeffrey Bolster, ed., *Cross-Grained and Wily Waters: A Guide to the Piscataqua Maritime Region* (Portsmouth, NH: Gundalow, 2002); Bourque and Whitehead, "Tarrentines and the Introduction of European Trade Goods"; Martin Pring, *The Voyage of Martin Pring, 1603*, ed. Henry Burrage (New York: Charles Scribner's Sons, 1906, American Journeys Collection AJ-040).

16. John Smith, *A Description of New England* (London: Printed by Humfrey Lownes for Robert Clerke, 1616, Zea E-Books in American Studies 3).

17. Karen E. Alexander et al., "Gulf of Maine Cod in 1861: Historical Analysis of Fishery Logbooks, with Ecosystem Implications," *Fish and Fisheries* 10, no. 4 (2009): 428–49; W. Jeffrey Bolster, "Putting the Ocean in Atlantic History: Maritime Communities and Marine Ecology in the Northwest Atlantic, 1500–1800," *American Historical Review* 113 (2008): 19–47; William Leavenworth, "The Changing Landscape of Maritime Resources in Seventeenth-Century New England," *International Journal of Maritime History* 20 (2008): 33–62.

18. Smith, *Description of New England*, 30.

19. Karen Alexander et al., "Catch Density: A New Approach to Shifting Baselines, Stock Assessment, and Ecosystem-Based Management," *Bulletin of Marine Science* 87 (2011): 213–34.

20. William D. Williamson, *History of the State of Maine; from Its First Discovery, A. D. 1602, to the Separation, A. D. 1820, Inclusive* (Hallowell, ME: Glaizier Masters, 1832; Maine History Documents 34); Jeremy Belknap, *The History of New-Hampshire (1784–1792)* (Philadelphia, PA: Robert Aitken, 1784, Internet Archive); Henrietta Marshall, *This Country of Ours: The Story of the United States* (New York: George H. Doran, 1917, University of Pennsylvania Digital Library).

21. Haven, *History of Grants*.

22. For more on Mason's biography as well as more broadly the early English colonial history of New-found-Land, see Peter E. Pope, *Fish into Wine: The Newfoundland Plantation in the Seventeenth Century* (Chapel Hill: University of North Carolina Press, 2004).

23. Leavenworth, "Changing Landscape of Maritime Resources."

24. Herbert C. Bell, "The West India Trade before the American Revolution," *American Historical Review* 22, no. 2 (1917): 272–87; Benjamin Woods Labaree, *America and the Sea: A Maritime History* (Mystic, CT: Mystic Seaport Museum, 1998).

25. Brian M. Fagan, *Fish on Friday: Feasting, Fasting, and the Discovery of the New World* (New York: Perseus Book Group, 2006).

26. Lisa Brooks, *Our Beloved Kin: A New History of King Philip's War* (New Haven, CT: Yale University Press, 2018), 3.

27. For more on settler colonialism, see Mahmood Mamdani, "Beyond Settler and Native as Political Identities: Overcoming the Political Legacy of Colonialism," *Comparative Studies in Society and History* 43, no. 4 (2001): 651–64; Kyle Powys Whyte, "Settler Colonialism, Ecology, and Environmental Injustice," *Environment and Society* 9, no. 1 (September 1, 2018): 125–44.

28. After 1630 and for the rest of the seventeenth century, the population of Massachusetts Bay was more than ten times that of New Hampshire and Maine. Learn more at the World Population Review website.

29. Neal Salisbury, *Manitou and Providence: Indians, Europeans, and the Making of New England, 1500–1643* (Oxford: Oxford University Press, 1984).

30. John Winthrop, "John Winthrop Dreams of a City on a Hill, 1630," American Yawp Reader.

31. Bruce Daniels, *New England Nation: The Country the Puritans Built* (New York: Palgrave Macmillan, 2012), 5.

32. William Hubbard, *A General History of New England: From the Discovery to MDCLXXX* (Cambridge, MA: C. C. Little and J. Brown, 1848, Internet Archive).

33. Trevor Burnard, *Planters, Merchants, and Slaves: Plantation Societies in British America, 1650–1820* (Chicago: University of Chicago Press, 2019).

34. Leavenworth, "Changing Landscape of Maritime Resources."

35. Williamson, *History of the State of Maine*.

36. Keith Basso, *Wisdom Sits in Places: Landscape and Language among the Western Apache* (Albuquerque: University of New Mexico Press, 1996), 110.

37. Ideas explored in detail in Basso, *Wisdom Sits in Places*.

38. The term *Place-thought* is one developed by Anishinaabeg scholar Vanessa Watts. See "Indigenous Place-Thought and Agency amongst Humans and Non Humans (First Woman and Sky Woman Go on a European World Tour!)," *Decolonization: Indigeneity, Education and Society* 2, no. 1 (2013), 20–34.

39. For more on the Little Ice Age, see Brian Fagan, *The Little Ice Age: How Climate Made History 1300–1850* (New York: Basic Books, 2001); Sam White, *A Cold Welcome: The Little Ice Age and Europe's Encounter with North America* (Cambridge, MA: Harvard University Press, 2017).

40. For a rich exploration of early colonial winter dynamics in the Northeast, see Thomas M. Wickman, *Snowshoe Country: An Environmental and Cultural History of Winter in the Early American Northeast* (Cambridge: Cambridge University Press, 2018).

41. Siobhan Senier, ed., *Dawnland Voices: An Anthology of Indigenous Writing from New England* (Lincoln: University of Nebraska Press, 2014).

42. Learn more by exploring the resources and the Story Map that includes Great Bay/P8bagok at the website of the Indigenous New Hampshire Collaborative Collective (INHCC). Possible other early Indigenous names for this river also include Beskategra and Pisgategwa, with a possible translation being "where the river divides."

43. P. Behm, R. Boumans, and Frederick Short, "Spatial Modeling of Eelgrass Distribution in Great Bay, New Hampshire," in *Landscape Simulation Modeling: A Spatially Explicit, Dynamic Approach*, ed. Robert Costanza and Alexey Voinov, 173–96 (New York: Springer-Verlag, 2004); Frederick Short, *The Ecology of the Great Bay Estuary, New Hampshire and Maine: An Estuarine Profile and Bibliography* (Durham, NH: Jackson Estuarine Laboratory, 1992).

44. Behm, Boumans, and Short, "Spatial Modeling of Eelgrass Distribution."

45. See NOAA's website for the Great Bay National Estuarine Reserve.

46. Jay Odell et al., "Great Bay Estuary Restoration Compendium," New Hampshire Coastal Program and New Hampshire Estuaries Project, 2006, 94; Short, *Ecology of the Great Bay Estuary.*

47. John Scott, *Pascatway River in New England*, British Library. To learn more about who John Scott was and his mapping practices, see David Allen, "John Scott and the Mapping of New England and New York," *Portolan*, Spring 2022, 23–33. Interestingly, in this recent article, Allen argues that it is likely that Scott also created *The Province of Mayne*, which opened this chapter. *The Province of Mayne*'s maker has long been a question, recorded in the archives as possibly William Hack (marked with a ?) because he was a well-known seventeenth-century English cartographer who worked on vellum.

48. John Scott, *Pascatway River in New England*, British Library.

49. Matthew Jenkinson, *Charles I's Killers in America: The Lives and Afterlives of Edward Whalley and William Goffe* (Oxford: Oxford University Press, 2019).

50. Richard D'Abate and Victor Konrad, "General Introduction," in *American Beginnings: Exploration, Culture and Cartography in the Land of Norumbega*, ed. Emerson Baker, et al., xix–1 (Lincoln: University of Nebraska Press, 1994).

51. Joseph Dow, *History of the Town of Hampton, New Hampshire, from Its Settlement in 1638, to the Autumn of 1892* (Salem, MA: Salem Press Pub. and Printing, 1893; University of Pennsylvania Digital Library).

52. Odell et al., "Great Bay Estuary Restoration Compendium," 36.

53. The estuary also provided a key locale for American eels, a species that leaves its freshwater habitat to spawn in the Sargasso Sea.

54. Portsmouth, the city located at the mouth of the Piscataqua River and the Atlantic Ocean, also claims 1623 as its founding date based on the arrival of David Thompson, who built his house known as *Pannaway* and who managed a fishery. Dover claims Hilton came earlier in 1623 than Thompson; today, the two cities each claim, and celebrate, being the "first settlement" in New Hampshire. Learn more about David Thompson, this date of 1623, and the debates around it in: J Dennis Robinson, *1623: Pilgrims, Pipe Dreams, Politics & the Founding of New Hampshire* (Portsmouth, NH: Harbortown Press, 2023). Also see John Scales, *Piscataqua Pioneers 1623–1775 Register of Members and Ancestors* (Dover, NH: Piscataqua Pioneers, 1919, Internet Archive).

55. John Scales, *History of Dover, New Hampshire* (Manchester, NH: John B. Clarke, 1923; Google Books), 1–4.

56. Alonzo Quint, "The First Church in Dover, and Its Pastor," *Granite Monthly: A Magazine of History, Biography, Literature and State Progress* 1, no. 7 (November 1877), Google Books.

57. Short, *Ecology of the Great Bay Estuary.*

58. Bolster, *Cross-Grained and Wily Waters*; James L. Garvin, "Small-Scale Brickmaking in New Hampshire," *IA. The Journal of the Society for Industrial Archeology* 20, no. 1/2 (1994): 19–31.

59. Bolster, *Cross-Grained and Wily Waters*; Short, *Ecology of the Great Bay Estuary.*

60. Joseph Goldenberg, *Shipbuilding in Colonial America* (Charlottesville: University of Virgina Press, 1976); Ben Ford, "Down by the Water's Edge: Modelling Shipyard Locations in Maryland, USA," *International Journal of Nautical Archaeology* 36, no. 1 (2007): 125–37.

61. Richard M Candee, "The Water Powered Sawmills of the Piscataqua," *Old Time New England*, 1970, 131–49.

62. Candee, "Water Powered Sawmills of the Piscataqua," 131.

63. Candee, "Water Powered Sawmills of the Piscataqua"; Emerson W. Baker and Nina Maurer, *Forgotten Frontier: Untold Stories of the Piscataqua* (exhibit catalog) (South Berwick, ME: Old Berwick Historical Society, 2018).

64. Odell et al., "Great Bay Estuary Restoration Compendium."

65. Gordon G. Whitney, *From Coastal Wilderness to Fruited Plain: A History of Environmental Change in Temperate North America from 1500 to the Present* (Cambridge: Cambridge University Press, 1996).

66. Tom Wessels, Brian D. Cohen, and Ann H. Zwinger, *Reading the Forested Landscape: A Natural History of New England* (Woodstock, VT: Countryman Press, 2005).

67. Belknap, *History of New-Hampshire*, 94.

68. Michael Gowell, "Piscataqua Gundalows," in Bolster, *Cross-Grained and Wily Waters.*

69. M. Bampton, "Deforestation and Siltation: A Historical and Ecological Look.," in Bolster, *Cross-Grained and Wily Waters*, 146.

70. Candee, "Water Powered Sawmills of the Piscataqua"; Bell, "West India Trade before the American Revolution."

71. Williamson, *History of the State of Maine*, 28–29.

72. Bridger is sometimes recorded as John Bridges.

73. William Cronon, *Changes in the Land: Indians, Colonists, and the Ecology of New England*, rev. ed. (New York: Hill and Wang, 2003); Jonathan R. Thompson et al., "Forest Loss in New England: A Projection of Recent Trends," *PLOS ONE* 12, no. 12 (2017): e0189636; Jonathan R. Thompson et al., "Four Centuries of Change in Northeastern United States Forests," *PLOS ONE* 8, no. 9 (2013): e72540; Sung Bae Jeon, Pontus Olofsson, and Curtis E. Woodcock, "Land Use Change in New England: A Reversal of the Forest Transition," *Journal of Land Use Science* 9, no. 1 (2014): 105–30.

74. For more on this modeling approach and how it relates to archaeological

survey and research, see Meghan C. L. Howey, Michael W. Palace, and Crystal H. McMichael, "Geospatial Modeling Approach to Monument Construction Using Michigan from A.D. 1000–1600 as a Case Study," *Proceedings of the National Academy of Sciences* 113, no. 27 (2016): 7443–48.

75. Diane's research has been essential to the success of GBAS. Her work is almost forensic; she has to put together vague pieces of information about land transfers and property lines, especially as we go back in time, when property lines were noted by statements such as "his land ran from the big rock to the large pine tree." She chased records down in state archives, county archives, library special collections, town records, and other, sometimes quite obscure, places.

76. In formal compliance archaeology terms, the narrowing of our research universe was akin to what is termed Phase IA in Section 106 compliance work and our shovel test surveying was akin to a Phase 1B. As an academic and community-based project, we did not have to cast our work in these contractual terms, but we followed standard professional guidelines and ethics.

Chapter 2

1. Eric R. Wolf, *Europe and the People without History* (Los Angeles: University of California Press, 1997).

2. The peopling of the New World is the subject of much ongoing debate in archaeology and beyond. No single, definitive answer has been established. One functional approach is to accept multiple models as likely valid. See Ben A. Potter et al., "Current Evidence Allows Multiple Models for the Peopling of the Americas," *Science Advances* 4, no. 8 (2018): eaat5473.

3. Neal Salisbury, "The Indians' Old World: Native Americans and the Coming of Europeans," *William and Mary Quarterly* 3 (1996): 435–58.

4. There is a robust school of colonial critique/postcolonial theory behind these ideas. Some influential works include Homi K. Bhabha, *The Location of Culture*, 2nd ed. (London: Routledge, 2004); Michel-Rolph Trouillot, *Global Transformations: Anthropology and the Modern World* (New York: Palgrave Macmillan, 2004); Edward W Said, *Orientalism* (New York: Pantheon Books, 1978); Michael Taussig, *Mimesis and Alterity: A Particular History of the Senses* (London: Routledge, 2017).

5. For more on the idea of material colonial entanglements, see Nicholas Thomas, *Entangled Objects: Exchange, Material Culture, and Colonialism in the Pacific* (Cambridge, MA: Harvard University Press, 2009).

6. Bhabha, *Location of Culture*, 53.

7. Taussig, *Mimesis and Alterity*, 129.

8. I draw here on the idea of New World people presented in Jennifer Reid, *Myth, Symbol and Colonial Encounter: British and Mi'kmaq in Acadia, 1700–1867* (Ottawa: University of Ottawa Press, 1995). And as she explored whether they wanted to become this or not, the process unfolded, carrying with it complex identities, alienation, acts of self-deception, and eventually devastating consequences.

9. Michael S. Nassaney, "Identity Formation at a French Colonial Outpost in the North American Interior," *International Journal of Historical Archaeology* 12, no. 4 (2008): 297–318; Craig N. Cipolla and Amélie Allard, "Recognizing River Power: Watery Views of Ontario's Fur Trade," *Journal of Archaeological Method and Theory* 26, no. 3 (2019): 1084–1105.

10. Or biographies, see Igor Kopytoff, "The Cultural Biography of Things: Commoditization as Process," in *The Social Life of Things: Commodities in Cultural Perspective*, ed. Arjun Appadurai, 64–94 (Cambridge: Cambridge University Press, 1986).

11. Diana DiPaolo Loren, "Considering Mimicry and Hybridity in Early Colonial New England: Health, Sin and the Body 'Behung with Beades,'" *Archaeological Review from Cambridge*, 2013, 151–68.

12. Margaret Robinson, "Animal Personhood in Mi'kmaq Perspective," *Societies* 4, no. 4 (2014): 672–88.

13. For many years, the precontact era in North America, including New England, has been called *prehistory*. Some archaeologists today use this term. The term *precontact* has its own shortcomings, but prehistory plays into colonial conceptions of North America being a land without history before Europeans graced its shores, and so I do not use that term. In his recent powerful, and award-winning, work, *The Rediscovery of America: Native Peoples and the Unmaking of U.S. History* (New Haven, CT: Yale University Press, 2023), Ned Blackhawk offers as his first figure a map of "Pre-contact (or pre-removal) Native Nations." The incorporation of "pre-removal" emphasizes the critical point that Native peoples were actively dispossessed of their land, and I am interested to see if this terminology becomes something archaeologists adopt in the future.

14. For a broad-brush view of precontact New England, see Dean R. Snow, *The Archaeology of New England* (Cambridge, MA: Academic Press, 1980). For more on precontact New Hampshire, see Robert Goodby, *A Deep Presence: 13,000 Years of Native American History* (Portsmouth, NH: Peter Randall Publisher, 2021); David R. Starbuck, *The Archeology of New Hampshire: Exploring 10,000 Years in the Granite State* (Durham: University of New Hampshire Press, 2006); Bruce J. Bourque, *Twelve Thousand Years: American Indians in Maine* (Lincoln: University of Nebraska Press, 2001).

15. Goodby, *Deep Presence*, 91.

16. There was likely more subsistence diversity than just caribou during the Paleo-Indian period, especially toward the end of the period as other game entered the Northeast. For more on the subsistence diversity of this period in the region, see Elizabeth Chilton, "Beyond 'Big': Gender, Age, and Subsistence Diversity in Paleo-Indian Societies," in *The Settlement of the American Continents: A Multidisciplinary Approach to Human Biogeography*, ed. C. Michael Barton et al., 162–72 (Tucson: University of Arizona Press, 2004); and chapter 4 in Matthew W. Betts and M. Gabriel Hrynick, *The Archaeology of the Atlantic Northeast* (Toronto: University of Toronto Press, 2021).

17. Brian Robinson et al., "Paleoindian Aggregation and Social Context at Bull Brook," *American Antiquity* 74 (2009): 423–47.

18. Dena Dincauze, *The Neville Site: 8,000 Years at Amoskeag, Manchester, New Hampshire* (Cambridge, MA: Peabody Museum Monographs 4, 1976).

19. Arthur E. Spiess and Robert A. Lewis, *The Turner Farm Fauna: 5000 Years of Hunting and Fishing in Penobscot Bay, Maine* (Augusta: Maine Archaeological Society, 2001).

20. Heike K. Lotze and Inka Milewski, "Two Centuries of Multiple Human Impacts and Successive Changes in a North Atlantic Food Web," *Ecological Applications* 14, no. 5 (2004): 1428–47; see also: Bruce J. Bourque, *Diversity and Complexity in Prehistoric Maritime Societies: A Gulf of Maine Perspective* (New York: Springer New York, 1995); Arthur E. Spiess and John Mosher, "Archaic Period Hunting and Fishing around the Gulf of Maine," in *The Archaic of the Far Northeast,* ed. David Sanger and M. A. P. Renouf (Orono: University of Maine Press, 2006).

21. Arthur E. Spiess, "People of the Clam: Shellfish and Diet in Coastal Maine Late Archaic and Ceramic Period Sites," *Journal of the North Atlantic* 10 (2017): 105–12.

22. See, for instance, the rather recent back and forth in *Nature Sustainability*: W. Wyatt Oswald et al., "Conservation Implications of Limited Native American Impacts in Pre-Contact New England," *Nature Sustainability* 3, no. 3 (2020): 241–46; Marc D. Abrams and Gregory J. Nowacki, "Native American Imprint in Palaeoecology," *Nature Sustainability* 3, no. 11 (2020): 896–97.

23. John Hart and Bernard Means, "Maize and Villages: A Summary and Critical Assessment of Current Northeast Early Late Prehistoric Evidence," in *Northeast Subsistence-Settlement Change: A.D. 700–1300*, ed. John Hart and Christina Rieth, 345–58 (Albany: New York State Museum, 2002).

24. Farming was not seen by Europeans farther north than the Saco River, but various explorers heard that it had been practiced along the more northern Kennebec River in Maine (Bourque, *Twelve Thousand Years*, 87).

25. Spiess, "People of the Clam."

26. Jennifer Birch, "Coalescent Communities: Settlement Aggregation and Social Integration in Iroquoian Ontario," *American Antiquity* 77, no. 4 (2012): 646–70; Hart and Means, "Maize and Villages"; Robert Hasenstab, "Agriculture, Warfare, and Tribalization in the Iroquois Homeland of New York: A G.I.S. Analysis of Late Woodland Settlement," PhD diss., University of Massachusetts, 1990.

27. Elizabeth S. Chilton, "Mobile Farmers of Pre-Contact Southern New England: The Archaeological and Ethnohistoric Evidence," in *Current Northeast Paleoethnobotany*, ed. John Hart, 157–76 (Albany: New York State Museum Bulletin 494,1999); Elizabeth S. Chilton, Tonya Largy, and Kathryn Curran, "Evidence for Prehistoric Maize Horticulture at the Pine Hill Site, Deerfield, Massachusetts," *Northeast Anthropology* 59 (1999): 23–46; Robert Hasenstab, "Fishing, Farming, and Finding the Village Sites: Centering Late Woodland New England Algonquians.,"

in *The Archaeological Northeast*, ed. Mary Ann Levine, Kenneth Sassaman, and Michael Nassaney,139–54 (Westport, CT: Bergin & Garvey, 1999).

28. Elizabeth Chilton, "'Towns They Have None': Diverse Subsistence and Settlement Strategies in Native New England," in *Northeast Subsistence-Settlement Change: A.D. 700–1300*, ed. John Hart and Christina Rieth, 289–300 (Albany: New York State Museum, 2002).

29. Hasenstab, "Fishing, Farming, and Finding the Village Sites."

30. Lisa Brooks, *The Common Pot: The Recovery of Native Space in the Northeast* (Minneapolis: University of Minnesota Press, 2008).

31. Robert Goodby, "Native American Life in the Piscataqua Region, 11,000–350 B.P," in *An Archaeological Site Investigation of the Pearl and Manning Street Wharves* (Portsmouth, NH: Strawbery Banke Museum, 1999).

32. Jeffery Maymon and Charles Bolian, "The Wadleigh Falls Site: An Early and Middle Archaic Period Site in Southeastern New Hampshire" in *Early Holocene Occupation in Northern New England*, ed. Brian Robinson, James Petersen, and Ann Robinson, 117–34 (Augusta: Occasional Publications in Maine Archaeology 9, 1992), 117–34; Laura Pope, "Wadleigh Falls Island NH 39-1: A Preliminary Site Report," *New Hampshire Archaeologist* 22 (1981): 8–15; David Skinas, "The Wadleigh Fall Site (NH 39-2): A Preliminary Report of the 1980 Excavations," *New Hampshire Archaeologist* 22 (1981): 16–30.

33. Harold Hecker, "Jasper Flakes and Jack's Reef Points at Adams Point: Speculations on Interregional Exchange in Late Middle Woodland Times in Coastal New Hampshire," *New Hampshire Archaeologist* 35 (1995): 61–83; the few shell midden sites found to date in the Great Bay are much smaller than the large shell heaps of coastal Maine, the most famous of which carries a name reflective of its large size, Whaleback Shell Midden State Historic Site, featured in Murray Carpenter, "Native American Secrets Lie Buried in Huge Shell Mounds," *New York Times*, October 19, 2017.

34. Eugene Finch, "The Great Bay Site," *New Hampshire Archaeologist* 15 (1969): 1–12.

35. Victoria Bunker, "New Hampshire's Prehistoric Settlement and Culture Chronology," *New Hampshire Archaeologist* 33/34 (1994): 20–28.

36. Funding for fieldwork was provided by the James H. and Claire Short Hayes Chair in the Humanities at the Center for the Humanities at the University of New Hampshire. This meant that GBAS was subject to UNH COVID protocols, which permitted at that time only a team of three for outdoor work and required us to test for COVID weekly to participate.

37. While empty of seventeenth-century materials, they did produce more recent nails and plow parts, which makes sense given that this meadow was plowed and farmed in the 1800s through the early 1900s.

38. Important archaeological projects have occurred in the region, and I do not intend to discount them. These include major excavations at the Chadborne house

led by Emerson W. Baker and the Old Berwick Historical Society, ongoing years of archaeology at Strawbery Banke, the Oyster River Environs Archaeology Project at Field-Bickford led by Craig Brown, strong cultural resource management work, and other projects, but given the size of this ecosystem, even these great projects represent a relatively limited scope of coverage archaeologically.

39. All AMS dating was done by Beta Analytic, sample #s Beta-595268 and Beta-609000 through 609006; for the radiometric date reports, please contact me.

40. We know this because when we dug out features, we took large soil samples and put each sample in water. Botanical remains in the soil floated to the top of the water, where we recovered them in a very fine mesh net. In archaeology, this is called conducting flotation. Our floatation samples were analyzed by a paleoethnobotanist Katie Reinhart, a specialist in identifying ancient plant remains in the Northeast.

41. John P. Hart and C. Margaret Scarry, "The Age of Common Beans (*Phaseolus Vulgaris*) in the Northeastern United States," *American Antiquity* 64, no. 4 (1999): 653–58.

42. Hart and Scarry, "Age of Common Beans"; Chilton, "'Towns They Have None'"; Bourque, *Twelve Thousand Years.*

43. Heidi Altman, Tanya Peres, and J. Matthew Compton, "Better than Butter: Yona Go'i, Bear Grease in Cherokee Culture," in *Bears: Archaeological and Ethnohistorical Perspectives in Native Eastern North America*, ed. Heather A. Lapham and Gregory A. Waselkov, 193–216 (Gainesville: University Press of Florida, 2020).

44. This whole ecosystem is home to many current restoration efforts, including ones focused on oysters. To learn more about oyster restoration efforts in Great Bay, see the Nature Conservancy's New Hampshire State website.

45. Findings from the Lomekwi site in Kenya, although controversial and up for debate, do seem to be pushing the world's oldest stone tools back to 3.3 million years ago.

46. Goodby, *Deep Presence.*

47. Wikipedia's entry on chert is a good place to go to start learning more about these lithic materials.

48. Goodby, *Deep Presence*, 30.

49. For more on precontact stone tool trade and exchange, see Goodby, *Deep Presence*; Bourque, *Twelve Thousand Years.*

50. Bourque, *Twelve Thousand Years.*

51. Barry C. Kent, "More on Gunflints," *Historical Archaeology* 17, no. 2 (1983): 27–40.

52. Matthew J. Gifford, "Everything Is Ballast: An Examination of Ballast Related Practices and Ballast Stones from the Emanuel Point Shipwrecks," master's thesis, University of West Florida, 2014.

53. Kent, "More on Gunflints."

54. John Walter Durel, "From Strawbery Banke to Puddle Dock: The Evolution of a Neighborhood, 1630–1850," PhD diss., University of New Hampshire, 1984, 99.

55. We identify this as a lead musket ball as the dimensions fit seventeenth-century musket shot dimensions, the seam indicates early production, the weight indicates that it is lead, and because of the patina, which if it were iron it would not have.

56. Bruce J. Bourque and Ruth Holmes Whitehead, "Tarrentines and the Introduction of European Trade Goods in the Gulf of Maine," *Ethnohistory* 32, no. 4 (1985): 327–41.

57. Kent, "More on Gunflints."

58. Nancy Kenmotsu, "Gunflints: A Study," *Historical Archaeology* 24, no. 2 (1990): 92–124; Todd Kristensen, "Flash in the Pan: The Archaeology of Gunflints in Alberta," *RETROactive* (blog), July 10, 2019.

59. Nassaney, "Identity Formation"; Kristensen, "Flash in the Pan."

60. It has a slight amber hue to it, a common color of French gun flints, but this is not as amber as one would expect for being a French gun flint, and having an amber hue is a noted part of English ballast flints. See Kent, "More on Gunflints."

61. Kent, "More on Gunflints," fig. 2.

62. Kent, "More on Gunflints"; Nassaney, "Identity Formation"; Kristensen, "Flash in the Pan." Gunflints have been found to be made from local cherts as well.

Chapter 3

1. For an extensive discussion of ground stone generally, see Jenny L. Adams, *Ground Stone Analysis* (Salt Lake City: University of Utah Press, 2014). For more on New Hampshire specifically, see chapter 3 in Robert Goodby, *A Deep Presence: 13,000 Years of Native American History* (Portsmouth, NH: Peter Randall Publisher, 2021). Also, the stones used to make ground stone tools are themselves ground stone tools: manufacturing tools such as polishers, abraders, hammerstones, and choppers.

2. Adams, *Ground Stone Analysis*, 3; Goodby, *Deep Presence*, 27.

3. Most bannerstones are highly polished stone items drilled down the center and are often thought to be ceremonial in nature. Some bannerstones are not highly polished and served as spear weights, filling more utilitarian functions. For more on eastern US bannerstones, see Kenneth E Sassaman and Asa R Randall, "The Cultural History of Bannerstones in the Savannah River Valley," *Southeastern Archaeology* 26, no. 2 (2007): 196–211.

4. Charles C. Willoughby, "The Adze and the Ungrooved Axe of the New England Indians," *American Anthropologist* 9, no. 2 (1907): 296–306.

5. Willoughby, "Adze and the Ungrooved Axe." This early publication shows helpful renderings of New England ungrooved axes and how they might have been hafted for some better reference.

6. Eric R. Wolf, *Europe and the People without History* (Los Angeles: University of California Press, 1997). Much of what we explore in chapter 2 and discuss here can be aptly appreciated as what Wolf characterizes as tactical or organizational power. This power controls the contexts in which people exhibit their capabilities

and interact with others, and this power can allow individuals or groups to direct and/or circumscribe the actions of others within determinate settings.

7. For more on the process of dispossession and colonial naturalization of concepts that support it, see Amy Den Ouden, *Beyond Conquest: Native Peoples and the Struggle for History in New England* (Lincoln: University of Nebraska Press, 2005).

8. Den Ouden, *Beyond Conquest.*

9. For a recent quantification and exploration of this land dispossession, see Justin Farrell et al., "Effects of Land Dispossession and Forced Migration on Indigenous Peoples in North America," *Science* 374, no. 6567 (2021).

10. In America in 2020, Black homeownership was 47 percent compared with 76 percent white homeownership. Of the United States' agricultural land base, white Americans own 98 percent of it, Black Americans 1.4 percent. See more on the USDA's website.

11. Dover underwent a series of rapid changes over the course of the 1630s. The Hiltons sold to the Bristol Company, which in turn sold it to Lords Saye and Brooke (1632). This area was referred to as Bristol when Capt. Thomas Wiggins, an agent of the Bristol Company and then of Lord Saye and Brooke, came with thirty settlers. He had the power of granting land to the settlers. Since the main objective was fishing and trading, each man received a grant of twenty acres, setting up a small compact community on Dover Neck. Rev. William Leveridge, a Puritan, was the first minister here. Over the next few years, there was much turmoil, and this was one reason these colonists agreed to join the Massachusetts Bay Colony on August 9, 1641. This history is explored more in chapter 4.

12. *Dover, NH Town Records: 1657–1753.* These are digitized and can be found under Historic Dover Records on the city of Dover's website.

13. Another unevenness that colonialism introduced was written records and archives. English colonists, with their emphasis on legitimacy and legality, have a trove of historical records associated with them. This allows us to talk about individuals in ways we cannot for the ancestral Abenaki/Pennacook peoples who lived through these changes. When we do meet individual Native peoples in the records, they are written about from the English perspective only. This means that as I take us to the English colonial site on the same landscape as the Indigenous site, as in chapter 2, I am able to layer in more specifics on individuals. I recognize this may contribute to a sense of the colonists being more real or alive. I want to be open about this limitation here and emphasize that while we, today, may not know the names of the Indigenous peoples who were living on this landscape, this does not mean their names are unknown; indeed they were once known, used, and remembered by their kin and community.

14. Rowles signed with Humphrey Chadborne in 1643; see Emerson W. Baker and Nina Maurer, *Forgotten Frontier: Untold Stories of the Piscataqua* (exhibit catalog) (South Berwick, ME: Old Berwick Historical Society, 2018). A note on "signed" deals: leadership, like property, was quite different from colonial and Indigenous

perspectives. The English interpreted S8gamo as something akin to "chief," a title conveying political power and authority. But, in N'dakinna, *S8gamo* meant "speaker," a symbolic community leader whose main role was to ensure resource distribution through his territory, via trade and exchange, by building, sustaining, and renewing relationships, often through ceremonial gatherings. S8gamo's were not positioned to "sell" land; this was an English interpretation/imposition. Also, the English only recognized male speakers in communities and so often missed the power female speakers held. For more on these leadership disconnects during the seventeenth century, see Lisa Brooks, *Our Beloved Kin: A New History of King Philip's War* (New Haven, CT: Yale University Press, 2018).

15. Various letters and lists from Gibbons to this end as well as complaints from Mason and his agents in England of not getting enough commodities from Gibbons, wishing he would still find "mines" at the lakes, and more are found in *Provincial Papers. Documents and Records Relating to the Province of New-Hampshire, from the Earliest Period of Its Settlement: 1623–1686*, vol. 1, compiled and ed. Nathaniel Bouton (Concord, NH: George E. Jenks, state printer, 1867, University of New Hampshire Scholars Repository), 61–99.

16. *Provincial Papers*, 62; See letter from Thomas Eyre to Gibbons in 1631: "I will now put on the sending of you the modell of a saw-mill, that you may have one going."

17. *Provincial Papers*, 61–99.

18. Baker and Maurer, *Forgotten Frontier*.

19. For example, Humphrey Chadborne, William Chadborne's son, bought his first land from Sagamore Rowles in 1643 and built his homestead on the neck of land where the Newichawannock and Asbenbedick Rivers converge and became very wealthy, acquiring more and more land over time as well. For more, see Baker and Maurer, *Forgotten Frontier*.

20. Mary Pickering Thompson, *Landmarks in Ancient Dover, New Hampshire* (Durham, NH: Concord Republican Press Association, 1892; Internet Archive), 181. See also *Provincial Papers*, 141.

21. These Scottish prisoners of war are an interesting presence here in this early colonial landscape, adding another layer to the mixture of peoples here in this emergent new world. When they were freed after five to seven years, they received land grants. By the end of the seventeenth century, all of the Scots who worked in Oyster River had left the area, many moving farther north up into what is today Maine. There is ongoing research on these Scots, including new efforts underway for learning more about them in Great Bay specifically. For more information on them, see Chris Gerrard et al., *Lost Lives, New Voices: Unlocking the Stories of the Scottish Soldiers at the Battle of Dunbar 1650* (Oxford: Oxbow Books, 2018); Carol Gardner, *The Involuntary American: A Scottish Prisoner's Journey to the New World* (Yardley, PA: Westholme Publishing, 2019); and the website of the Scottish Prisoners of War Society.

22. Everett Stackpole and Lucien Thompson, *History of the Town of Durham New Hampshire (Oyster River Plantation) with Genealogical Notes*, vol. 1 (Durham, NH: Town of Durham, 1913, University of New Hampshire's Scholars Repository), 40. *Dover, NH Town Records*, Section 3:10; *Provincial Papers*, vol. 1:441; see also Thompson, *Landmarks in Ancient Dover, New Hampshire*, 170.

23. The document was signed on May 12, 1657, by Henry Sherborn and recorded on May 13, 1657; copied from the original, November 19, 1683; *Rockingham County Registry of Deeds*, vol. 7: 441–442; The phrase *to have and to hold*, common today in wedding vows, was old English property law indicting continuance of possession.

24. Bristol today is reckoning with this history, like many places across the globe. In 2020 a statue of a seventeenth-century chattel slavery trader from Bristol was taken down during protests.

25. C. M. Senior, *A Nation of Pirates: English Piracy in Its Heydey* (London: David and Charles, 1875, Bristol Record Society).

26. Gordon Harris, "The Great Colonial Hurricane and the Wreck of the Angel Gabriel," *Historic Ipswich* (blog), October 24, 2021.

27. Thompson, *Landmarks in Ancient Dover, New Hampshire*, 180–83.

28. *History of Wages in the United States From Colonial Times to 1928* (Washington, DC: Bulletin of the United States Bureau of Labor Statistics, No. 499, 1929.)

29. Woodman Institute, founded 1916, is now the Woodman Museum of Dover, New Hampshire.

30. Emerson W. Baker, "Formerly Machegonne, Dartmouth, York, Stogummor, Casco, and Falmouth: Portland as a Contested Frontier in the Seventeenth Century," in *Creating Portland: History and Place in Northern New England*, ed. Joseph A. Conforti, 12–13 (Lebanon NH: University Press of New England, 2005).

31. For some examples of garrisons' embeddedness in Dover today, I point to a few examples: Garrison Elementary School, Garrison City Beer Works, and the local youth soccer league named Garrison City Soccer.

32. See chapter 7 of Christine M. DeLucia, "The Memory Frontier: Geographies of Violence and Regeneration in Colonial New England and the Native Northeast after King Philip's War. (Garrisoned Piscataqua Pp. 484–618)," PhD diss., Yale University, 2012.

33. *Yankee* is a term for descendants of original English colonial New England settlers.

34. Alea Henle refers to these institutions as "historical cultures" in *Rescued from Oblivion: Historical Cultures in the Early United States* (Amherst: University of Massachusetts Press, 2020).

35. See various area town histories of the 1800s and early 1900s and popular poems such as those of Sarah Orne Jewett, including her poem "York Garrison, 1640," and more. These tended to default to the term *garrison* to describe most early colonial homesteads, regardless of fortification history of these structures, which helped advance a sense of fortifying and protecting and overcoming

Indigenous-driven violence, among other challenges, as central to the experience of colonists here.

36. Thompson, *Landmarks in Ancient Dover, New Hampshire.*

37. Thompson, *Landmarks in Ancient Dover, New Hampshire*, 181.

38. Thompson, *Landmarks in Ancient Dover, New Hampshire*, 181.

39. Thompson, in *Landmarks in Ancient Dover, New Hampshire*, explains both views, whereas Stackpole and Thompson, *History of the Town of Durham New Hampshire*, suggest Burnham over Gibbons.

40. The axe would have been whole in its use-life, but as we only excavated half this feature, we only recovered a portion of the whole tool.

41. *Rockingham County Registry of Deeds*, Probate #498 Inventory of Jeremiah Burnham.

42. Moose appears in many mythologies in N'dakinna. See Siobhan Senier, ed., *Dawnland Voices: An Anthology of Indigenous Writing from New England* (Lincoln: University of Nebraska Press, 2014).

43. On the distribution of moose today in New Hampshire, see the website of New Hampshire Fish and Game Department.

44. "Determining Age and Growth through Stable Isotopes," 2020, NOAA Fisheries (website).

45. *Rockingham County Registry of Deeds*, Probate #498 Inventory of Jeremiah Burnham.

46. *Rockingham County Registry of Deeds*, vol 9: 111.

Chapter 4

1. George Wadleigh, *Notable Events in the History of Dover, New Hampshire: From the First Settlement in 1623 to 1865* (Dover, NH: Tufts College Press, 1913, Library of Congress), 21.

2. In these early decades of English colonial presence in this estuary, colonial populations were low density and spread out far and wide with often large landholdings, so much so that some described the area in the 1630s as "almost without English inhabitants," John Gorham Palfrey, *History of New England* (Carlisle, MA: Applewood Books, 1858, Google Books), 523.

3. In general, the exact sequence of colonial events and claims on Dover Neck are murky, including the transfer of Dover Neck from the Hilton's to Bristol. For early twentieth-century efforts to sort this out in Dover, see *Historical Sketch, Views and Business Directory of Dover, NH* (Dover, NH: Dover Grange, 1926, no. 225).

4. Women could not own or inherit property under English law, except widows could be granted what was known as the widow's third of their deceased husband's property.

5. Michael E. Leveridge, *A Godly Minister: The Reverend William Leverich of Great Britain, New England and New York* (Cambridge: Self-published by Michael E. Leveridge in collaboration with Thomas Leverich, 2008).

6. Alonzo Quint, "The First Church in Dover, and Its Pastor," *Granite Monthly: A Magazine of History, Biography, Literature and State Progress* 1, no. 7 (November 1877), Google Books.

7. Wadleigh, *Notable Events in the History of Dover*, 151.

8. Royalists were being promoted at the time in England by William Laud, who was executed at the end of the First English Civil war in 1645 for his devotion to the Church of England; see John Scales, *History of Dover, New Hampshire* (Manchester, NH: John B. Clarke, 1923, Google Books), 106.

9. Quint, "First Church in Dover, and Its Pastor."

10. Scales, *History of Dover, New Hampshire*, 107.

11. Scales, *History of Dover, New Hampshire*, 107.

12. For more on Ann Hutchinson, see: Marilyn J. Westerkamp, *The Passion of Anne Hutchinson: An Extraordinary Woman, the Puritan Patriarchs, and the World They Made and Lost* (Oxford: Oxford University Press, 2021).

13. J. R. Graves, James Pendleton, and A. C. Dayton, "Hanserd Knollys in America," in *Southern Baptist Review Journal*, 1858, 465–73; Scales, *History of Dover, New Hampshire*, 109.

14. Graves, Pendleton, and Dayton, "Hanserd Knollys in America."

15. He also changed the name of the town to Northam, although this did not last a year.

16. The agreement was by males only, seemingly of some level of landownership.

17. Perhaps reflective of Dover's early history, the exact location of the originally written combination is murky. In *Notable Events in the History of Dover*, Wadleigh provides a transcript of a copy of the Dover Combination made by Governor Cranfield in 1682 found in the Public Record Office in London (page 18). This is the version of the combination published today on Dover public websites.

18. Wadleigh, *Notable Events in the History of Dover*, 21.

19. Scales, *History of Dover, New Hampshire*, 111.

20. Wadleigh, *Notable Events in the History of Dover*, 21.

21. Alonzo Hall Quint, *Historical Memoranda Concerning Persons and Places in Old Dover, New Hampshire*, ed. John Scales (Dover, NH: Dover Enquirer, 1900, Internet Archive), 20.

22. Wadleigh, *Notable Events in the History of Dover*; Mary Pickering Thompson, *Landmarks in Ancient Dover, New Hampshire* (Durham, NH: Concord Republican Press Association, 1892, Internet Archive).

23. Wadleigh, *Notable Events in the History of Dover*, 21.

24. Quint, *Historical Memoranda Concerning Persons and Places*, 22.

25. John Scales, *History of Strafford County, New Hampshire and Representative Citizens* (Chicago: Richmond-Arnold Publishing, 1914, Internet Archive), 172.

26. Quint, *Historical Memoranda Concerning Persons and Places*, 22.

27. Waldron is also often written as Walderne.

28. Local Indigenous leaders and community groups combined efforts at recasting

Waldron's history and legacy have been powerful. A new historical marker titled "Native Retribution against Maj. Waldron" was dedicated in a prominent location in downtown Dover, New Hampshire, in August 2023. An accompanying educational short documentary film has also been created, *Pennacook Retribution: Who Shall Judge the Indians Now?* This film has been shown in many public and educational contexts in the region and is available through the Indigenous New Hampshire Collaborative Collective's YouTube channel.

29. Paul Wainwright et al., *A Space for Faith: The Colonial Meetinghouses of New England* (Portsmouth, NH: UNKNO, 2010).

30. This colonial-era path was eventually turned into a road and has been variously called High Street, Main Highway, and today is Dover Point Road.

31. *Dover, NH, Town Records: 1657–1753*, Historic Dover Records, City of Dover, NH (original spellings); see also Wadleigh, *Notable Events in the History of Dover*, 35.

32. *Dover, NH Town Records.*

33. Meghan C. L. Howey and Christine M. DeLucia, "Spectacles of Settler Colonial Memory: Archaeological Findings from an Early Twentieth-Century 'First' Settlement Pageant and Other Commemorative Terrain in New England," *International Journal of Historical Archaeology* 26 (2022): 974–1007.

34. Wadleigh, *Notable Events in the History of Dover*, 70.

35. For recent work on these violences, see Lisa Brooks, *Our Beloved Kin: A New History of King Philip's War* (New Haven, CT: Yale University Press, 2018); Christine M. DeLucia, *Memory Lands: King Philip's War and the Place of Violence in the Northeast* (New Haven, CT: Yale University Press, 2018). I engage with some of the impacts of this southern New England violence in this northern frontier in chapter 6.

36. Wadleigh, *Notable Events in the History of Dover*, 70.

37. Howey and DeLucia, "Spectacles of Settler Colonial Memory."

38. René Chartrand, *The Forts of Colonial North America: British, Dutch and Swedish Colonies*, illustrated edition (Oxford: Osprey Publishing, 2011); Charles Orser, *An Archaeology of the English Atlantic World, 1600–1700* (Cambridge: Cambridge University Press, 2018).

39. Orser, *Archaeology of the English Atlantic World*, 265.

40. See chapter 6 in Orser, *Archaeology of the English Atlantic World*, for more on many of these, from Fort St. George in what is today Maine to Charles Towne in what is today South Carolina.

41. See Orser, *Archaeology of the English Atlantic World*, fig. 6.1.

42. The last known event in the 1654 meetinghouse was a proprietors' meeting in 1722; *Dover, NH Town Records*. The structure may have been recycled into other structures, but this is unconfirmed.

43. In 1908 a stone wall and iron fence were installed around the site by the Daughters of the American Revolution (DAR.), a heritage organization that engaged in many regional and national activities focused on colonial origins and genealogical descent.

44. See the Principles of Archaeological Ethics laid out by the leading archaeological society, the Society of American Archaeology, at the organization's website.

45. Donald Bryant and David R. Starbuck, "First Parish Church—Dover Point Site," National Register of Historic Places Nomination, Inventory Form, National Park Service, 1983.

46. Peter Leach, *A Theory Primer and Field Guide for Archaeological, Cemetery, and Forensic Surveys with Ground Penetrating Radar* (Nashua, NH: Geophysical Survey Systems, Inc., 2021).

47. The watchtower berm on the southeast has been damaged somewhat.

48. For more on what this structure most likely was and what it meant, see Howey and DeLucia, "Spectacles of Settler Colonial Memory."

49. The 1908 fence is in the ditch, so it created a functional barrier to the extent of our test excavations.

50. Orser, *Archaeology of the English Atlantic World*, 276.

51. While I have discussed religious plurality in this frontier zone, it was all variations on Christian theology.

52. This orientation was also found during the rough survey of the site done for the National Registrar nomination: Bryant and Starbuck, "First Parish Church."

53. See Natural Resources Conservation Services Soil Survey for more on the soil on this site, Hinckley loamy sand.

54. James L. Garvin, "Small-Scale Brickmaking in New Hampshire," *IA. The Journal of the Society for Industrial Archeology* 20, no. 1/2 (1994): 19–31.

55. "The Origin of the Troy Ounce," *Provident Metals* (blog), July 27, 2017.

56. The avoirdupois system, based on sixteen-ounce pounds, was also in use at same time in England, and merchants gravitated more to this division system, which we have inherited in the United States still today from our colonial English roots.

57. W. G. Sumner, "The Spanish Dollar and the Colonial Shilling," *American Historical Review* 3, no. 4 (1898): 607–19; Michael Barbieri, "The Dollar in Revolutionary America," *Journal of the American Revolution*, September 27, 2016.

58. In the 1800s, the United States adopted the troy weight system to measure precious metals and gunpowder and this is still in use today.

59. See Ivor Noël Hume, *A Guide to the Artifacts of Colonial America* (Philadelphia: University of Pennsylvania Press, 2001 [1969]). Tobacco was an export from Indigenous North America to Europe, likely introduced from the Spanish first, but established practice in England in the 1500s. Pipe smoking became widespread and traveled to the English colonies in the Americas, and in England, pipe making became an export trade industry to colonial America.

60. The classic piece on dating pipe stems was J Harrington, "Dating Stem Fragments of Seventeenth and Eighteenth Century Clay Tobacco Pipes," *Quarterly Bulletin of the Archaeological Society of Virginia* 9, no. 1 (1954): 10–14. Debate and other histograms ensued. See Lewis Binford, "A New Method of Calculating Dates from Kaolin Pipe Stem Samples," *Southeastern Archaeology* 9, no. 1 (1962): 19–21; James

Deetz, "Harrington Histograms versus Binford Mean Dates as a Technique for Establishing the Occupational Sequence of Sites at Flowerdew Hundred, Virginia," *American Archaeology* 6, no. 1 (1987): 62–68. For a recent assessment, see Lauren K McMillan, "An Evaluation of Tobacco Pipe Stem Dating Formulas," *Northeast Historical Archaeology* 45 (2016): 67–91.

Chapter 5

1. Sean M. Rafferty and Rob Mann, eds., *Smoking and Culture: The Archaeology of Tobacco Pipes in Eastern North America* (Knoxville: University of Tennessee Press, 2004); Shannon Tushingham et al., "Biomolecular Archaeology Reveals Ancient Origins of Indigenous Tobacco Smoking in North American Plateau," *Proceedings of the National Academy of Sciences* 115, no. 46 (2018): 11742–47; Elizabeth Bollwerk and Shannon Tushingham, eds., *Perspectives on the Archaeology of Pipes, Tobacco and Other Smoke Plants in the Ancient Americas* (Cham: Springer International, 2016).

2. Christoph Strobel, *The Global Atlantic: 1400 to 1900* (London: Routledge, 2015), 140.

3. Kaolin is often called china clay. Mining of it lasted through the 1800s and came with notable environmental impacts of its own. See Wheal Martyn Clay Works, "Discover Wheal Martyn and the China Clay Story," 2020.

4. Charles Orser, *An Archaeology of the English Atlantic World, 1600–1700* (Cambridge: Cambridge University Press, 2018), 96.

5. Kenan Heidtke, "Jamaican Red Clay Tobacco Pipes," master's thesis, Texas A&M, 1992.

6. Heidtke, "Jamaican Red Clay Tobacco Pipes."

7. J. Cameron Monroe and Seth Mallios, "A Seventeenth-Century Colonial Cottage Industry: New Evidence and a Dating Formula for Colono Tobacco Pipes in the Chesapeake," *Historical Archaeology* 38, no. 2 (2004): 68–82.

8. Monroe and Mallios, "Seventeenth-Century Colonial Cottage Industry." It appears that enslaved Africans produced red clay pipes in the British colony of Jamacia as well. See Heidtke, "Jamaican Red Clay Tobacco Pipes," for more.

9. Neill DePaoli, "Pemaquid, Maine: Preliminary Reconstruction of a Seventeenth Century Coastal Community's Domestic and International Trade Connections," *Bulletin of Massachusetts Archaeological Society* 45, no. 1 (1984): 24–40.

10. Patricia Capone and Elinor Downs, "Red Clay Tobacco Pipes: Petrographic Window into Seventeenth-Century Economics at Jamestown, Virginia, and New England," in Rafferty and Mann, *Smoking and Culture*, 305–16.

11. Petrographic analysis showed no centralized production center but multiple local New England productions locales (see Capone and Downs, "Red Clay Tobacco Pipes"). I state that these are English products, but I cannot rule out use by Indigenous peoples of N'dakinna, and/or we may find other redware pipe craft traditions in the future. This is what we know currently, which I would be excited to see expand and evolve as more research and archaeology are done.

12. Sherene Baugher and Robert W. Venables, "Ceramics as Indicators of Status and Class in Eighteenth-Century New York," in *Consumer Choice in Historical Archaeology*, ed. Suzanne M. Spencer-Wood, 31–53 (New York: Plenum Press 1987).

13. Terry L. Anderson and Robert Paul Thomas, "White Population, Labor Force and Extensive Growth of the New England Economy in the Seventeenth Century. *Journal of Economic History* 33, no. 3 (1973): 647, 651; Baugher and Venables, "Ceramics as Indicators of Status and Class," 34.

14. DePaoli, "Pemaquid, Maine."

15. Craig Brown, Richard Lunt, and Peter Sablock, "Hard by the Water's Edge: A Preliminary Report of the Darby Field Homestead-Bickford Garrison (27-ST-71) Excavations," *New Hampshire Archaeologist* 54 (2014): 14–38.

16. A rich resource on colonial and postcolonial era historic ceramics for readers interested in more ware details is hosted by the Maryland Department of Planning's Jefferson Patterson Park and Museum with a website Diagnostic Artifacts in Maryland.

17. Orser, *Archaeology of the English Atlantic World*, 83.

18. David R. M. Gaimster, *German Stoneware, 1200–1900: Archaeology and Cultural History: Containing a Guide to the Collections of the British Museum, Victoria & Albert Museum, and Museum of London* (London: British Museum Press, 1997).

19. Orser, *Archaeology of the English Atlantic World*, 86.

20. Timothy Brook, *Vermeer's Hat: The Seventeenth Century and the Dawn of the Global World*, Illustrated edition (New York: Bloomsbury Publishing, 2009); Strobel, *Global Atlantic*.

21. Strobel, *Global Atlantic*, 143. English potteries started eventually trying to produce porcelain as well in the 1700s.

22. Brook, *Vermeer's Hat*.

23. Orser, *Archaeology of the English Atlantic World*; Brook, *Vermeer's Hat*.

24. Orser, *Archaeology of the English Atlantic World*, 93.

25. Orser, *Archaeology of the English Atlantic World*.

26. These shifting regulations from England make ceramic wares found at sites important dating materials as well. For a time sequence of colonial ceramics, see the website Diagnostic Artifacts in Maryland.

27. To learn more about these ceramics, visit Historic Jamestown's online catalog, look under "Bartmann Jugs." Occasionally, molded sprig arms stretching down were added, transforming the jug into a man holding his belly.

28. Baugher and Venables, "Ceramics as Indicators of Status and Class"; Megan Victor, "Under the Tavern Table: Excavations at the Tavern on Smuttynose Island, Maine and Implications for Commensal Politics and Informal Economy," *International Journal of Historical Archaeology* 23, no. 1 (2019): 34–56.

29. Ivor Noël Hume, *A Guide to the Artifacts of Colonial America* (Philadelphia: University of Pennsylvania Press, 2001 [1969]).

30. When we are unsure whether something is an artifact, we err on the side of overcollecting and keep questionable items for further assessment in the lab.

31. Neil Brodie, Morag Kersel, and Kathryn Walker Tubb, "Museum Acquisitions: Responsibilities for the Illicit Traffic in Antiquities," in *Archaeology, Cultural Heritage, and the Antiquities Trade,* ed. Neil Brodie et al., 245–57 (Gainesville: University Press of Florida, 2006).

32. For a classic introduction to analyzing archaeological ceramics, see Carla M. Sinopoli, *Approaches to Archaeological Ceramics* (New York: Plenum Press, 1991).

33. This site was excavated by Craig Brown as part of the state of New Hampshire's Rescue Archaeology program (SCRAP). We at GBAS acquired the collections from this site in a salvage situation as state archaeologists changed and the state was pushing for reduced collections in their possession. Given the proximity and significance of this as one of a handful of systematically excavated seventeenth-century sites in Great Bay, these collections are now part of the University of New Hampshire's permanent collection. For more on that fieldwork, see Brown, Lunt, and Sablock, "Hard by The Water's Edge."

34. Our MNV method followed closely the procedure laid out in Barbara L Voss and Rebecca Allen, "Guide to Ceramic MNV Calculation Qualitative and Quantitative Analysis," *Technical Briefs in Historical Archaeology* 5 (2010): 1–9. See fig. 1 in this publication for a helpful guide to what a minimum vessel looks like. This resource is available online.

35. Given the fragmentary nature of ceramic sherds, not all minimum vessels could have the same information recorded. A detailed accounting of our MNV process and coding is beyond the scope of this chapter, where my aim is to make some more overarching points about colonial community formation playing out on the ground in the Great Bay Estuary, but plans are underway to make details and data available in a more technical publication.

36. Staffordshire was the most common English fine earthenware, but assemblages also included North Devon Sgraffito and more utilitarian English earthenware also from North Devon, as well as Border wares. A full fleshing out of the ceramic analysis is beyond the scope of this chapter but, again, is in prep for a more technical publication.

37. Sarah Peabody Turnbaugh, "17th and 18th Century Lead-Glazed Redwares in the Massachusetts Bay Colony," *Historical Archaeology* 17, no. 1 (1983): 3–17.

38. DePaoli, "Pemaquid, Maine"; Turnbaugh, "17th and 18th Century Lead-Glazed Redwares in the Massachusetts Bay Colony."

39. Lura Watkins, *Early New England Potters and Their Wares* (Cambridge, MA: Harvard University Press, 1950).

40. Watkins, *Early New England Potters and Their Wares*, 15.

41. Watkins, *Early New England Potters and Their Wares.*

42. Turnbaugh, "17th and 18th Century Lead-Glazed Redwares," 10.

43. James L. Garvin, "Small-Scale Brickmaking in New Hampshire," *IA. The Journal of the Society for Industrial Archeology* 20, no. 1/2 (1994): 19–31.

44. In Portsmouth, Samuel Marshall is listed as a potter in 1729; in Hampton,

Henry Moulton started potting in the 1720s; and in Exeter, Nathaniel Libby established a pottery in 1742/43. For more, see chapter 14 in Watkins, *Early New England Potters and Their Wares*.

45. Turnbaugh, "17th and 18th Century Lead-Glazed Redwares," 13.

46. Baugher and Venables, "Ceramics as Indicators of Status and Class."

47. Turnbaugh, "17th and 18th Century Lead-Glazed Redwares."

48. Jane Pettigrew and Bruce Richardson, *A Social History of Tea: Tea's Influence on Commerce, Culture and Community* (Chicago: Benjamin Press, 2013).

49. Victor, "Under the Tavern Table."

50. Nineteen of the twenty-four tankards were at the Field-Bickford site, which reflects that this site likely had a tavern at this location at one time, something that should be unpacked in its own right in a separate analysis. This chapter looks at overarching patterns, but there are many inter- and intrasite analyses that can be done with these ceramic data in the future.

51. For some examples from American archaeology, see Craig N. Cipolla, ed., *Foreign Objects: Rethinking Indigenous Consumption in American Archaeology* (Tucson: University of Arizona Press, 2017).

52. For more on the evolution of utensils in colonial America, see Lydia Barrett Blackmore, "'Just IMPORTED and to Be SOLD': Methods of Acquisition and Use of Knives, Forks, and Silver Spoons in Eighteenth-Century Virginia," honors thesis, William and Mary, 2010.

53. Seal-top spoons were at first functional inventions, so people traveling could have their own utensils and also have something that could double as a wax seal, but in the seventeenth century in England they began making these spoon balusters much more decorative. You can see a well-preserved example of a whole spoon with a highly similar seal that was found in Chichester, England, at the Fishing Industry Protocol for Archaeological Discoveries website ("17th Century Seal-Top Spoon").

Chapter 6

1. For a rich account of this event, see this work, which I draw on throughout this chapter: Craig Brown, "The Great Massacre of 1694: Understanding the Destruction of Oyster River Plantation," *Historical New Hampshire*, 1998, 69–90. See also Emerson W. Baker, "Trouble to the Eastward: The Failure of Anglo-Indian Relations in Early Maine," PhD diss., Willam and Mary, 1986; Christine M. DeLucia, "The Memory Frontier: Geographies of Violence and Regeneration in Colonial New England and the Native Northeast after King Philip's War. (Garrisoned Piscataqua Pp. 484–618)," PhD diss., Yale University, 2012.

2. For more on this broad concept, see Michel-Rolph Trouillot, *Silencing the Past: Power and the Production of History* (Boston: Beacon Press, 1995).

3. This concept of colonial contemporary memory and narratives of violence is eloquently developed and explored in Christine M. DeLucia, *Memory Lands: King*

Philip's War and the Place of Violence in the Northeast (New Haven, CT: Yale University Press, 2018).

4. DeLucia, *Memory Lands*, 2.

5. For more on material commemorations and issues around place making and colonial history in New England, see DeLucia, *Memory Lands*; Randall Handsman, "Landscapes of Memory in Wampanoag Country and the Monuments upon Them," in *Archaeologies of Placemaking: Monuments, Memories, and Engagement in Native North America*, ed. Patricia Rubertone, 161–93 (Walnut Creek, CA: Left Coast Press, 2008); Patricia Rubertone, "Engaging Monuments, Memories, and Archaeology," in *Archaeologies of Placemaking: Monuments, Memories, and Engagement in Native North America*, ed. Patricia Rubertone, 13–34 (Walnut Creek, CA: Left Coast Press, 2008); Lisa Blee and Jean M. O'Brien, *Monumental Mobility: The Memory Work of Massasoit* (Chapel Hill: University of North Carolina Press, 2019).

6. Again, we can think of it as a wake that we live in and that lives in us, as explained by Christina Elizabeth Sharpe, *In the Wake: On Blackness and Being* (Durham, NC: Duke University Press, 2016).

7. John Pike, *Journal of the Rev. John Pike, of Dover, N.H.* (Cambridge: Massachusetts Historical Society, 1876, Library of Congress), 16.

8. See Francis Parkman, *Francis Parkman: France and England in North America*, vol. 2: *Count Frontenac and New France under Louis XIV, a Half-Century of Conflict, Montcalm and Wolfe* (New York: Library of America, 1983 [1877]); Everett Stackpole and Lucien Thompson, *History of the Town of Durham New Hampshire (Oyster River Plantation) with Genealogical Notes*, vol. 1 (Durham, NH: Town of Durham, 1913, University of New Hampshire's Scholars Repository); Mary Pickering Thompson, *Landmarks in Ancient Dover, New Hampshire* (Durham, NH: Concord Republican Press Association, 1892, Internet Archive). Jeremy Belknap in his *The History of New-Hampshire (1784–1792)* (Philadelphia, PA: Robert Aitken, 1784, Internet Archive) details this event for seven pages (215–222), and he uses more flourishing words to describe the Native actors in this ("their bloody work"), but even he does not use the term "massacre" to describe this event; this happens in later historical narratives and accounts.

9. *Raid* is the preferred term by the committees' Indigenous leaders, and they have gone on record in the press noting this term as their preference.

10. Rasles is also variously Rale, Rasle. This episode has its own compelling and complexly layered story, and exploring those details is beyond this book. I bring it up to offer an important counter to word selection in historical commemoration. Interestingly, Indigenous peoples from this village were part of the Oyster River raiding party, so like much in the colonial landscape, there were webs of connection all around.

11. Brown, "Great Massacre of 1694."

12. Michael G. Laramie, *King William's War: The First Contest for North America, 1689–1697* (Yardley, PA: Westholme Publishing, 2017).

13. W. E. Daugherty, "Maritime Indian Treaties in Historical Perspective," Treaties

and Historical Research Centres, Department of Indian and Northern Affairs Canada, 1983, 11.

14. Lisa Brooks, *Our Beloved Kin: A New History of King Philip's War* (New Haven, CT: Yale University Press, 2018), 8.

15. Captain John Underhill, whom we met in chapter 4, helped lead the Battle of Mystic Fort for the English.

16. Robust scholarship has been published on King Phillip's War. One of the most important of these is the recent, and award-winning, work by Abenaki historian Lisa Brooks, *Our Beloved Kin*, in which she systematically retells the history of this war from an Indigenous perspective.

17. Brooks, *Our Beloved Kin*, 207.

18. This boundary was breached routinely by the English who went farther north and east into Maine. See Emerson Baker, "Trouble To the Eastward." Recently, the Upstander Project made a short film on the impacts of this colonial-era bounty hunting called *Bounty* (open access on their website).

19. Stackpole and Thompson, *History of the Town of Durham*, 86. There was also a story of an Irishman taken captive.

20. For more from Maine on King Phillip's War impacts, see Emerson Baker, "Trouble to the Eastward." For more on such an imposed, and damaging, Massachusetts Bay Colony episode in Saco, see Brooks, *Our Beloved Kin*, 207–9.

21. This event is commonly reported as being a sham battle, but ongoing historical research indicates that this was not what was planned or understood by the attendees. The outcome of the event is more consistently reported.

22. John Scales, *History of Dover, New Hampshire* (Manchester, NH: John B. Clarke, 1923, Google Books); Belknap, *History of New-Hampshire*; Baker, "Trouble To the Eastward"; Brooks, *Our Beloved Kin*.

23. Belknap, *History of New-Hampshire*; DeLucia, *Memory Lands*.

24. As also noted in chapter 4, local Indigenous leaders and community partners have been successful in actively recasting the Waldron story, including a new historical marker in downtown Dover, New Hampshire titled Native Retribution against Maj. Waldron and a documentary film, *Pennacook Retribution: Who Shall Judge the Indians Now?*, available on Indigenous New Hampshire Collaborative Collective's YouTube channel.

25. In 1675–78, saw mills were burned in Saco and Scarboro. In 1689, again mills burned in Dover, and in 1690, mills burned at Salmon Falls. See Pike, *Journal*. Resistance against ecological devastation continued into the 1700s in northern colonial zones. For more on this, see Lisa Brooks and Cassandra Brooks, "The Reciprocity Principle and Traditional Ecological Knowledge: Understanding the Significance of Indigenous Protest on the Presumpscot River," *International Journal of Critical Indigenous Studies* 11 (2010): 1837–44.

26. Brown, "Great Massacre of 1694," 71. See also Pike, *Journal*, on the raid on Salmon Falls.

27. Daugherty, "Maritime Indian Treaties in Historical Perspective," 10.

28. Daugherty, "Maritime Indian Treaties in Historical Perspective," 11.

29. Brooks, *Our Beloved Kin.*

30. Brown, "Great Massacre of 1694," 73.

31. Daugherty, "Maritime Indian Treaties in Historical Perspective"; Brown, "Great Massacre of 1694"; Stackpole and Thompson, *History of the Town of Durham.*

32. Brown, "Great Massacre of 1694," 81.

33. Belknap, *History of New-Hampshire*, 217.

34. For an account from one captive, Ann Jenkins, see Stackpole and Thompson, *History of the Town of Durham*, 91–2.

35. Craig Brown, Richard Lunt, and Peter Sablock, "Hard by the Water's Edge: A Preliminary Report of the Darby Field Homestead-Bickford Garrison (27-ST-71) Excavations," *New Hampshire Archaeologist* 54 (2014): 14–38.

36. Belknap, *History of New-Hampshire*, 218; Stackpole and Thompson, *History of the Town of Durham*, 91.

37. Stackpole and Thompson, *History of the Town of Durham,* 89.

38. The Meader Garrison was burned, see Thompson, *Landmarks in Ancient Dover, New Hampshire*, 175.

39. James L. Garvin, "Small-Scale Brickmaking in New Hampshire," *IA. The Journal of the Society for Industrial Archeology* 20, no. 1/2 (1994): 19–31.

40. C. W. Kanolt, "Melting Points of Fire Bricks," Technologic Papers of the Bureau of Standards, no. 10, 1912, National Bureau of Standards, Washington, DC.

41. Stackpole and Thompson, *History of the Town of Durham*, 96.

42. The story also states that one Abenaki warrior was shot, but not killed, from long range in this meadow. Where this shot came from is pretty murky; some accounts give no specific location (Stackpole and Thompson, *History of the Town of Durham*, 96.) and others state that it was from a sentry box (Belknap, *History of New Hampshire*, 220). The Burnham garrison itself, up on the hill overlooking this field, is never named or suggested as the origin point. This was right after the attacks up and down the river, when colonists all over the river were reeling and in defensive mode.

43. Again, interior landscapes were particularly powerful places in winter as the English struggled to adapt to the snow of this continental climate. See Thomas M. Wickman, *Snowshoe Country: An Environmental and Cultural History of Winter in the Early American Northeast* (Cambridge: Cambridge University Press, 2018).

44. Keith Basso, *Wisdom Sits in Places: Landscape and Language Among the Western Apache* (Albuquerque: University of New Mexico Press, 1996).

45. Lisa Brooks, *The Common Pot: The Recovery of Native Space in the Northeast* (Minneapolis: University of Minnesota Press, 2008); Handsman, "Landscapes of Memory in Wampanoag Country."

46. This is the boundary shown in *The Province of Mayne* (see fig. 1.1). These boundaries were obviously fought over and won over by the English in subsequent

conflicts, with the line eventually along Quebec providence and the Maritimes where it is today.

47. Again, this was more than just a European or European colonial conflict; it should also be seen as part of the broadly expanding, and northeastwardly moving, arc of Indigenous resistance to settler colonialism. In fact, Indigenous groups signed their own peace treaty in 1713 with New England's colonial government in Portsmouth on the mouth of the Piscataqua River, with representatives from several sovereign Native groups traveling here from more inland and northeasterly villages to find a path forward. For more on this war here and this treaty, see the website developed for the treaties' three hundredth anniversary, Portsmouth Peace Treaty of 1713.

48. Daniel Vickers, *Farmers and Fishermen: Two Centuries of Work in Essex County, Massachusetts, 1630–1850* (Chapel Hill: University of North Carolina Press, 1994).

49. Kathryn Yusoff, *A Billion Black Anthropocenes or None* (Minneapolis: University of Minnesota Press, 2018); Sharpe, *In the Wake*; Amy Den Ouden, *Beyond Conquest: Native Peoples and the Struggle for History in New England* (Lincoln: University of Nebraska Press, 2005).

50. Christian Weller and Lily Roberts, "Eliminating the Black-White Wealth Gap Is a Generational Challenge," *Center for American Progress Reports*, March 19, 2021.

51. One of the properties he bought was neighboring Cutt's land and Pittman's land as w: Inv. of Ezekiel Pitman; *Rockingham County Registry of Deeds*, vol 9: 436 (signed June 18, 1716; Rec: July 7, 1716).

52. *Rockingham County Registry of Deeds*, vol 8: 307, Order: Division of Jerimiah's Estate.

53. *Rockingham County Registry of Deeds*, vol 8: 307, and vol 10: 121, Administration of Jeremiah Burnham's Estate and Inventory (died 1718; RC Probate #498).

54. Yusoff, *Billion Black Anthropocenes or None.*

55. For more on this unfolding process in colonial New England, see Vickers, *Farmers and Fishermen*. Also, the land being turned into property was Indigenous homelands.

56. Mark Sammons and Valerie Cunningham, *Black Portsmouth: Three Centuries of African-American Heritage* (Durham: University of New Hampshire Press, 2004); Jody R Fernald, "Slavery in New Hampshire: Profitable Godliness to Racial Consciousness," master's thesis, History, University of New Hampshire, 2007.

57. These indentured Scots, as noted briefly in chapter 3, are another interesting thread of early colonial dynamism that is often overlooked and whose stories have gone untold. There is active, ongoing research on indentured Scots and their place in the early colonial story.

58. For more on this still too often overlooked history in New England, see Dinah Mayo-Bobee, "Servile Discontents: Slavery and Resistance in Colonial New Hampshire, 1645–1785," *Slavery and Abolition* 30, no. 3 (2009): 339–60; Fernald, "Slavery in New Hampshire"; Wendy Warren, *New England Bound: Slavery and Colonization*

in Early America, (New York: Liveright, 2017); Sammons and Cunningham, *Black Portsmouth*. See also the robust community resources raising the profile of these histories, particularly the Black Heritage Trail of New Hampshire.

59. Fernald, "Slavery in New Hampshire," 15.

60. Mayo-Bobee, "Servile Discontents"; Sammons and Cunningham, *Black Portsmouth*, chapter 2.

61. A series of deeds, transfers, acquisitions recovered from archival records show significant Burnham lands running from the Oyster River all the way back to the Lamprey River, constituting numerous hectares.

62. Stackpole and Thompson, *History of the Town of Durham*, 250; Thompson, *Landmarks in Ancient Dover, New Hampshire*, 162.

63. A marriage is recorded between Belmont and Venus and they had seven children: Aenon, Caesar, Jubal, Titus, Peter, Candace, and another daughter. The point out on Oyster River on Burnham land they lived on is derisively, historically called N***er point. Thompson, *Landmarks in Ancient Dover, New Hampshire*.

64. For the groundbreaking study that showed changes in headstone carving style tracked shifting religious, economic, and social developments in historic New England, see James Deetz, *In Small Things Forgotten: An Archaeology of Early American Life* (New York: Knopf Doubleday Publishing Group, 1996).

Conclusion

1. Ned Blackhawk, *The Rediscovery of America: Native Peoples and the Unmaking of U.S. History* (New Haven, CT: Yale University Press, 2023), 49.

2. As explored in some detail in the recent article, Meghan C. L. Howey and Christine M. DeLucia, "Spectacles of Settler Colonial Memory: Archaeological Findings from an Early Twentieth-Century 'First' Settlement Pageant and Other Commemorative Terrain in New England," *International Journal of Historical Archaeology*, 26 (2022): 974–1007.

3. For a small sampling of work documenting the threat of sea level rise to cultural heritage sites across the globe, see David G. Anderson et al., "Sea-Level Rise and Archaeological Site Destruction: An Example from the Southeastern United States Using DINAA (Digital Index of North American Archaeology)," *PLOS ONE* 12, no. 11 (2017): e0188142; Mark D. McCoy, "The Race to Document Archaeological Sites Ahead of Rising Sea Levels: Recent Applications of Geospatial Technologies in the Archaeology of Polynesia," *Sustainability* 10, no. 1 (2018): 185; Lena Reimann et al., "Mediterranean UNESCO World Heritage at Risk from Coastal Flooding and Erosion Due to Sea-Level Rise," *Nature Communications* 9, no. 1 (2018): 4161.

4. NASA has a live monitor of climate change's impacts, including sea level rise, on their global climate website.

5. See Cameron Wake et al., "New Hampshire Coastal Flood Risk Summary Part 1: Science," New Hampshire Coastal Flood Risk Science and Technical Advisory Panel, 2019.

6. Cameron Wake et al., "Climate Change in the Piscataqua/Great Bay Region: Past, Present, and Future," Carbon Solutions New England, 2011.

7. For details of this analysis, see Meghan C. L. Howey, "Harnessing Remote Sensing Derived Sea Level Rise Models to Assess Cultural Heritage Vulnerability: A Case Study from the Northwest Atlantic Ocean," *Sustainability* 12, no. 22 (2020): 9429.

8. New Hampshire Coastal Risk and Hazards Commission, *Preparing New Hampshire for Projected Storm Surge, Sea-Level Rise and Extreme Precipitation*, 2016.

9. I want to be careful here to avoid traps of "discovery"; of course Indigenous places were once known by the peoples who used them and valued them, and indeed some are known still and shared in oral traditions. When I refer to them "waiting to be found," it is in terms of official, Western-oriented practice and recording.

10. I draw here from the beautiful and powerful lecture for the Nobel Prize in Literature by Derek Walcott about postcolonial landscapes in the Antilles, *The Antilles: Fragments of Epic Memory* (1992).

BIBLIOGRAPHY

Abrams, Marc D., and Gregory J. Nowacki. "Native American Imprint in Palaeoecology." *Nature Sustainability* 3, no. 11 (2020): 896–97.

Adams, Jenny L. *Ground Stone Analysis*. Salt Lake City: University of Utah Press, 2014.

Alexander, Karen, William Leavenworth, S. Claesson, and W. Jeffrey Bolster. "Catch Density: A New Approach to Shifting Baselines, Stock Assessment, and Ecosystem-Based Management." *Bulletin of Marine Science* 87 (2011): 213–34.

Alexander, Karen E., William B. Leavenworth, Jamie Cournane, Andrew B. Cooper, Stefan Claesson, Stephen Brennan, Gwynna Smith, et al. "Gulf of Maine Cod in 1861: Historical Analysis of Fishery Logbooks, with Ecosystem Implications." *Fish and Fisheries* 10, no. 4 (2009): 428–49.

Allen, David. "John Scott and the Mapping of New England and New York." *Portolan*, Spring 2022, 23–33

Altman, Heidi, Tanya Peres, and J. Matthew Compton. "Better than Butter: Yona Go'i, Bear Grease in Cherokee Culture." In *Bears*, edited by Heather A. Lapham and Gregory A. Waselkov, 193–216. Gainesville: University Press of Florida, 2020.

Anderson, David G., Thaddeus G. Bissett, Stephen J. Yerka, Joshua J. Wells, Eric C. Kansa, Sarah W. Kansa, Kelsey Noack Myers, R. Carl DeMuth, and Devin A. White. "Sea-Level Rise and Archaeological Site Destruction: An Example from the Southeastern United States Using DINAA (Digital Index of North American Archaeology)." *PLOS ONE* 12, no. 11 (2017): e0188142.

Anderson, Terry L. and Robert Paul Thomas. "White Population, Labor Force and

Extensive Growth of the New England Economy in the Seventeenth Century." *Journal of Economic History* 33, no. 3 (1973): 634–67.

Angus, Ian. "Anthropocene: What's in a Name?" *Climate & Capitalism*, 2015.

Baker, Emerson. "Formerly Machegonne, Dartmouth, York, Stogummor, Casco, and Falmouth: Portland as a Contested Frontier in the Seventeenth Century." In *Creating Portland: History and Place in Northern New England*, edited by Joseph A. Contori, 12–13. Lebanon, NH: University Press of New England, 2005.

———. "Trouble to the Eastward: The Failure of Anglo-Indian Relations in Early Maine." PhD diss., Willam and Mary, 1986.

Baker, Emerson W., and Nina Maurer. *Forgotten Frontier: Untold Stories of the Piscataqua* (exhibit catalog). South Berwick, ME: Old Berwick Historical Society, 2018.

Bampton, M. "Deforestation and Siltation: A Historical and Ecological Look." In Bolster, *Cross-Grained and Wily Waters*, 145–47.

Barbieri, Michael. "The Dollar in Revolutionary America." *Journal of the American Revolution*, September 27, 2016.

Baron, William R. "Historical Climates of the Northeastern United States." In *Holocene Human Ecology in Northeastern North America*, edited by George P. Nicholas, 29–46. Boston, MA: Springer US, 1988.

Basso, Keith. *Wisdom Sits in Places: Landscape and Language among the Western Apache*. Albuquerque: University of New Mexico Press, 1996.

Baugher, Sherene, and Robert W. Venables. "Ceramics as Indicators of Status and Class in Eighteenth-Century New York." In *Consumer Choice in Historical Archaeology*, edited by Suzanne M. Spencer-Wood, 31–53. New York: Plenum Press, 1987.

Behm, P., R. Boumans, and Frederick Short. "Spatial Modeling of Eelgrass Distribution in Great Bay, New Hampshire." In *Landscape Simulation Modeling: A Spatially Explicit, Dynamic Approach*, edited by Robert Costanza and Alexey Voinov, 173–96. New York: Springer-Verlag, 2004.

Belknap, Jeremy. *The History of New-Hampshire (1784–1792)*. Philadelphia, PA: Robert Aitken, 1784, Internet Archive.

Bell, Herbert C. "The West India Trade before the American Revolution." *American Historical Review* 22, no. 2 (1917): 272–87.

Betts, Matthew W., and M. Gabriel Hrynick. *The Archaeology of the Atlantic Northeast*. Toronto: University of Toronto Press, 2021.

Bhabha, Homi K. *The Location of Culture*. 2nd ed. London: Routledge, 2004.

Binford, Lewis. "A New Method of Calculating Dates from Kaolin Pipe Stem Samples." *Southeastern Archaeology* 9, no. 1 (1962): 19–21.

Birch, Jennifer. "Coalescent Communities: Settlement Aggregation and Social Integration in Iroquoian Ontario." *American Antiquity* 77, no. 4 (2012): 646–70.

Blackhawk, Ned. *The Rediscovery of America: Native Peoples and the Unmaking of U.S. History*. New Haven, CT: Yale University Press, 2023.

Blackmore, Lydia Barrett. "'Just IMPORTED and to Be SOLD': Methods of

Acquisition and Use of Knives, Forks, and Silver Spoons in Eighteenth-Century Virginia," Honors thesis, William and Mary, 2010.

Blee, Lisa, and Jean M. O'Brien. *Monumental Mobility: The Memory Work of Massasoit*. Chapel Hill: University of North Carolina Press, 2019.

Bollwerk, Elizabeth, and Shannon Tushingham, eds. *Perspectives on the Archaeology of Pipes, Tobacco and Other Smoke Plants in the Ancient Americas*. Cham: Springer International, 2016.

Bolster, W. Jeffrey, ed. *Cross-Grained and Wily Waters: A Guide to the Piscataqua Maritime Region*. Portsmouth, NH: Gundalow, 2002.

———. *The Mortal Sea: Fishing the Atlantic in the Age of Sail*. Cambridge, MA: Harvard University Press, 2012.

———. "Putting the Ocean in Atlantic History: Maritime Communities and Marine Ecology in the Northwest Atlantic, 1500–1800." *American Historical Review* 113 (2008): 19–47.

Bonneuil, Christophe, and Jean-Baptiste Fressoz. *The Shock of the Anthropocene: The Earth, History and Us*. Translated by David Fernbach. London: Verso, 2016.

Bostic, Heidi, and Meghan Howey. "To Address the Anthropocene, Engage the Liberal Arts." *Anthropocene* 18 (2017): 105.

Bosworth, Kai. "Feminist Geography in the Anthropocene: Sciences, Bodies, Futures." In *Routledge Handbook of Gender and Feminist Geographies*, edited by Anindita Datta, Peter Hopkins, Lynda Johnston, Elixabeth Olson, and Joseli Maria Silva, 445–54. London: Routledge, 2020.

Bourque, Bruce J. *Diversity and Complexity in Prehistoric Maritime Societies: A Gulf of Maine Perspective*. New York: Springer New York, 1995.

———. *Twelve Thousand Years: American Indians in Maine*. Lincoln: University of Nebraska Press, 2001.

Bourque, Bruce J., and Ruth Holmes Whitehead. "Tarrentines and the Introduction of European Trade Goods in the Gulf of Maine." *Ethnohistory* 32, no. 4 (1985): 327–41.

British Library. "Pascatway River in New England." British Library Catalog (online).

Brodie, Neil, Morag Kersel, and Kathryn Walker Tubb. "Museum Acquisitions: Responsibilities for the Illicit Traffic in Antiquities." In *Archaeology, Cultural Heritage, and the Antiquities Trade*, edited by Neil Brodie, Morag Kersel, Christina Luke, and Kathryn Walker Tubb, 245–57. Gainesville: University Press of Florida, 2006.

Brondizio, Eduardo S., Karen O'Brien, Xuemei Bai, Frank Biermann, Will Steffen, Frans Berkhout, Christophe Cudennec, et al. "Re-Conceptualizing the Anthropocene: A Call for Collaboration." *Global Environmental Change* 39 (2016): 318–27.

Brook, Timothy. *Vermeer's Hat: The Seventeenth Century and the Dawn of the Global World*. New York: Bloomsbury Publishing, 2009.

Brooks, Lisa. *The Common Pot: The Recovery of Native Space in the Northeast*. Minneapolis: University of Minnesota Press, 2008

———. *Our Beloved Kin: A New History of King Philip's War*. New Haven, CT: Yale University Press, 2018.

———. “Turning the Looking Glass on King Philip’s War: Locating American Literature in Native Space.” *American Literary History* 25, no. 4 (2013): 718–50.

Brooks, Lisa, and Cassandra Brooks. “The Reciprocity Principle and Traditional Ecological Knowledge: Understanding the Significance of Indigenous Protest on the Presumpscot River.” *International Journal of Critical Indigenous Studies* 3 no. 2 (2010): 11–28.

Brown, Craig “The Great Massacre of 1694: Understanding the Destruction of Oyster River Plantation.” *Historical New Hampshire*, 1998, 69–90.

Brown, Craig, Richard Lunt, and Peter Sablock. “Hard by the Water’s Edge: A Preliminary Report of the Darby Field Homestead-Bickford Garrison (27-ST-71) Excavations.” *New Hampshire Archaeologist* 54 (2014): 14–38.

Bryant, Donald, and David R. Starbuck. “First Parish Church—Dover Point Site.” National Register of Historic Places Nomination, Inventory Form, National Park Service, 1983.

Bunker, Victoria. “New Hampshire’s Prehistoric Settlement and Culture Chronology.” *New Hampshire Archaeologist* 33/34 (1994): 20–28.

Burnard, Trevor. *Planters, Merchants, and Slaves: Plantation Societies in British America, 1650–1820*. Chicago: University of Chicago Press, 2019.

Calloway, Colin G. *The American Revolution in Indian Country: Crisis and Diversity in Native American Communities*. Cambridge: Cambridge University Press, 1995.

Candee, Richard M. “The Water Powered Sawmills of the Piscataqua.” *Old Time New England*, 1970, 131–49.

Capone, Patricia, and Elinor Downs. “Red Clay Tobacco Pipes: Petrographic Window into Seventeenth-Century Economics at Jamestown, Virginia, and New England.” In Rafferty and Mann, *Smoking and Culture*, 305–16.

Carpenter, Murray. “Native American Secrets Lie Buried in Huge Shell Mounds.” *New York Times*, October 19, 2017.

Castree, Noel. “The Anthropocene and Geography I: The Back Story.” *Geography Compass* 8, no. 7 (2014): 436–49.

———. “Framing, Deframing and Reframing the Anthropocene.” *Ambio* 50, no. 10 (2021): 1788–92.

Chakrabarty, Dipesh. “The Climate of History: Four Theses.” *Critical Inquiry* 35, no. 2 (2009): 197–222.

Champlain, Samuel de. *The Voyages and Explorations of Samuel de Champlain, 1604–1616*. 2 vols. Translated by C. Pomery Otis. Boston: Prince Society, 1878, Canadiana.

Chartrand, René. *The Forts of Colonial North America: British, Dutch and Swedish Colonies*. Oxford: Osprey Publishing, 2011.

Chen, Xianyao, Xuebin Zhang, John A. Church, Christopher S. Watson, Matt A. King, Didier Monselesan, Benoit Legresy, and Christopher Harig. “The Increasing Rate of Global Mean Sea-Level Rise during 1993–2014.” *Nature Climate Change* 7, no. 7 (2017): 492–95.

Chilton, Elizabeth S. “Beyond ‘Big’: Gender, Age, and Subsistence Diversity in

Paleo-Indian Societies." In *The Settlement of the American Continents: A Multidisciplinary Approach to Human Biogeography*, edited by C. Michael Barton, Geoggrey Clark, David Yesner, and Georges Pearson, 162–72. Tucson: University of Arizona Press, 2004.

———. "Mobile Farmers of Pre-Contact Southern New England: The Archaeological and Ethnohistoric Evidence." In *Current Northeast Paleoethnobotany*, edited by John Hart, 157–76. Albany: New York State Museum Bulletin 494, 1999.

———. "'Towns They Have None': Diverse Subsistence and Settlement Strategies in Native New England." In *Northeast Subsistence-Settlement Change: A.D. 700–1300*, edited by John Hart and Christina Rieth, 289–300. Albany: New York State Museum, 2002.

Chilton, Elizabeth S., Tonya Largy, and Kathryn Curran. "Evidence for Prehistoric Maize Horticulture at the Pine Hill Site, Deerfield, Massachusetts." *Northeast Anthropology* 59 (1999): 23–46.

Cipolla, Craig N., ed. *Foreign Objects: Rethinking Indigenous Consumption in American Archaeology*. Tucson: University of Arizona Press, 2017.

Cipolla, Craig N., and Amélie Allard. "Recognizing River Power: Watery Views of Ontario's Fur Trade." *Journal of Archaeological Method and Theory* 26, no. 3 (2019): 1084–1105.

Cronon, William. *Changes in the Land: Indians, Colonists, and the Ecology of New England*. Rev. ed. New York: Hill and Wang, 2003.

Crutzen, Paul J. "Geology of Mankind." *Nature* 415, no. 6867 (2002): 23.

Crutzen, Paul J., and E. F. Stoermer. "The Anthropocene." *IGBP Newsletter* 41 (2000): 17–18.

D'Abate, Richard, and Victor Konrad. "General Introduction." In *American Beginnings: Exploration, Culture and Cartography in the Land of Norumbega*, edited by Emerson W. Baker, Edwin Churchill, Richard D'Abate, Kristine Jones, Victor Konrad, and Harald Prins, xix–1. Lincoln: University of Nebraska Press, 1994.

Daniels, Bruce. *New England Nation: The Country the Puritans Built*. New York: Palgrave Macmillan, 2012.

Daugherty, W. E. "Maritime Indian Treaties in Historical Perspective." Treaties and Historical Research Centres, Department of Indian and Northern Affairs Canada, 1983.

Davis, Heather, and Zoe Todd. "On the Importance of a Date, or, Decolonizing the Anthropocene." *ACME: An International Journal for Critical Geographies* 16, no. 4 (2017): 761–80.

Deetz, James. "Harrington Histograms versus Binford Mean Dates as a Technique for Establishing the Occupational Sequence of Sites at Flowerdew Hundred, Virginia." *American Archaeology* 6, no. 1 (1987): 62–68.

———. *In Small Things Forgotten: An Archaeology of Early American Life*. New York: Knopf Doubleday Publishing Group, 1996.

DeLucia, Christine M. "The Memory Frontier: Geographies of Violence and

Regeneration in Colonial New England and the Native Northeast after King Philip's War. (Garrisoned Piscataqua Pp. 484–618)." PhD diss., Yale University, 2012.

———. *Memory Lands: King Philip's War and the Place of Violence in the Northeast.* New Haven, CT: Yale University Press, 2018.

Den Ouden, Amy. *Beyond Conquest: Native Peoples and the Struggle for History in New England.* Lincoln: University of Nebraska Press, 2005.

DePaoli, Neill. "Pemaquid, Maine: Preliminary Reconstruction of a Seventeenth Century Coastal Community's Domestic and International Trade Connections." *Bulletin of Massachusetts Archaeological Society* 45, no. 1 (1984): 24–40.

Dincauze, Dena. *The Neville Site: 8,000 Years at Amoskeag, Manchester, New Hampshire.* Cambridge, MA: Peabody Museum Monographs 4, 1976.

Dover, NH, Town Records: 1657–1753. Historic Dover Records, City of Dover, NH.

Dow, Joseph. *History of the Town of Hampton, New Hampshire, from Its Settlement in 1638, to the Autumn of 1892.* Salem, MA: Salem Press Pub. and Printing, 1893, University of Pennsylvania Digital Library.

Durel, John Walter. "From Strawbery Banke to Puddle Dock: The Evolution of a Neighborhood, 1630–1850." PhD diss., University of New Hampshire, 1984.

Edney, Matthew H., and Mary Sponberg Pedley, eds. *The History of Cartography.* Vol. 4: *Cartography in the European Enlightenment.* Chicago: University of Chicago Press, 2020.

Elhacham, Emily, Liad Ben-Uri, Jonathan Grozovski, Yinon M. Bar-On, and Ron Milo. "Global Human-Made Mass Exceeds All Living Biomass." *Nature* 588, no. 7838 (2020): 442–44.

Ellis, Erle C. *Anthropocene: A Very Short Introduction.* Oxford: Oxford University Press, 2018.

Ethridge, Robbie, and Sheri M. Shuck-Hall, eds. *Mapping the Mississippian Shatter Zone: The Colonial Indian Slave Trade and Regional Instability in the American South.* Lincoln: University of Nebraska Press, 2009.

Fagan, Brian. *Fish on Friday: Feasting, Fasting, and the Discovery of the New World.* New York: Perseus Book Group, 2006.

———. *The Little Ice Age: How Climate Made History 1300–1850.* New York: Basic Books, 2001.

Farrell, Justin, Paul Berne Burrow, Kathryn McConnell, Kyle Whyte, and Gal Koss. "Effects of Land Dispossession and Forced Migration on Indigenous Peoples in North America." *Science* 374, eabe4943 (2021).

Fernald, Jody R. "Slavery in New Hampshire: Profitable Godliness to Racial Consciousness." Master's thesis, University of New Hampshire, 2007.

Finch, Eugene. "The Great Bay Site." *New Hampshire Archaeologist* 15 (1969): 1–12.

Ford, Ben. "Down by the Water's Edge: Modelling Shipyard Locations in Maryland, USA." *International Journal of Nautical Archaeology* 36, no. 1 (2007): 125–37.

Gaimster, David R. M. *German Stoneware, 1200–1900: Archaeology and Cultural*

History: Containing a Guide to the Collections of the British Museum, Victoria & Albert Museum, and Museum of London. London: British Museum Press, 1997.

Gardner, Carol. *The Involuntary American: A Scottish Prisoner's Journey to the New World.* Yardley, PA: Westholme Publishing, 2019.

Garvin, James L. "Small-Scale Brickmaking in New Hampshire." *IA. The Journal of the Society for Industrial Archeology* 20, no. 1/2 (1994): 19–31.

Gerrard, Chris, Pam Graves, Andrew Millard, Richard Annis, and Anwen Caffell. *Lost Lives, New Voices: Unlocking the Stories of the Scottish Soldiers at the Battle of Dunbar 1650.* Oxford: Oxbow Books, 2018.

Gifford, Matthew J. "Everything Is Ballast: An Examination of Ballast Related Practices and Ballast Stones from the Emanuel Point Shipwrecks." Master's thesis, University of West Florida, 2014.

Goldenberg, Joseph. *Shipbuilding in Colonial America.* Charlottesville: University of Virgina Press, 1976.

Goodby, Robert. *A Deep Presence: 13,000 Years of Native American History.* Portsmouth, NH: Peter Randall Publisher, 2021.

———. "Native American Life in the Piscataqua Region, 11,000–350 B.P." In *An Archaeological Site Investigation of the Pearl and Manning Street Wharves.* Portsmouth, NH: Strawbery Banke Museum, 1999.

Gowell, Michael. "Piscataqua Gundalows." In Bolster, *Cross-Grained and Wily Waters,* 111–12.

Graves, J. R., James Pendleton, and A. C. Dayton. "Hanserd Knollys in America." *Southern Baptist Review Journal,* 1858, 465–73.

Handsman, Randall. "Landscapes of Memory in Wampanoag Country and the Monuments upon Them." In *Archaeologies of Placemaking: Monuments, Memories, and Engagement in Native North America,* edited by Patricia Rubertone, 161–93. Walnut Creek, CA: Left Coast Press, 2008.

Harrington, J. "Dating Stem Fragments of Seventeenth and Eighteenth Century Clay Tobacco Pipes." *Quarterly Bulletin of the Archaeological Society of Virginia* 9, no. 1 (1954): 10–14.

Harris, Gordon. "The Great Colonial Hurricane and the Wreck of the Angel Gabriel." *Historic Ipswich* (blog), October 24, 2021.

Hart, John, and Bernard Means. "Maize and Villages: A Summary and Critical Assessment of Current Northeast Early Late Prehistoric Evidence." In *Northeast Subsistence-Settlement Change: A.D. 700–1300,* edited by John Hart and Christina Rieth, 345–58. Albany: New York State Museum, 2002.

Hart, John P., and C. Margaret Scarry. "The Age of Common Beans (*Phaseolus Vulgaris*) in the Northeastern United States." *American Antiquity* 64, no. 4 (1999): 653–58.

Hasenstab, Robert. "Agriculture, Warfare, and Tribalization in the Iroquois Homeland of New York: A G.I.S. Analysis of Late Woodland Settlement." PhD diss., University of Massachusetts, 1990.

———. "Fishing, Farming, and Finding the Village Sites: Centering Late Woodland New England Algonquians." In *The Archaeological Northeast*, edited by Mary Ann Levine, Kenneth Sassaman, and Michael Nassaney,139–54. Westport, CT: Bergin & Garvey, 1999.

Haven, Samuel Foster. *History of Grants under the Great Council for New England, a Lecture of a Course by Members of the Massachusetts Historical Society.* Boston: Press of John Wilson and Son, 1869, Internet Archive.

Hecker, Harold. "Jasper Flakes and Jack's Reef Points at Adams Point: Speculations on Interregional Exchange in Late Middle Woodland Times in Coastal New Hampshire." *New Hampshire Archaeologist* 35 (1995): 61–83.

Heidtke, Kenan. "Jamaican Red Clay Tobacco Pipes." Master's thesis, Texas A&M, 1992.

Henle, Alea. *Rescued from Oblivion: Historical Cultures in the Early United States.* Amherst: University of Massachusetts Press, 2020.

Heritage Newfoundland and Labrador. "The International Fishery of the 16th Century." 1997.

Historical Sketch, Views and Business Directory of Dover, NH. Dover, NH: Dover Grange, 1926, no. 225.

History of Wages in the United States from Colonial Times to 1928. Washington, DC: Bulletin of the United States Bureau of Labor Statistics, No. 499, 1929.

Holm, Poul, Francis Ludlow, Cordula Scherer, Charles Travis, Bernard Allaire, Cristina Brito, Patrick W. Hayes, et al. "The North Atlantic Fish Revolution (ca. AD 1500)." *Quaternary Research* 108 (2022): 92–106.

Howey, Meghan C. L. "Harnessing Remote Sensing Derived Sea Level Rise Models to Assess Cultural Heritage Vulnerability: A Case Study from the Northwest Atlantic Ocean." *Sustainability* 12, no. 22 (2020): 9429.

Howey, Meghan C. L., and Christine M. DeLucia. "Spectacles of Settler Colonial Memory: Archaeological Findings from an Early Twentieth-Century 'First' Settlement Pageant and Other Commemorative Terrain in New England." *International Journal of Historical Archaeology* 26 (2022): 974–1007.

Howey, Meghan C. L., Michael W. Palace, and Crystal H. McMichael. "Geospatial Modeling Approach to Monument Construction Using Michigan from A.D. 1000–1600 as a Case Study." *Proceedings of the National Academy of Sciences* 113, no. 27 (2016): 7443–48.

Hubbard, William. *A General History of New England: From the Discovery to MDCLXXX.* Cambridge, MA: C. C. Little and J. Brown, 1848, Internet Archive.

Hume, Ivor Noël. *A Guide to the Artifacts of Colonial America.* Philadelphia: University of Pennsylvania Press, 2001 [1969].

Intergovernmental Panel on Climate Change (IPCC). *Climate Change 2021: The Physical Science Basis (6th Assessment Report of the Intergovernmental Panel on Climate Change).* IPCC, 2021.

Jackson, Jeremy B. C., Michael X. Kirby, Wolfgang H. Berger, Karen A. Bjorndal, Louis W. Botsford, Bruce J. Bourque, Roger H. Bradbury, et al. "Historical Overfishing and the Recent Collapse of Coastal Ecosystems." *Science* 293, no. 5530 (2001): 629–38.

Jenkinson, Matthew. *Charles I's Killers in America: The Lives and Afterlives of Edward Whalley and William Goffe*. Oxford: Oxford University Press, 2019.

Jeon, Sung Bae, Pontus Olofsson, and Curtis E. Woodcock. "Land Use Change in New England: A Reversal of the Forest Transition." *Journal of Land Use Science* 9, no. 1 (2014): 105–30.

Kanolt, C. W. "Melting Points of Fire Bricks." Technologic Papers of the Bureau of Standards, no. 10, 1912. National Bureau of Standards, Washington, DC.

Kenmotsu, Nancy. "Gunflints: A Study." *Historical Archaeology* 24, no. 2 (1990): 92–124.

Kent, Barry C. "More on Gunflints." *Historical Archaeology* 17, no. 2 (1983): 27–40.

Kirch, Patrick. "Archaeology and Global Change: The Holocene Record." *Arer* 30 (2005): 409.

Kopytoff, Igor. "The Cultural Biography of Things: Commoditization as Process." In *The Social Life of Things: Commodities in Cultural Perspective*, edited by Arjun Appadurai, 64–94. Cambridge: Cambridge University Press, 1986.

Kristensen. "Flash in the Pan: The Archaeology of Gunflints in Alberta." *RETROactive* (blog), July 10, 2019.

Kurlansky, Mark. *Cod: A Biography of the Fish That Changed the World*. New York: Penguin Books, 1998.

Labaree, Benjamin Woods. *America and the Sea: A Maritime History*. Mystic, CT: Mystic Seaport Museum, 1998.

Langston, Nancy. *Climate Ghosts: Migratory Species in the Anthropocene*. Waltham, MA: Brandeis University Press, 2021.

Laramie, Michael G. *King William's War: The First Contest for North America, 1689–1697*. Yardley, PA: Westholme Publishing, 2017.

Latour, Bruno. *Facing Gaia: Eight Lectures on the New Climatic Regime*. Translated by Catherine Porter. Cambridge: Polity Books, 2017.

Leach, Peter. *A Theory Primer and Field Guide for Archaeological, Cemetery, and Forensic Surveys with Ground Penetrating Radar*. Nashua, NH: Geophysical Survey Systems, Inc. (GSSI), 2021.

Leavenworth, William. "The Changing Landscape of Maritime Resources in Seventeenth-Century New England." *International Journal of Maritime History* 20 (2008): 33–62.

Lepore, Jill. *The Name of War: King Philip's War and the Origins of American Identity*. New York: Vintage Books, 1998.

Leveridge, Michael E. *A Godly Minister: The Reverend William Leverich of Great Britain, New England and New York*. Cambridge: Self-published by Michael E. Leveridge in collaboration with Thomas Leverich, 2008.

Lewis, Simon L., and Mark A. Maslin. "Defining the Anthropocene." *Nature* 519, no. 7542 (2015): 171–80.

———. *The Human Planet: How We Created the Anthropocene*. New Haven, CT: Yale University Press, 2018.

Lightfoot, Kent G., Lee M. Panich, Tsim D. Schneider, and Sara L. Gonzalez. "European Colonialism and the Anthropocene: A View from the Pacific Coast of North America." *Anthropocene* 4 (2013): 101–15.

Loren, Diana DiPaolo. "Considering Mimicry and Hybridity in Early Colonial New England: Health, Sin and the Body 'Behung with Beades.'" *Archaeological Review from Cambridge*, 2013, 151–68.

Lotze, Heike K., and Inka Milewski. "Two Centuries of Multiple Human Impacts and Successive Changes in a North Atlantic Food Web." *Ecological Applications* 14, no. 5 (2004): 1428–47.

Luciano, Dana. "The Inhuman Anthropocene." *Avidly* (blog), 2015.

Lyell, Charles. *Principles of Geology, Being an Attempt to Explain the Former Changes of the Earth's Surface, by Reference to Causes Now in Operation*. Vol. 3. London: John Murray, 1833, Google Books.

Mamdani, Mahmood. "Beyond Settler and Native as Political Identities: Overcoming the Political Legacy of Colonialism." *Comparative Studies in Society and History* 43, no. 4 (2001): 651–64.

Marshall, Henrietta. *This Country of Ours: The Story of the United States*. New York: George H. Doran, 1917, University of Pennsylvania Digital Library.

Maymon, Jeffery, and Charles Bolian. "The Wadleigh Falls Site: An Early and Middle Archaic Period Site in Southeastern New Hampshire." In *Early Holocene Occupation in Northern New England*, edited by Brian Robinson, James Petersen, and Ann Robinson, 117–34. Augusta: Occasional Publications in Maine Archaeology no. 9, 1992.

Mayo-Bobee, Dinah. "Servile Discontents: Slavery and Resistance in Colonial New Hampshire, 1645–1785." *Slavery and Abolition* 30, no. 3 (2009): 339–60.

McCoy, Mark D. "The Race to Document Archaeological Sites ahead of Rising Sea Levels: Recent Applications of Geospatial Technologies in the Archaeology of Polynesia." *Sustainability* 10, no. 1 (2018): 185.

McMillan, Lauren K. "An Evaluation of Tobacco Pipe Stem Dating Formulas." *Northeast Historical Archaeology* 45 (2016): 67–91.

Mentz, Steve. *Break Up the Anthropocene*. Minneapolis: University of Minnesota Press, 2019.

———. *Shipwreck Modernity: Ecologies of Globalization, 1550–1719*. Minneapolis: University of Minnesota Press, 2015.

Milstein, Cindy, ed. *Rebellious Mourning: The Collective Work of Grief*. Chico, CA: AK Press, 2017.

Mitchell, John Hanson. *The Paradise of All These Parts: A Natural History of Boston*. Boston: Beacon Press, 2009.

Monroe, J. Cameron, and Seth Mallios. "A Seventeenth-Century Colonial Cottage

Industry: New Evidence and a Dating Formula for Colono Tobacco Pipes in the Chesapeake." *Historical Archaeology* 38, no. 2 (2004): 68–82.

Nassaney, Michael S. "Identity Formation at a French Colonial Outpost in the North American Interior." *International Journal of Historical Archaeology* 12, no. 4 (2008): 297–318.

New Hampshire Coastal Risk and Hazards Commission. *Preparing New Hampshire for Projected Storm Surge, Sea-Level Rise and Extreme Precipitation*, 2016.

O'Brien, Jean M. *Firsting and Lasting: Writing Indians Out of Existence in New England.* Minneapolis: University of Minnesota Press, 2010.

Odell, Jay, Alyson L Eberhardt, David M Burdick, and Pete Ingraham. "Great Bay Estuary Restoration Compendium." New Hampshire Coastal Program and the New Hampshire Estuaries Project, 2006.

"The Origin of the Troy Ounce." *Provident Metals* (blog), July 27, 2017.

Orser, Charles. *An Archaeology of the English Atlantic World, 1600–1700.* Cambridge: Cambridge University Press, 2018.

Oswald, W. Wyatt, David R. Foster, Bryan N. Shuman, Elizabeth S. Chilton, Dianna L. Doucette, and Deena L. Duranleau. "Conservation Implications of Limited Native American Impacts in Pre-Contact New England." *Nature Sustainability* 3, no. 3 (2020): 241–46.

Palfrey, John Gorham. *History of New England.* Carlisle, MA: Applewood Books, 1858, Google Books.

Parkman, Francis. *Francis Parkman: France and England in North America.* Vol. 2: *Count Frontenac and New France under Louis XIV, a Half-Century of Conflict, Montcalm and Wolfe.* New York: Library of America, 1983 [1877].

Pettigrew, Jane, and Bruce Richardson. *A Social History of Tea: Tea's Influence on Commerce, Culture and Community.* Chicago: Benjamin Press, 2013.

Pike, John. *Journal of the Rev. John Pike, of Dover, N.H.* Cambridge: Massachusetts Historical Society, 1876, Library of Congress.

Pope, Laura. "Wadleigh Falls Island NH 39-1: A Preliminary Site Report." *New Hampshire Archaeologist* 22 (1981): 8–15.

Pope, Peter E. *Fish into Wine: The Newfoundland Plantation in the Seventeenth Century.* Chapel Hill: University of North Carolina Press, 2004.

Potter, Ben A., James F. Baichtal, Alwynne B. Beaudoin, Lars Fehren-Schmitz, C. Vance Haynes, Vance T. Holliday, Charles E. Holmes, et al. "Current Evidence Allows Multiple Models for the Peopling of the Americas." *Science Advances* 4, no. 8 (2018): eaat5473.

Pring, Martin. *The Voyage of Martin Pring, 1603.* Edited by Henry Burrage. New York: Charles Scribner's Sons, 1906, American Journeys Collection AJ-040.

Provincial Papers. Documents and Records Relating to the Province of New-Hampshire, from the Earliest Period of Its Settlement: 1623–1686. Vol 1. Compiled and edited by Nathaniel Bouton. Concord, NH: George E. Jenks, state printer, 1867, University of New Hampshire Scholars Repository.

Quint, Alonzo. "The First Church in Dover, and Its Pastor." *Granite Monthly: A Magazine of History, Biography, Literature and State Progress*, 1, no. 7 (November 1877), Google Books.

———. *Historical Memoranda Concerning Persons and Places in Old Dover, New Hampshire*. Edited by John Scales. Dover NH: Dover Enquirer, 1900, Internet Archive.

Rafferty, Sean M., and Rob Mann, eds. *Smoking and Culture: The Archaeology of Tobacco Pipes in Eastern North America*. Knoxville: University of Tennessee Press, 2004.

Reid, Jennifer. *Myth, Symbol and Colonial Encounter: British and Mi'kmaq in Acadia, 1700–1867*. Ottawa: University of Ottawa Press, 1995.

Reimann, Lena, Athanasios T. Vafeidis, Sally Brown, Jochen Hinkel, and Richard S. J. Tol. "Mediterranean UNESCO World Heritage at Risk from Coastal Flooding and Erosion Due to Sea-Level Rise." *Nature Communications* 9, no. 1 (2018): 4161.

Robinson, Brian, Jennifer Ort, William Eldridge, Adrian Burke, and Bertrand Pelletier. "Paleoindian Aggregation and Social Context at Bull Brook." *American Antiquity* 74 (2009): 423–47.

Robinson, J Dennis. 1623: Pilgrims, Pipe Dreams, Politics & the Founding of New Hampshire Portsmouth, NH: Harbortown Press, 2023.

Robinson, Margaret. "Animal Personhood in Mi'kmaq Perspective." *Societies* 4, no. 4 (2014): 672–88.

Rockingham County Registry of Deeds. Rockingham County Offices, Brentwood, NH.

Rubertone, Patricia. "Engaging Monuments, Memories, and Archaeology." In *Archaeologies of Placemaking: Monuments, Memories, and Engagement in Native North America*, edited by Patricia Rubertone, 13–34. Walnut Creek, CA: Left Coast Press, 2008.

Ruddiman, Will, Erle C. Ellis, Jed Kaplan, and Dorian Fuller. "Defining the Epoch We Live In." *Science* 348 (2015): 38–39.

Said, Edward W. *Orientalism*. New York: Pantheon Books, 1978.

Salisbury, Neal. *The Indians of New England: A Critical Bibliography*. Bloomington: Indiana University Press, 1982.

———. "The Indians' Old World: Native Americans and the Coming of Europeans." *William and Mary Quarterly* 3 (1996): 435–58.

———. *Manitou and Providence: Indians, Europeans, and the Making of New England, 1500–1643*. Oxford: Oxford University Press, 1984.

Sammons, Mark, and Valerie Cunningham. *Black Portsmouth: Three Centuries of African-American Heritage*. Durham: University of New Hampshire Press, 2004.

Sassaman, Kenneth E., and Asa R Randall. "The Cultural History of Bannerstones in the Savannah River Valley." *Southeastern Archaeology* 26, no. 2 (2007): 196–211.

Scales, John. *History of Dover, New Hampshire*. Manchester, NH: John B. Clarke, 1923, Google Books.

———. *History of Strafford County, New Hampshire and Representative Citizens*. Chicago: Richmond-Arnold Publishing, 1914, Internet Archive.

——. *Piscataqua Pioneers 1623–1775 Register of Members and Ancestors*. Dover, NH: Piscataqua Pioneers, 1919, Internet Archives.

Schmidt, Benjamin. "Mapping an Empire: Cartographic and Colonial Rivalry in Seventeenth-Century Dutch and English North America." *William and Mary Quarterly* 54, no. 3 (1997): 549–78.

Senier, Siobhan, ed. *Dawnland Voices: An Anthology of Indigenous Writing from New England*. Lincoln: University of Nebraska Press, 2014.

Senior, C. M. *A Nation of Pirates: English Piracy in Its Heydey*. London: David and Charles, 1875, Bristol Record Society.

Sharpe, Christina Elizabeth. *In the Wake: On Blackness and Being*. Durham, NC: Duke University Press, 2016.

Short, Frederick. *The Ecology of the Great Bay Estuary, New Hampshire and Maine: An Estuarine Profile and Bibliography*. Durham, NH: Jackson Estuarine Laboratory, 1992.

Sinopoli, Carla M. *Approaches to Archaeological Ceramics*. New York: Plenum Press, 1991.

Skinas, David. "The Wadleigh Fall Site (NH 39–2): A Preliminary Report of the 1980 Excavations." *New Hampshire Archaeologist* 22 (1981): 16–30.

Smith, Bruce D., and Melinda A. Zeder. "The Onset of the Anthropocene." *Anthropocene*, When Humans Dominated the Earth: Archeological Perspectives on the Anthropocene, 4 (2013): 8–13..

Smith, David C., William R. Baron, Anne E. Bridges, Harold W. Borns Jr, and Janet K. TeBrake. "Climate Fluctuation and Agricultural Change in Southern and Central New England, 1765–1880." *Maine History* 21 (1982): 179–200.

Smith, John. *A Description of New England*. London: Printed by Humfrey Lownes for Robert Clerke, 1616, Zea E-Books in American Studies 3.

Snow, Dean R. *The Archaeology of New England*. Cambridge, MA: Academic Press, 1980.

Spiess, Arthur E. "People of the Clam: Shellfish and Diet in Coastal Maine Late Archaic and Ceramic Period Sites." *Journal of the North Atlantic* 10 (2017): 105–12.

Spiess, Arthur E., and Robert A. Lewis. *The Turner Farm Fauna: 5000 Years of Hunting and Fishing in Penobscot Bay, Maine*. Augusta: Maine Archaeological Society, 2001.

Spiess, Arthur E., and John Mosher. "Archaic Period Hunting and Fishing around the Gulf of Maine." In *The Archaic of the Far Northeast*, edited by David Sanger and M. A .P. Renouf. Orono: University of Maine Press, 2006.

Stackpole, Everett, and Lucien Thompson. *History of the Town of Durham New Hampshire (Oyster River Plantation) with Genealogical Notes*. Vol. 1. Durham: Town of Durham, 1913, University of New Hampshire's Scholars Repository.

Starbuck, David R. *The Archeology of New Hampshire: Exploring 10,000 Years in the Granite State*. Durham: University of New Hampshire Press, 2006.

Steffen, Will, Wendy Broadgate, Lisa Deutsch, Owen Gaffney, and Cornelia Ludwig.

"The Trajectory of the Anthropocene: The Great Acceleration." *Anthropocene Review* 2, no. 1 (2015): 81–98.

Strobel, Christoph. *The Global Atlantic: 1400 to 1900*. London: Routledge, 2015.

Sumner, W. G. "The Spanish Dollar and the Colonial Shilling." *American Historical Review* 3, no. 4 (1898): 607–19.

Taussig, Michael. *Mimesis and Alterity: A Particular History of the Senses*. London: Routledge, 2017.

Thomas, Nicholas. *Entangled Objects: Exchange, Material Culture, and Colonialism in the Pacific*. Cambridge, MA: Harvard University Press, 2009.

Thompson, Colleen. *State of the Gulf of Maine Report: The Gulf of Maine in Context*. Nova Scotia: Gulf of Maine Council on the Marine Environment, 2010.

Thompson, Jonathan R., Dunbar N. Carpenter, Charles V. Cogbill, and David R. Foster. "Four Centuries of Change in Northeastern United States Forests." *PLOS ONE* 8, no. 9 (2013): e72540.

Thompson, Jonathan R., Joshua S. Plisinski, Pontus Olofsson, Christopher E. Holden, and Matthew J. Duveneck. "Forest Loss in New England: A Projection of Recent Trends." *PLOS ONE* 12, no. 12 (2017): e0189636.

Thompson, Mary Pickering. *Landmarks in Ancient Dover, New Hampshire*. Durham, NH: Concord Republican Press Association, 1892, Internet Archive.

Trouillot, Michel-Rolph. *Global Transformations: Anthropology and the Modern World*. New York: Palgrave Macmillan, 2004.

———. *Silencing the Past: Power and the Production of History*. Boston: Beacon Press, 1995.

Tsing, Anna Lowenhaupt. *The Mushroom at the End of the World*. Princeton, NJ: Princeton University Press, 2015.

Tsing, Anna Lowenhaupt, Andrew S. Mathews, and Nils Bubandt. "Patchy Anthropocene: Landscape Structure, Multispecies History, and the Retooling of Anthropology: An Introduction to Supplement 20." *Current Anthropology* 60, no. S20 (2019): S186–97.

Turnbaugh, Sarah Peabody. "17th and 18th Century Lead-Glazed Redwares in the Massachusetts Bay Colony." *Historical Archaeology* 17, no. 1 (1983): 3–17.

Tushingham, Shannon, Charles M. Snyder, Korey J. Brownstein, William J. Damitio, and David R. Gang. "Biomolecular Archaeology Reveals Ancient Origins of Indigenous Tobacco Smoking in North American Plateau." *Proceedings of the National Academy of Sciences* 115, no. 46 (2018): 11742–47.

Vickers, Daniel. *Farmers and Fishermen: Two Centuries of Work in Essex County, Massachusetts, 1630–1850*. Chapel Hill: University of North Carolina Press, 1994.

Victor, Megan. "Under the Tavern Table: Excavations at the Tavern on Smuttynose Island, Maine and Implications for Commensal Politics and Informal Economy." *International Journal of Historical Archaeology* 23, no. 1 (2019): 34–56.

Voss, Barbara L., and Rebecca Allen. "Guide to Ceramic MNV Calculation Qualitative and Quantitative Analysis." *Technical Briefs in Historical Archaeology* 5 (2010): 1–9.

Wadleigh, George. *Notable Events in the History of Dover, New Hampshire: From the First Settlement in 1623 to 1865*. Dover NH: Tufts College Press, 1913, Library of Congress.

Wainwright, Paul, Peter Benes, William E. Williams, and Brent D. Glass. *A Space for Faith: The Colonial Meetinghouses of New England*. Portsmouth, NH: UNKNO, 2010.

Wake, Cameron, Elizabeth Burakowski, Eric Kelsey, Katherine Hayhoe, Anne Stoner, Chris Watson, and Ellen Douglas. "Climate Change in the Piscataqua/Great Bay Region: Past, Present, and Future." Carbon Solutions New England, 2011.

Wake, Cameron, Jayne Knott, Thomas Lippmann, Mary Stampone, Thomas Ballestero, David Bjerklle, Elizabeth Burakowski, Stanley Glidden, Iman Hosseini-Shakib, and Jennifer Jacobs. "New Hampshire Coastal Flood Risk Summary Part 1: Science." New Hampshire Coastal Flood Risk Science and Technical Advisory Panel, 2019.

Walcott, Derek, "The Antilles: Fragments of Epic Memory." Nobel Prize in Literature Lecture, 1992.

Warren, Wendy. *New England Bound: Slavery and Colonization in Early America*. New York: Liveright, 2017.

Watkins, Lura. *Early New England Potters and Their Wares*. Cambridge, MA: Harvard University Press, 1950.

Watts, Vanessa. "Indigenous Place-Thought and Agency amongst Humans and Non Humans (First Woman and Sky Woman Go on a European World Tour!)." *Decolonization: Indigeneity, Education and Society* 2, no. 1 (2013): 20–34.

Weizman, Eyal. *The Conflict Shoreline: Colonization as Climate Change in the Negev Desert*. Göttingen: Steidl, 2015.

Weller, Christian, and Lily Roberts, "Eliminating the Black-White Wealth Gap Is a Generational Challenge." *Center for American Progress Reports*, March 19, 2021.\\ uc0\\u8221{} {\\i{}Center for American Progress} (blog

Wessels, Tom, Brian D. Cohen, and Ann H. Zwinger. *Reading the Forested Landscape: A Natural History of New England*. Woodstock, VT: Countryman Press, 2005.

Westerkamp, Marilyn J. *The Passion of Anne Hutchinson: An Extraordinary Woman, the Puritan Patriarchs, and the World They Made and Lost*. Oxford: Oxford University Press, 2021.

Wheal Martyn Clay Works. "Discover Wheal Martyn and the China Clay Story." 2020.

White, Sam. *A Cold Welcome: The Little Ice Age and Europe's Encounter with North America*. Cambridge, MA: Harvard University Press, 2017.

Whitehead, Ruth Holmes. *Nova Scotia: The Protohistoric Period 1500–1630*. Halifax: Nova Scotia Museum, 1993, Curatorial Report #75.

Whitney, Gordon G. *From Coastal Wilderness to Fruited Plain: A History of Environmental Change in Temperate North America from 1500 to the Present*. Cambridge: Cambridge University Press, 1996.

Whyte, Kyle Powys. "Settler Colonialism, Ecology, and Environmental Injustice." *Environment and Society* 9, no. 1 (September 1, 2018): 125–44.

Wickman, Thomas M. *Snowshoe Country: An Environmental and Cultural History of Winter in the Early American Northeast*. Cambridge: Cambridge University Press, 2018.

Williamson, William D. *History of the State of Maine; from Its First Discovery, A. D. 1602, to the Separation, A. D. 1820, Inclusive*. Hallowell, ME: Glaizier Masters, 1832, Maine History Documents 34.

Willoughby, Charles C. "The Adze and the Ungrooved Axe of the New England Indians." *American Anthropologist* 9, no. 2 (1907): 296–306.

Winthrop, John. "John Winthrop Dreams of a City on a Hill, 1630." American Yawp Reader.

Wolf, Eric R. *Europe and the People without History*. Los Angeles: University of California Press, 1997.

Yusoff, Kathryn. *A Billion Black Anthropocenes or None*. Minneapolis: University of Minnesota Press, 2018.

INDEX

Page numbers in italics refer to figures.